Dilemmas of Difference, Inclusion and Disability

Inclusion has become very influential internationally in the field of schooling. This has involved the introduction of policies that pursue more provision for, and acceptance of, students with special educational needs or disabilities in ordinary school settings. However, these policies represent different and often conflicting values and approaches to education.

The basic dilemma of difference is whether to recognise or not to recognise differences, as either way there are negative implications or risks associated with stigma, devaluation, rejection or denial of relevant opportunities. This is the first book to examine ideas about these dilemmas from a range of disciplines and fields about the nature and origins of such dilemmas as they apply to special and inclusive education. In particular these dilemmas are about:

- identification – whether to identify students as having special educational needs/disabilities or not?
- curriculum – how much of a common curriculum is relevant to these students?
- placement – can appropriate learning take place in ordinary schools and classes or not?

This ground-breaking book examines the perspectives of professional educators and administrators at national and local authority level across three countries: England, the USA and the Netherlands, and questions how they recognise tensions or dilemmas in responding to student differences. Of interest to researchers, students, academics and professionals, this study will provide a much needed balanced and powerful contribution to the inclusion debate.

Brahm Norwich is Professor of Educational Psychology and Special Educational Needs at the University of Exeter, UK.

Dilemmas of Difference, Inclusion and Disability

International perspectives
and future directions

Brahm Norwich

Routledge
Taylor & Francis Group

LONDON AND NEW YORK

First published 2008
by Routledge
2 Park Square, Milton Park, Abingdon, Oxon OX14 4RN

Simultaneously published in the USA and Canada
by Routledge
270 Madison Ave, New York, NY 10016

Transferred to Digital Printing 2008

Routledge is an imprint of the Taylor & Francis Group, an informa business

© 2008 Brahm Norwich

Typeset in Times New Roman by
Book Now Ltd, London
Printed and bound in Great Britain by
Antony Rowe, Chippenham, Wiltshire

British Library Cataloguing in Publication Data
A catalogue record for this book is available from the British Library

Library of Congress Cataloging in Publication Data
A catalog record has been requested for this book

ISBN10: 0–415–39846–0 (hbk)
ISBN10: 0–415–39847–9 (pbk)
ISBN10: 0–415–93886–0 (ebk)

ISBN13: 978–0–415–39846–6 (hbk)
ISBN13: 978–0–415–39847–3 (pbk)
ISBN13: 978–0–415–93886–7 (ebk)

Contents

Illustrations

Tables

Figures

Acknowledgements

I am very grateful to all those who agreed to be interviewed for this study, without whose time and interest it would not have happened. I also appreciate the advice and help of Professor Phil Burke, USA and Professor Sip Jan Pijl, Netherlands, and the help of my colleagues Professor Rupert Wigerif and Margie Tunbridge for reading some drafts.

Chapter I

Introduction

Dilemmas of difference, inclusion and disability

> ... dilemmas are revealed as fundamentally born out of a culture which produces more than one possible ideal world, ... social beings are confronted by and deal with dilemmatic situations as a condition of their humanity.
>
> (Billig *et al.*, 1988: p. 163)

Introduction

The book examines theoretical and empirical aspects about dilemmas of difference as they apply to education and specifically to the area of disability (special educational needs). The basic dilemma is whether to recognise and respond or not to recognise and respond to differences, as either way there are some negative implications or risks associated with stigma, devaluation, rejection or denial of relevant and quality opportunities. The specific notion of dilemmas of difference has its origins in socio-legal studies (Minow, 1985) about how difference or diversity is handled in the US legal system, but has applicability to other systems to the extent that they are committed to democratic and egalitarian values. As such, the notion has had a wide relevance to other aspects of diversity, such as gender and ethnicity as well as disability, and in areas of society, such as employment and housing as well as education. My interest in policy and practice dilemmas arose from within the field of special and inclusive education (Norwich, 1990) and led me to consider wider policy dilemmas of an ideological nature, what some have called ideological dilemmas (Billig *et al.*, 1988). Though there has been some work on the concept of dilemmas of difference in making sense of the special and inclusive educational policy and practice matters, this is the first book which focuses specifically on dilemmas of difference in a particular aspect of education on this scale.

What is novel about this book is its examination of theoretical ideas relevant to dilemmas of difference from philosophical, political, sociological, historical, psychological and educational perspectives. It will draw on theoretical perspectives in other areas of difference, to inform the development of theoretical perspectives to differences in educational terms. The book also contains a detailed analysis of a three country international study of perspectives to dilemmas of difference in the field of disability and learning difficulties in education that follows up an earlier two country study done just over ten years ago (Norwich, 1993b). Not only can some comparison be made between perspectives over this period of time, but this book-length account makes it possible to present these cross-disciplinary theoretical aspects and the recent three country study in considerably more detail and complexity than the earlier study. Both studies are based on an analysis which identifies dilemmas of difference or differentiation relevant to children with disabilities in three related areas: (i) identification (whether to identify children as having a disability/difficulty relevant to education or not); (ii) curriculum (whether to provide a common curriculum to all children or not); and (iii) placement or location (to what extent children with more severe difficulties/disabilities will learn in ordinary or general schools and classes or not). These three areas are central to the field of special and inclusive education and, as later chapters show, also have relevance to general educational policy and practice matters.

The purpose of this book is therefore to bring together disparate work that reflects on dilemmas of difference as they apply specifically to the field of disability in education. However, in doing so, it is also expected that this will have implications for the relevance of this framework to general education and other social policy areas in this and similar countries. It is clear that the stance of the book derives from my particular context – policy and practice in England and the United Kingdom. But, the focus is clearly to consider and analyse policy and practice experiences in other countries to see where there are similarities and differences. Differences can be related to historical, political and social contexts while similarities can be conceptualised in terms of what is shared as regards the field and common political and educational issues. Like other comparative studies, the cross-country stance opens up variations in conceptualisation, policy and practices that are not evident in an examination of the system in a single country.

The choice of the three countries, the USA, the Netherlands and England, was made partly for theoretical and partly pragmatic reasons. Through its civil rights traditions the USA has been one of the countries which first developed legislation to assure education provision for children with difficulties and disabilities. This can be seen to have had international influence on other Western-style countries and through its special cultural links particular influence on the UK system. This is why the USA was chosen for the earlier 1990s comparative study and was chosen again for the more recent one. Pijl and Meijer (1991) in their comparison of special education systems in Europe and America distinguish between three categories of systems: (i) two-track-oriented (separate special education and general education systems); (ii) one-track-oriented (strong efforts to avoid separate segregated systems); and (iii) continuum of provision-oriented (range of separate and inclusive systems). They identify the USA and United Kingdom as having continuum-oriented systems compared to the Netherlands as having a two-track system. The Netherlands was chosen in this study to represent a European country with a different political and educational tradition to the United Kingdom. The Netherlands special education system has been historically segregated though there have been recent political moves towards greater inclusion. Educationalists in the Netherlands with inclusion interests have also recently looked to the USA and United Kingdom for specific models of inclusive education policy and practice. Another reason for choosing the Netherlands was that this specific research involved in-depth interviewing of policy-makers, administrators and teachers and this was made possible because most Netherlands teachers and administrators are fluent in English.

Arriving at a dilemmatic framework

There has been a notable lack of interest in the analysis of educational matters from the perspective of dilemmas. Though the term 'dilemma' is often seen in educational policy, theory and research, this use is just as an alternative way of referring to problems or issues. In this kind of use the term 'dilemma' can be replaced by the term 'issue' or 'question' without any loss of meaning. But, the term 'dilemma' refers to something more specific, a situation when there is a choice between alternatives which are unfavourable. There have been few educationalists who have developed and used a dilemmatic framework in a systematic and analytic way. Others may have used the term and found it useful in a limited way but not developed its use nor connected the analysis with wider analyses of social and political values and systems.

It is the contrast between the value of this framework and its relative neglect by others in the special and inclusive education field that has prompted my continuing interest in it. Perhaps the dilemmas of difference or other kind of dilemmas, such as control versus autonomy, are regarded as resolved and therefore as false dilemmas. Alternatively a neglect of dilemmatic analysis may be because dilemmas do not have definitive solutions. Their resolution involves some balancing, perhaps some compromise and therefore some giving up or loss of valued principles or outcomes. As Isaiah Berlin has explained, in these situations there is some loss and the approach can be seen as undermining passionate commitment to policies and practices (Berlin, 1990). The dilemmatic framework accepts some inescapability of conflict and the necessity of tragic choice. Perhaps this is behind the occasional query about the validity of dilemmas. For example, Clough (2006) in his review of a previous book of mine about moderate learning difficulties, which used the dilemmatic framework, questioned whether assumptions about dilemmas of difference were testable. In this way he was casting doubt on the validity of these dilemmas. One of my personal reasons for writing this book has been to reaffirm with further evidence that assumptions about dilemmas of difference are testable and useful.

The trail that I have followed towards dilemmas of difference arose from my professional experience and practice as teacher, educationalist and professional psychologist. Special educational needs or special needs education in the United Kingdom in the 1980s was characterised by conflicting, oversimplified and polarised models and theoretical perspectives. By 1990 I felt that there was a need for an approach which went beyond the practical know-how texts or the critical ones that managed to focus mainly on negative aspects of current systems. This was an approach which aimed to 'present difficulties and dilemmas', which at the time implied a need to reappraise the special needs education system (Norwich, 1990). Sometimes solutions or useful ways forward could be identified, but sometimes there were hard choices and no easy solutions. In a subsequent analysis of whether the term 'special educational needs' had outlived its usefulness it seemed that the way to address hard choices was to find ways of resolving dilemmas about identifying children seen as having SEN or in need of special education (Norwich, 1993a). At that time I had not come across the notion of dilemmas of difference, as used by Minow (1985) in her socio-legal analyses of US legislation and court judgments. However, I had become familiar with Billig's notion of ideological dilemmas as applied to various social spheres, including teaching in primary classrooms (Billig *et al.*, 1988). These ideological dilemmas were about control versus autonomy and commonality versus differentiation and on the basis of this theoretical analysis I designed the 1993 international study of ideological dilemmas.

It was when I was interviewing teachers in the USA that I came across Minow's (1985) analysis of dilemmas of difference and saw the clear connection with what I had been developing. Although Minow's more substantial analysis in her 1990 book had already been published then (Minow, 1990), I did not find it till I started systematic searching for the recent study about 18 months ago. However, I had already started to see links between the kind of dilemmatic analysis that seemed to be relevant to the special needs and inclusive education field and the political analyses of Isaiah Berlin about the balancing of political values in finding resolutions to policy dilemmas (Berlin, 1990). My current position is one where dilemmas of difference, which are relevant to various aspects of human difference, can be seen as ideological dilemmas that arise in systems which are committed to egalitarian values and principles amongst other values and principles. This is where Robert Dahl's (1982) analysis of the dilemmas of plural democracy was relevant. The involvement of egalitarian values in these ideological dilemmas is also why the notion of progressive dilemmas is relevant

(Goodhart, 2004). Dilemmas of difference, which have particular relevance to the difference of disability or learning difficulties, is not the only dimension of difference relevant to education or special education. However, it is a key one and the one that is the focus of this book.

Organisation of the book

This book is organised into eight chapters. The second chapter sets out the background theoretical, policy and research considerations relevant to dilemmas of difference in relation to education, inclusion, disability and special educational needs. This starts with a presentation of Minow's analyses of dilemmas of difference from a legal studies perspective with a particular focus on her treatment of special education legislation and court judgments. There is also a critical discussion of her philosophical attempt to question several key assumptions that give rise to these dilemmas and her argument that questioning these assumptions resolves the dilemmas. The chapter then moves on to political analyses about conflicts of political values and how these have come to be identified as dilemmas of plural democracy (Dahl, 1982) and progressive dilemmas (Goodhart, 2004). The focus then turns to various tensions about inclusive education which set the scene for an account of how others have used a dilemmatic framework to make sense of educational questions. This leads into a discussion of dilemmas in special education with the chapter ending with a summary of the earlier 1993 USA–England comparative study of ideological dilemmas in special needs education.

The third chapter presents a brief overview of some of the key aspects of the systems of educational provision for students with difficulties and disabilities in the USA, the Netherlands and England. These accounts are based on available statistics and overviews of various aspects of the wider school system and the place of special education within these systems.

The fourth chapter sets out details about the specific aims design and carrying out of the study. It provides basic information about the participants and the settings and areas in which they worked. The specific methods used in generating the data and in analysing them are explained and justified. Some of the practical problems in carrying out the study and the ethical issues involved are also discussed.

Chapters 5, 6 and 7 focus in turn on each of the three dilemmas that are examined in this study: identification, curriculum and location. These chapters examine participants' perspectives across each of the three countries which enables cross-country similarities and differences to be identified. The organisation and coverage of each chapter is the same: an analysis of dilemma recognition and resolution ratings, an analysis of ratings by professional role and then a breakdown of the 1st and 2nd level themes used to explain recognition and resolution positions. These chapters also include direct excerpts from the interviews to illustrate how participants in each country explained their recognition and resolution positions.

It is in the final chapter, Chapter 8, that the findings in each country group will be related to the national policy and practice context. This will analyse the findings about the three dilemmas in each country in terms of policy and practice in that country, as presented in Chapter 3. How the current findings relate to what was found in the 1993 study will also be analysed and interpreted in terms of some possible continuities or changes over a decade in two of the countries, the USA and England. Chapter 8 also shows how the findings fit a dilemmatic framework. It is clear from this overview of the book that it is possible for readers to select specific parts or chapters depending on their interests. However, for an overview of how the different aspects fit together and an appreciation of the full evidence and argument, reading the book all through is needed.

Chapter 2

Thinking through dilemmas

> When does treating people differently emphasize their differences and stigmatise or hinder them on that basis? And when does treating people the same become insensitive to their difference and likely to stigmatise or hinder them on that basis?
>
> (Minow, 1990: p. 20)

Introduction

In this chapter I set the theoretical and research scene for an exploration of dilemmas of difference in this book. Ideas from various related disciplines are integrated into an account which starts with work in the legal studies field about dilemmas of difference which goes beyond the educational field. This perspective leads into a discussion of political ideas about political and values conflicts, what have come to be called progressive dilemmas, because they relate to dilemmas that arise from a commitment to egalitarian values. This focus on difference and diversity is pursued by a more specific focus on educational questions, in particular about tensions in inclusive education. From there the discussion picks up specific studies and theories about dilemmas in education generally and then goes on to dilemmas in special education. The final section deals directly with the study which I conducted in the early 1990s in terms of ideological dilemmas in special needs education (Norwich, 1993b).

It will become clear from this analysis that dilemmas are not just difficulties or issues, they represent a particular decision-oriented view about hard choices where options all have some unfavourable consequences. Different authors focus on different kinds of dilemmas. 'Dilemmas of plural democracy' (Dahl, 1982) connects with the commonality–differentiation tensions represented by Minow's 'dilemmas of difference' (Minow, 1985, 1990, 2005), but relates more centrally to dilemmas about control and autonomy. The notion of 'progressive dilemmas' (Goodhart, 2004) has closer links to Dahl's notions because of its wider focus than just difference or diversity. My use of 'ideological dilemmas' in the 1993 study drew on Billig's notion

(Billig *et al.*, 1988) and went wider than difference dilemmas. It will be argued that we can organise these dilemmas in terms of dilemmas of plural democracy that might also, in contemporary terms, be called progressive dilemmas. Amongst these progressive dilemmas are ones about control versus autonomy and commonality versus differentiation (relating to ethnicity, gender and disability, for instance). So, dilemmas of difference can be seen as a form of progressive dilemma and relate to various aspects of difference, including disability.

Dilemmas of difference: a legal studies perspective

Martha Minow in her 1990 book on dilemmas of difference notes the irony of the difference in policy-makers' approaches during the 1970s and 80s in the USA to special education for students with disabilities and students for whom English was not their first language. There was a move to at least part-time bilingual withdrawal programmes for students for whom English was not their first language, while for students with disabilities the move was towards mainstream classrooms and the 'least restrictive environment'. Her point is that despite this seeming difference there is an underlying similarity in these moves; in both areas, there was a struggle to deal with children who were seen as 'different' without stigmatising them or denying them relevant opportunities. From this perspective, the problems of inequality can be aggravated either by treating members of a minority as the same as the majority or by treating them as different. Put in other terms the dilemma of difference can be seen to reflect the choice between integration versus segregation, similar versus special treatment or neutrality versus accommodations. As a legal theorist, Minow's point is that dilemmas of difference go well beyond the areas of special and bilingual education. These questions of similar versus special treatment also apply to other areas of difference. For example, for religious differences, religiously observant students may request to use school time to engage in religious activities or students from certain religious backgrounds may seek to be exempt from certain courses which conflict with their religious beliefs. As regards gender differences, there is the question of when women's biological differences from men are used to justify special benefits in the workplace, such as maternity leave and whether this helps or harms them? Special benefits can be used to reinforce stereotypes that have been used to exclude women from jobs or hold them back in competition with men for promotion. Where legal rules have adopted a position of neutrality between men and women, as Minow argues, this supposed neutrality presents women with a situation where the workplace is designed for men. If they wish their needs to be taken into account, then they are requesting a departure from a legal position of neutrality.

Minow's analysis of the pervasiveness of the dilemmas of difference in the US context shows how these hard questions and choices are reflected in constitutional matters with respect to equal protection, due process and statutory interpretations of civil rights. She points out how these controversies extend beyond the legal sphere into the world of education, employment, housing etc.:

> These controversies enact the political dramas of a diverse society committed to equality and pluralism. I suggest that the dilemma of difference is not an accidental problem in this society. The dilemma of difference grows from the ways in which this society assigns individuals to categories and, on that basis, determines whom to exclude from political, social and economic activities.
>
> (Minow, 1990: p. 21)

Kennedy (1999) exemplifies Minow's analysis through a discussion of US history to illustrate the presence of dilemmas of difference in black–white conflicts. He argues that those who have benefited from racial oppression tended to ignore its consequences and assume that once formal discrimination ceased, all members would be on an equal footing. He compares the formal abandoning of apartheid in South Africa to the situation in the USA when the first civil rights legislation (later to become the Civil Rights Act of 1866) was vetoed by the then President, Andrew Johnson. Johnson's grounds for vetoing were that this kind of legislation was special legislation that would give black people discriminating protection that went beyond what was given to white people. Johnson, as Kennedy shows, minimised the impact of slavery by asserting that blacks and whites had equal power in their social and economic interactions. Johnson's reasoning is relevant to this discussion of dilemmas of differences because it shows the historical continuity and significance of the issues that are relevant to this set of dilemmas.

Minow's stance to the dilemma of difference is not only to point to the pervasiveness of the dilemma, but to the source of the dilemma in a way that will offer productive responses to challenge it. So, not only is difference recreated through colour or gender or disability blindness and in affirmative action, it can also be reflected in Government neutrality and Government preferences. In asking why dilemmas of difference appear unresolvable, she argues that as long as difference carries stigma it precludes equality:

> Difference is linked to stigma or deviance and sameness is a pre-requisite for equality. Perhaps these assumptions must be identified and assessed if we are to escape or transcend dilemmas of difference.
>
> (Minow, 1990: p. 50)

Minow then sets out five unstated assumptions as underlying the difference dilemma, that need to be made explicit and questioned from what she calls a relational perspective. In so doing she contends that other choices and responses to difference are made possible, so challenging or renovating the dilemmas.

Assumption 1: difference is intrinsic, not a comparison

This assumption responds to the question of who is different by claiming that it depends on discovering intrinsic features, in which people are neatly pigeon-holed into sharply drawn categories. She is critical of this view, that difference is based on some essential difference, preferring a relational model in which differences result from comparisons of similarities and differences. Historically, difference has been associated with social hierarchies of superiority–inferiority. This leads to the second assumption to be challenged.

Assumption 2: the norm need not be stated

According to Minow, when the comparisons are made they are often done in terms of unstated norms. It has been the case historically that these norms have been those of the more established and powerful members of society, for example, male, white and middle/upper class backgrounds. This connects with the next assumption, that of neutrality.

Assumption 3: the observer can see without a perspective

This assumption is that impartial observers can make unbiased judgements of these differences without the influence of social context. However, Minow is not proposing a strong version of subjectivity nor denouncing an aspiration to impartiality, but rather cautioning against simplistic assumptions of objectivity. Judgements of difference need to take into account that our interests and social contexts can influence what differences are perceived.

Assumption 4: other perspectives are irrelevant

If observations and judgements are assumed to be objective, then there is no need to take account of others' perspectives. One way of examining whether judgements are influenced by interests and contexts is to examine how others observe and judge issues. Others' perspectives will be seen as irrelevant if its assumed that those in charge adopt universal and superior perspectives.

Assumption 5: the status quo is natural, uncoerced and good

This assumption leads to several other positions that need to be questioned, according to Minow. For example, there is a difference between Government actions that change the status quo and those that maintain it by omission or failure. She uses the example of buildings that are not constructed for wheelchair access to argue that institutional arrangements, which are not simply neutral and natural, affect access.

In making these five assumptions explicit and then questioning them, she intends to show that the differences that lead to dilemmas arise from relationships in social contexts which are alterable. Her position is that this is the way to introduce new possibilities for change, but she does also recognise that making these assumptions explicit in specific cases and situations is more difficult than an abstract presentation of them. Here is an example of how she uses a case in the area of special education to illustrate her approach to the dilemma of difference.

The case was the first to come to the US Supreme Court under the Education for All Handicapped Children Act (1975), the precursor of the present Individuals with Disabilities Education Act (IDEA) legislation in the USA. It concerned Amy Rowley who had a profound hearing impairment that was developed before she learned language. She went to a publicly funded regular school that came under the Federal legislation that assured a 'free appropriate public education' for all 'handicapped children'. As part of her individual educational plan (IEP), her regular classroom experience was supplemented by teaching from a tutor for one hour a day and speech therapy three hours per week. Her parents objected that the plan did not give her what was 'appropriate', as she needed, according to them, a sign language interpreter in all her classes. The school response was that this was not needed as she was succeeding in all respects without this assistance. Though the Court judged that the State had complied with the required procedures and that the IEP had produced some educational benefits for Amy, Minow notes that the parents and the authorities, despite their other differences, agreed that the problem had been Amy's, because she was different from other children. In Minow's terms, both sides used the unstated norm of the hearing child, rather than considering another norm around which provision might be organised.

There was the possibility for Amy to go to a special school or class for hearing impaired children, as some advocated, which may have provided better social experiences and more sensitivity to individual needs. Such special provision would take the hearing impaired child as the norm and use sign language in class teaching. However, that option was not deemed acceptable given the Government's legislation that stipulated regular class provision to the maximum extent possible. Also, Amy had been shown to progress in a regular class, so segregated provision would not be acceptable. Minow notes that the litigation did not consider a third option which questioned the unstated assumption that the hearing child was the norm in terms of mode of teaching and accepted the use of oral communication teaching methods as a given. By questioning this assumption she suggests that the teacher teach her class in both sign language and oral language. In adopting this stance, the problem becomes one for the whole class and not just for Amy, so that the hearing children could also learn sign language and use this to communicate with Amy.

It is clear that this approach does address the dilemma of difference in Amy's situation. The dilemma applied to Amy might go like this: If Amy is taught via oral communication methods and with minimal use of signing in a regular class setting, then she will not have the same experiences as other children. But, if she is taught full time by signing methods through an interpreter, she would be isolated from her peers and perhaps marked out as different in a negative way. This can be seen as a tension between relevant learning experiences versus isolation and stigma, a case of inclusion versus exclusion within a regular class setting. However, Minow's proposed resolution of changing the teaching mode norm to include both oral and signing methods and to have the hearing children fluent in sign language, though promising educational and wider social benefit terms for all, has practical requirements which need to be addressed. Minow does not address these practical questions, even though the initial Supreme Court case was partly over whether the school should provide a full-time signing interpreter, which is a practical question. If it is challenging to have a full-time sign interpreter for Amy, it would be even more complex and costly to have the regular class teacher also fluent in signing for teaching purposes and all the hearing children able to use signing for social communication purposes. In considering these options in greater detail, it is clear that more questions and issues are raised than the simple switching of the norm of teaching mode to be inclusive of an hearing impaired child.

Minow's social constructionist or social relations turn, does open up promising ways of approaching dilemmas of difference. However, tensions seem to persist, though perhaps less sharply. It is notable that in her afterword to the 1990 book, she recognises that her approach only goes so far, as she talks about the dilemma becoming 'less paralysing' (p. 375) if we try to look at the issues from another point of view. She argues that it is possible to 'replace a norm that excludes with a norm that includes' (p. 377), but then admits that the 'resolution is not a solution, but a shift in assumptions' (p. 383). There is also some recognition by her that there are continuing tensions associated with 'difference' in her approach to the political philosophical basis in the argument. She wishes to defend both a liberal rights and relational strategy in her framework, and does not see this as contradictory as she rejects either/or solutions. Her commitment is to combining different approaches and seeing how a relational strategy can contribute to enhancing the traditional rights-based analysis. By concluding in this way, Minow can be interpreted as adopting a position similar to some political philosophies that recognise the interplay and tensions that exist between different values.

Political and value conflict: progressive dilemmas

We would expect the tensions implicit in dilemmas of difference to be reflected in political analyses around the questions of democracy and equality. In this section I show how this dilemma about difference or diversity is connected to analyses from a different disciplinary background. One way into this is to consider the analysis undertaken by Dahl (1982) of what he calls the dilemmas of pluralist democracy. He argues that in a plural democracy, individuals and organisations (which he treats as interchangeable for his argument) ought to have some autonomy, but at the same time also be controlled, as they have the potential to increase injustice, to foster egoism and even weaken democracy. This is the basic problem in democracy of any scale, as he argues, leading to fundamental dilemmas in plural democracies. Dahl identifies six forms of this dilemma:

i   Rights versus utility: are solutions to be judged in terms of utilitarian grounds (for example, happiness, well-being, satisfaction of wants, etc.) or in terms of rights that are independent of utility?

ii   A more exclusive versus more inclusive demos: no demos has ever included all human beings, every demos is exclusive to some extent. So the question becomes why this demos rather than another. This is an often ignored and embarrassing question which is usually answered in practice in terms affiliations and attachments and sometimes with a hidden utilitarian assumption that some demoses lead to greater well-being, for example.

iii Equality among individuals versus equality among organisations: in terms of equality of voting, there are issues concerned with whether this applies to individuals or to organisations. The principle of equality of individual voting is violated if organisations (provinces, states, units, etc.) are granted equal votes. Unless there are equal numbers of individuals in units granted equal votes, voting equality for units/organisations means inequality among citizens.

iv   Uniformity versus diversity: diversity is to be protected in democracies as good in itself and for its results. It can be justified on rights and utilitarian grounds. It is an easy and appealing position. Uniformity may have negative connotations and may be better referred to as commonality. Though it may still seem to be less appealing than diversity, commonality is also desirable because all differences are not matters either of rights nor do all have good consequences.

v   Centralisation versus decentralisation: though this dilemma is not the same as the previous one, uniformity often requires some centralisation and diversity assumes some decentralisation. This dilemma is over the location of controls, but also has implications for communications between units in an organisation. Decentralisation can reduce lines of communication and jamming in the centre, but it may prevent an over-view of the system from developing as each unit decides without aware-ness of what is going on elsewhere.

vi Concentration versus dispersal of power and political resources: this dilemma has links to the previous two dilemmas as diversity, decentrali-sation and dispersal often go together. Dahl suggests that this last dilemma may seem lopsided in the USA where there is such a commit-ment to the programme of classical liberalism. However, even in the USA liberalism conceded some of its commitment to dispersal in the development of progressive liberalism. Dahl shows that when uniform application of a policy is desirable and it cannot be attained without some centralisation, some concentration of power and resources is required.

The tensions implicit in the dilemmas of difference, as analysed by Minow, can be seen as part of wider political dilemmas about plural democ-racy. What Dahl refers to as uniformity versus diversity might better be phrased as the tension between commonality and difference. Dahl does not take the dilemmas that he outlines as any justification for inaction, but as 'considerations to be taken into account in clarifying alternatives before us' (p. 107). But what he does not focus on are the implications and losses asso-ciated with his dilemmatic views. This is where the political analyses of Isaiah Berlin are relevant as they acknowledge the agonising over alterna-tives in value dilemmas (Berlin, 1990). Berlin's position is that not all human values either now or in the past are necessarily compatible with each other. For him this means that there are no final solutions where tensions and conflicts are resolved once and for all:

> The notion of the perfect whole, the ultimate solution, in which all good things coexist, seems to be not merely unattainable – that is a truism – but conceptually incoherent; I do not know what is meant by harmony of this kind. Some of the Great goods cannot live together. That is a conceptual truth. We are doomed to choose, and every choice may entail an irreparable loss.
>
> (p. 13)

Berlin's insistence on being critical of those who deny the 'collision of values' and who continue to hold out the prospect of the removal of these contradictions in some future perfect world is one that he dismisses in these terms:

Happy are those who live under a discipline which they accept without question, who freely obey the orders of leaders, spiritual and temporal, whose word is fully acceptable as unbreakable law; or those who have, by their own methods, arrived at clear and unshakeable convictions about what to do and what to be brooks no possible doubt. I can only say that those who rest on such comfortable beds of dogma are victims of forms of self-induced myopia, blinkers that may make for contentment, but not for understanding of what it is to be human.

(pp. 13–14)

Berlin's recognition of social and political collisions that arise from the conflict of positive values has relevance to the considerations of this book overall in his recognition of the tensions that can arise from pursuing liberty and equality. Liberty for the powerful can threaten the 'right to a decent existence for the weak and less gifted' (p. 12). This resembles the tensions between autonomy and control described above, as analysed by Dahl (1982). Berlin's responses to these tensions is to advocate 'trade-offs' in which 'rules, values and principles must yield to each other in varying degrees in specific situations' (p. 17):

They [these conflicts] can be minimised by promoting and preserving an uneasy equilibrium which is constantly threatened and in constant need of repair – that alone, I repeat, is the precondition of decent societies and morally acceptable behaviour, otherwise we are bound to lose our way.

(p. 19)

Not only is Berlin's position one that recognises that these value conflicts can be experienced as agonising, but it accepts that resolutions involve balancing, lead to uneasy balances and that there is some loss involved in the process. However, Berlin acknowledges that this approach might be seen as 'dull' and 'not the stuff of which calls to heroic action by inspired leaders are made' (p. 19). It is notable that Berlin does not analyse the implications of what has to be given up in this approach for its appeal and adoption. As Ignatieff (1998) commented, in his biography of Berlin, this was a statement of the inescapability of moral conflict and the necessity of tragic choice. Berlin was by no means the first to consider pluralism, but his assertion that pluralism entailed liberalism was original. However, there has been criticism of his argument that if there is disagreement about basic values, a liberal system would enable the adjudication and compromises between these values. As Gray (1989) has argued, giving liberty priority is inconsistent with pluralism and contradicts Berlin's argument that 'equality may demand the restraint of liberty' (Berlin, 1990, p. 12).

How these different values interact and play out is a key issue in the contemporary world both for values within Western societies and for the interaction of different religious and secular world views internationally. The relevance of value conflicts to understanding contemporary political and social issues has been evident in the theme of progressive dilemmas which has been discussed recently by Goodhart (2004). His analysis has focused on the tensions between diversity and solidarity, involving particular aspects of diversities (ethnic and religious), rather than others (gender and disability), that pose dilemmas for Western-style democracies in the context of globalisation and mass immigration. These dilemmas are seen as progressive because they arise for those who support progressive political positions. Goodhart's position is that a conflict between sharing/solidarity and diversity can arise because people have come not only to live amongst strangers more than before, but are expected to share with them. The tensions are seen to arise from progressive support for greater diversity, which can undermine a consensus on which welfare states rest. This dilemma assumes that there is a historic clash over the basis for the mutual obligations necessary in society: whether in terms of local groups and communities with shared values and histories or whether in terms of universal liberal principles which extend obligations beyond the group, community and nation. Goodhart's argument is that if the universality position denies that humans are group based with some constraints of their willingness to share, then various policies become hard to defend. For example, national expenditure on health would be at similar levels to overseas development aid and no immigration controls would be justifiable.

Goodhart's analysis, like Berlin's, places the tensions in a historical context and suggests that modern societies have found ways of accommodating these tensions. For example, modern ideas of citizenship do not have an ethnic basis, but are grounded on legal, political and social rights and duties. So even if policy and politics is about negotiating this tension:

> the logic of solidarity, with its tendency to draw boundaries, and the logic of diversity, with its tendency to cross boundaries, do at times pull apart.
>
> (Goodhart, 2004: p. 32)

Analyses of plural and conflicting values

In focusing on questions about value conflicts and dilemmas, attention is drawn to the nature of these value conflicts. One question which philosophers of ethics have analysed, relevant to social and political conflicts, is whether it can be obligatory to do something even though it is wrong and shameful? This is sometimes called the question of 'dirty hands' and can be found in situations, such as: Can it be justified to torture someone to reveal information which will save innocent life? Stocker (1990) has argued that despite a widespread view that there are conceptual difficulties with this kind of situation (some have even identified 'dirty hands' as contradictory), it is possible to show that these situations are unproblematic conceptually. Stocker assumes that 'dirty hands' situations are situations of conflicts between what is justified/obligatory and what is wrong. Some may call these conflicts dilemmas, but he prefers the term dilemma for situations when options are all wrong.

A problem that arises from recognising value conflicts is that either one rejects the possibility of conflicts, which implies that ethics is irrelevant and impractical, or accepts that there are conflicts, which implies that ethics is incomplete. Stocker rejects these options because they assume that all evaluations have direct implications for guiding actions. His analysis is that some evaluations do not guide actions, which presents a third option. He gives the example of a conflict experienced by a university teacher about teaching a programme to students who are not adequately prepared to or ready to understand. The teacher may come to the decision that she/he has to suspend teaching this course and focus on a remedial programme to enable the students to become ready for the initial course. In doing so s/he may be quite clear that this is the right way to proceed, but still regret and be angry about having to do this. These emotions will give rise to evaluations and conflict over this way of proceeding. For Stocker these evaluations of the action are not ones that guide actions. Conflicts in his analysis involve tensions between evaluations that guide an act with evaluations that do not directly guide an act.

His analysis of conflicts can be applied more closely to educational situations that involve children with special educational needs/disabilities. Imagine, for example, a primary teacher has been teaching a class where there is a boy who has presented serious challenging behaviours with adults and peers over a period of two years. After trying many in-class interventions based on the support of specialists in behaviour problems, the teacher comes to consider the option of having the boy spend half of his classroom time in a separate unit in the school. The teacher may judge that it is the right action for him to spend time in the unit, despite all the effort to engage him and adapt an ordinary class setting, because he will be in a setting where (i) adaptations can be more geared to his social–emotional needs, (ii) he has more prospect of cognitive learning, (iii) others in the class will be less disrupted by incidents, and (iv) others will have attention from the teacher they did not have before. These reasons relate to the boy's needs as well as those of his ordinary class peers. Although the teacher may evaluate this course of action as right, he may regret the actions, feel defeated and upset that the boy may feel rejected by this move and worry about the appropriateness of the provision in the unit and the boy's future prospects. In Stocker's scheme these concerns will lead to negative evaluations about the placement, but these evaluations do not guide or affect the placement decision. This kind of example, according to Stocker, shows that it is possible to give an account about the nature of conflicts that is based on a complete and realistic system of values. Stocker's position is quite straightforward, that values are just plural and that if this poses some difficulties for sound judgements, then these just have to be faced. Plural values are also, he argues, the rule and pervasive in everyday life.

Tensions in inclusive schooling

In some current analyses about inclusion in education there is a recognition of tensions that link with the above themes about equality and difference. For example, Campbell *et al.* (2002) identify a tension between:

> a perception of an 'inclusive school' as meeting the needs of all children in a similar manner and the need to develop differential practices relating to different forms of inclusionary and exclusionary pressures, for example linked to social disadvantage or identified special educational needs.
>
> (p. 150)

Though there are some references to same versus difference tensions, like the above quote, these are not analysed in much detail, nor do they feature as frequently as references in the literature to the tensions between the promotion of inclusion and the drive for standards through market strategies (e.g. Florian and Rouse, 2001 for the United Kingdom and the USA, Thomas and Loxley, 2001, for the United Kingdom, and Hursh, 2005 for the USA). Much of the literature about inclusion, particularly in the United Kingdom goes no further than recognise the differences in perspectives about inclusion. This diversity is recognised by Clough and Corbett (2000), for example, in their statement that 'there is finally no enduring version which pervades the history of inclusive education' (p. 6). Dyson (2000) also talks about inclusions and not inclusion. Cole (2005) along similar lines, argues that though inclusion is hard to define, the focus should not be on what inclusion means, but rather on the meanings of inclusion. The meanings of inclusion clearly need to be understood in their diversity, but it is evident that none of these authors go on to examine the possible tensions between these different conceptions, nor how these tensions might be resolved.

The notion of inclusive education has many conceptual and value threads that need to be identified. It is a term that owes its force partly to it replacing the term integration. Though many practitioners might see the terms as interchangeable, many of the proponents attach considerable conceptual and value significance to the notion of inclusion. This is partly because inclusion has been constructed to have a more embracing and universalist meaning; it does not set boundaries between different areas of 'vulnerability'. So integration is said to be about those with special educational needs or disabilities, but inclusion goes beyond to reference others who experience social exclusion, for example, including those from socioeconomically disadvantaged backgrounds and ethnic minorities. Inclusion is also said to have a more systemic and social meaning, in that it is about restructuring ordinary or regular schools to have the capacity to accommodate all children. Integration is seen to be more about placing the individual child in a system which assimilates the child without adapting itself to accommodate the child. So, inclusion is described as being about participation, not just placement or location. As argued in Norwich and Kelly (2004), a distinction between inclusion and integration does not justify detaching the concepts from each other and treating integration in a negative way. In the United Kingdom, when integration was used in the 1980s, it referred not just to the placement or location of children, but to social and functional aspects of bringing children with and without special educational needs together. Strongly connected with functional integration was the notion of whole school policies and practices, in which schools would restructure in order to accommodate children (Thomas and Feiler, 1988). It is notable that authors who supported whole school policies then, came to support inclusive education more recently (Thomas and Loxley, 2001).

Not only is there continuity and connection between integration and inclusion, but the construction of inclusion as a universal concept representing a 'pure' value, that accepts no degrees, conditions or limits, leads to a conceptual dead end. Recognising the diversity of interpretations of inclusive education is one step, but if these interpretations are incompatible, then a response is required. Campbell (2002) not only recognises that inclusion lacks clarity, but that its complexity leads to confusion. She identifies, following Lunt and Norwich (1999), that inclusive schooling can refer to (i) a recognition of individual needs, (ii) a recognition of individual achievement, (iii) an appreciation of diversity (as normal and positive), (iv) the physical location of children in schools, (v) the educational experience of children, and (vi) the emotional well-being and social interaction of children. Campbell also recognises that associated with these different aspects of 'inclusion' are some debates about what is implied by inclusion:

a   What is the balance between individual needs and the needs of the majority?
b   How far inclusion is about the active participation of children and to what extent is it about inclusion as 'done to' children?
c   Is inclusion a state of affairs or an on-going process?
d   How is inclusion related to exclusion?

(Campbell, 2002: p. 13)

It is evident from the above analysis that as regards children with special educational needs or disabilities, there is a key question about whether a commitment to inclusive education means what has been called 'full inclusion'? Does inclusion mean that children with severe and complex difficulties are not educated in separate classes, units or special schools (Kaufman and Hallahan, 1995)? Another issue that arises from the complexity of terms is that there is also little clarity about what participation refers to in attempts to define inclusive education in participatory terms (Booth *et al.*, 2000). Is it participation in the 'cultures, curricula and communities of local schools' (Booth *et al.*, 2000, p. 12), is it in ordinary or regular classrooms or does it just mean participation in the education system (Warnock, 2005)?

Part of what has been called a 'purist' version of inclusion is that inclusion is about children's rights and involves a move away from the language of needs (Thomas and Loxley, 2001). But, as with other versions of inclusion, this is an incomplete position, as the connections with rights and social justice raises as many issues as it answers. Though the Salamanca Statement about inclusive education (UNESCO, 1994) makes strong recommendations about inclusive schooling, it only asserts a fundamental right to education, not to an inclusive education. Given the different aspects of inclusive education, as outlined above, it can be argued that children may have several, conflicting rights and there is scope for disagreement about which should take priority. For example, Lunt and Norwich (1999) distinguished between:

i   a right to participate in an ordinary school
ii   a right to acceptance and respect
iii a right to individually relevant learning
iv   a right to engage in common learning opportunities
v   a right to active involvement and choice in the matter.

A further distinction can be added to this list – a right to participate not just in an ordinary school, but in an ordinary classroom. For example, a right to individually relevant learning may not always be compatible with a right to participate in an ordinary classroom. Put in this way it is possible to see the links between rights issues and conceptual questions about what is involved in participation, as discussed above. For example, if inclusion means participating in the same learning programmes in the same location and being accepted and respected there, then *any* separate provision, say, in a part-time withdrawal setting, could be considered exclusionary, whether or not it provides opportunities to engage in common or relevant learning for an individual child.

Not only does the above analysis indicate that seeking clarity about inclusive education through reference to human rights perpetuates the problems, so does the quest to anchor inclusive education in notions of justice without a well-formulated conception of social justice. The diversity of interpretations and positions about inclusive education are reproduced in different conceptions about justice in educational studies (Gewirtz, 2002). This would be expected in light of the analyses and discussions about political values and democracy in the early sections of this chapter. Gewirtz distinguishes between distributional and relational justice. The former refers to how goods are distributed in society and the latter to the nature of relationships between individuals and groups within society. Distributional questions are central to political analyses about equality of opportunity, equality of outcomes and equity as a fair distribution. Some aspects of these will be touched on later in this chapter in the discussion about Sen's political philosophy, which takes a position about equality of capabilities as it relates to dilemmas of difference (Sen, 1992). For Gewirtz, relational justice is linked to 'justice as recognition', which is about the recognition of differences between groups and individual in terms of various identities. In arguing for the importance of both aspects of justice, Gewirtz notes that the distributional aspect is individualistic in its focus on what individuals are due, while the relational aspect is more holistic and social with its focus on the inter-connections between individuals and groups; it is about solidarity. This is a useful distinction, partly because it reminds us that there is both an individualistic and a social solidarity or community aspect to ideas about inclusive education.

Inclusive education is often justified in terms of promoting an inclusive society and at least a society which aims to reduce social exclusion. The introduction of the terms inclusive education and schooling in the early 1990s coincided with wider international and particularly European interest in social exclusion. The replacement of the term integration and its assumed limitations may stem from the wider social and policy analysis of that time. Social exclusion like other related terms has been multi-faceted, covering the distribution of goods, such as financial resources, knowledge and skills, as well as relational aspects, such as recognition, respect, care and social inter-connections. How far inclusive schooling can go in promoting a socially inclusive society goes back to questions about whether schools can compensate for society (Bernstein, 1970). What the brief analysis in this section has shown is that though ideas and values within education about inclusion have been elaborated and developed over the last two decades, they raise questions about the nature of differences, human rights and a just and fair society. But, there have been relatively few analyses which recognise some of the basic tensions which underlie the complexity of the issues confronted. Some of these are discussed in the next section.

Dilemmas in education

In this section I discuss some attempts to understand diverse issues within education in terms of dilemmas and their resolutions, before moving on to a discussion of dilemmas in special education. Judge (1981) in an analysis of education identified five dilemmas surrounding the purposes of schooling. He defended the idea that 'our purposes are conflicting, contradictory and largely unexamined' (p. 111). Judge also makes the point, made in the introductory chapter of this book, that the term dilemma can sometimes be used as a way of talking about a difficulty or an issue. However, he means something more specific than this, as a situation when there is choice between alternatives when neither is favourable. His dilemmas are:

1   Utility versus culture – where utility is about individual and collective economic prosperity, and culture refers to individual and fulfilment and social harmony.
2   Fair selection versus comprehensiveness and universality in school examinations – though designed to support fairness and efficiency in selection when favour and influence ruled in selection decisions, the systems once generalised across a population risks alienating those who do not succeed at them.
3   Common versus diverse school curriculum – the common curriculum relates to ideas about equal provision, opportunity and the support for community, whereas diversity relates to optional programmes that follow interests and provides a counter to imposed curricula.
4   Management versus autonomy – this is about the division of power between central and local government, between local government and schools and within schools between professionals and users of education services – parents, employers and community.
5   Function versus profession as regards teachers' roles – this relates to the above dilemma in that employers represent the management focus on defining minimum functions, while teachers seek autonomy to pursue their ideas about professionalism, with the risks of becoming narrow in their interests.

What is relevant about Judge's analysis, although it is more than 25 years old, is that he adopts a line of argument that resembles later dilemmatic views – that tensions need to be addressed, not avoided, that they need to be thought through and that the form the tension takes reflects historical factors. He argues that it is healthy to recognise contradictions and that:

> because choices cannot, of course, be absolute, I have tried to present them in terms of 'dilemmas' and to argue in each of the five cases, that we could if we chose adjust the balance in the respect which we accord to pairs of opposing principles and that if we did, there would be consequences in policy and action
>
> (Judge, 1981: p. 115)

The other point to note about Judge's analysis is that his dilemmas map closely to Dahl's dilemmas of plural democracy. Though Judge does not refer to these political analyses, this is an example of where major themes come to be represented in different disciplines.

At about the same time as Judge's analysis, Berlak and Berlak (1981) wrote a book about dilemmas of schooling which used the same language and assumptions. Here were two Americans, from St Louis, Missouri, who developed an analysis of everyday primary teaching issues from a study of British primary schools. Their aim was to represent the process of classroom teaching and learning in terms of a number of dilemmas and their resolutions. These authors came to the United Kingdom at the time of US interest in open education to find out how the British system of informal primary schools worked and what lessons it had for developments in the USA. What they found was that their experiences of the UK primary schools did not correspond with the literature about informal and open educational practices. Their difficulty in finding a way to represent the complexity of what they experienced led them to use the language of dilemmas. Their study is a demonstration of how three sets of dilemmas help to make sense of the context, issues and processes of teaching that they observed while in the United Kingdom. They identified 16 distinct dilemmas that they organised into three broad sets, in terms of (i) control, (ii) curriculum and (iii) societal themes. Below are examples from each broad set of dilemmas:

Control set

Teacher versus child control (standards) – this relates to whether the teacher sets the standard by which work is assessed and monitors and maintains that standard or whether the child sets the standard.

Curriculum set

Each child unique versus children have shared characteristics – this relates to the assumption about organising learning activities, whether children share characteristics and be taught in mainly similar ways with some variations, say in pace and standards, or whether they are unique and needing a unique pattern of activities.

Societal set

Equal versus differential allocation of resources – this relates to the distribution of resources, whether an equal allocation because this is fair versus differential allocation, as some start with disadvantages and equal allocations preserve inequalities.

These teaching dilemmas differ from Judge's set which relate to a systemic level.

However, both sets identify control dilemmas, though one with a systemic focus and the other a teaching focus. The Berlaks' analysis is interesting theoretically as it provides a dialectical account of teacher action based on the symbolic interactionism of Mead (1934). They argue that a dilemmatic approach can represent the thought and action of teachers as the ongoing dynamic of behaviour and consciousness in an educational context. Their view is that dilemmas imply a focus on acts and their consequences. They connect this to Mead's concept of a person as a conscious being who is both an object who is acted upon, and a subject, as an initiator of actions. Where these authors contribute to Meadian theory relates to his analysis of the 'I', the 'Me' and the 'generalised other'. The 'I' represents the initiating active agent, the 'Me', the view of oneself as an object in the environment, which is developed from others' perspectives. These other perspectives can become generalised into the 'generalised other' from which the person internalises generalised perspectives, values and norms. The Berlaks argue that the 'generalised other' need not involve shared and common perspectives and values, but may also involve perspectives and values that conflict. This means that the person may internalise generalised perspectives and values that are in tension. The dilemmas that they identify are therefore seen to represent contradictions which reside in the individual, the situation and the wider society.

This Meadian approach to dilemmas in education has similarities to a more recent social psychological attempt to understand everyday thinking, including that of teachers, in terms of ideological dilemmas (Billig *et al.*, 1988). Billig's approach resembles the Berlaks' in that he also rejects the sociological view that individuals are simply shaped by ideology, the view that individuals bear the received ideological tradition and act unthinkingly. Billig assumes that individuals are not only acted on, but also think and initiate actions. They think about ideological matters which involve basic values, and this includes considering the contrary and conflicting aspects of this thinking. Billig's view is that formalised ideologies are positions which are extracted from an argumentative dialogue about education (or some other social practice). Each ideology is therefore not a separate self-contained conception, but is formulated in response and contradiction to other positions which are part of the same scheme of discourse. So, these different positions, while being part of an argumentative dialogue, are not as mutually exclusive of each other as their self-contained and purist formulations might suggest. Billig illustrates his position by considering how and what teachers think in practice. He drew on the work of Edwards and Mercer (1987), which explored the thinking and practice of 'progressive' primary school teachers. This study showed that teachers tended to draw on elements of the opposing ideologies, at times from a discourse of exploratory and experiential learning, and at others, from a discourse which attributed failure to innate, personal and social factors, not to inappropriate teaching and learning conditions. The point that Billig draws from this work is that there are no clear-cut distinctions to be drawn from alternative educational ideologies. There are dilemmas about how to 'bring out' of learners what is not there to begin with, and how to ensure that they 'discover' what they are meant to.

Burbules (1997) is another author who has examined some dilemmas that accompany discussions of difference in education. His approach is philosophical, descriptive and critical of the variety of ways in which difference has been debated in educational circles. He suggests that there are tensions about difference, in his recognition that 'difference in these senses seems to be both an opportunity and a problem' (p. 2), but does not elaborate on the dilemmatic aspects. He identifies 'a tension between sameness and diversity' in education theory and practice in these terms:

> On one hand a desire to use education to make people more alike (whether this is in regards to a 'melting pot' of citizenship values and beliefs, the essential texts of 'cultural literacy', the factual knowledge and skills that can be measured by standardised tests, or the establishment of uniform national standards across the curriculum), and on the other hand, a desire to seek the different learning styles and needs, the different cultural orientations and the different aspirations toward work and living represented by the diverse populations of students in public schools.
>
> (p. 2)

Though he recognises these tensions, he restricts his analysis to an elucidation of how difference is used as a term, not to the key question of resolutions. His starting point is that 'difference' has emerged in current thinking because of the political trend for groups to argue for their distinctiveness, linked to the politics of identity, and from a post-modern suspicion of generalities and unifying themes.

Raveaud (2005) has recently undertaken a study of differentiation in classrooms for children aged 4–7 years in English and French primary schools. Though the study was not formulated in terms of dilemmas of difference, its focus on differentiation and its cross-country comparison are relevant to this discussion of dilemmas of difference in education. The study showed that there was systematic ability grouping and differentiation by task in English classrooms compared to an equal entitlement approach in the French classrooms, a difference which was related to ideological commitments in the two countries. There has been an attachment in France to the republican ideals of offering all children equal opportunities and integration into French society. In England there has been a more diverse set of historic ideals, amongst which there have been progressive child-centred ideals. Though Raveaud is cautious about generalising from this small sample, the analysis of differentiation at this stage of schooling reflects the social and historic context of schooling. The core educational values in France are republican ideals about emancipation and social justice, while in England the core values are more about developing the potential of each child's happiness and balance. Mixed ability is dealt with in French classes by varying the means of learning (time and teacher and peer support), while in England differentiation is practised by varying tasks. Differentiation by task is seen as a last resort in France, especially for those with exceptional needs. The concept of the pupil in France is of a social being entitled to equal expectations with peers, while in England the pupil is to be a happy well-balanced child with their full potential to be realised. The source of self-esteem in France is, therefore, about being included in a common curriculum, while in England, it is from individual success at tasks. The French see the English differentiated approach at this stage of schooling as perpetuating social inequalities, while the English see French universalism as lacking in respect for individual needs and self-esteem, presenting little challenge for the very able and excessive demands for the less able. It is interesting that Raveaud notes that there is:

> a profound dilemma here, which is not often made explicit, between a genuine concern to protect self esteem and avoid disaffection, on one hand, and a reification of initial academic differences due to social and cultural background.

> (p. 474)

Raveaud does not relate this dilemma to the dilemmas of difference, but it is clear that what she has identified can be seen as an instance of such dilemmas.

Dilemmas in special education

Artiles has been someone who has drawn attention in the USA to a silence about other dimensions of difference within special educational research circles (Artiles, 2000). Over a 20-year period ending in the mid-1990s he found only 3 per cent of published research in peer reviewed journals examined data across ethnic and social class lines. In doing so, he has drawn on Minow's notion of a dilemma of difference (Artiles, 1998) and has also highlighted a point she made in Minow (1990) about the contrary responses to ethnic and linguistic differences. For ethnic minorities school segregation was deemed unfair, whereas linguistic minorities fought initially for differential treatment in the form of bilingual education programmes. Artiles also draws on Minow's response to the dilemmas of difference in terms of her five assumptions about difference that need to be questioned. He asserts that her approach will make it possible to 'transcend the traditional dilemmas of difference' (Artiles, 1998: p. 17). But, there is no explanation of how this would work and how far this would go in resolving these dilemmas of difference. This is a fairly uncritical reading of dilemmas of difference and their resolution.

From a UK perspective, Dyson has also used a dilemmatic perspective to make sense of special education policy and practice historically (Dyson and Millward, 2000; Dyson, 2001). Drawing on Norwich (1994) and Artiles (1998) he identifies a basic contradiction within liberal democracies:

> between an intention to treat all learners as essentially the same and an
> equal and opposite intention to treat them as different.
>
> (Dyson, 2001: p. 25)

Dyson sees these dilemmas as going beyond the field of special education in his recognition that it is in special education that these tensions have been historically most acute. Dyson sees the dilemmatic perspective as providing an approach to the history of the field of special education that is neither a 'story of uninterrupted progress, nor of a doomed struggle against over-whelming odds' (p. 25). Policy and practice is therefore seen as the attempted resolutions to these dilemmas, which can turn out to be unstable. Past resolutions are different from current and future ones, though the basic tensions remain.

Dyson's use of the dilemma of difference is interesting because of its focus on a historical perspective and the way he traces recent historical developments over the last quarter century in the United Kingdom. He identifies resolutions that emphasise commonality as having become domi-nant, perhaps because of their adoption by Governments, as then leading to backlashes that emphasise difference. However, there may be some doubt about whether this is an accurate historical account. Government and other organisations may promote commonality resolutions, but still see limits to these resolutions. For example, the Government's Green Paper in England (DfEE, 1997), while promoting more inclusive schools, did recognise a future for some special schools. Other organisations may promote common-ality resolutions but not be clear about any limits. Resolutions to dilemmas like these differ in the extent to which those proposing and enacting them see them as definitive solutions or as resolutions that contain some elements of other less favoured options. As resolutions are applied in practice and depending on their outcomes, they may be evaluated more or less favour-ably, leading to different resolutions. What Dyson does not deal with in his analysis of historical trends in terms of the dilemmas of difference is this distinction between solutions and resolutions.

This is where the work of Croll and Moses (2000) in England is relevant to thinking about tensions and dilemmas in special educational needs and inclusion. Based on a study of professional and administrators' views about inclusion, they focus on the divergence between expressions of support for the principle of inclusion and the continuing level of support for separate school provision. They found widespread support for inclusion as an educational ideal amongst those more directly involved in special education, on one hand, but what they call a 'pragmatic' view, on the other. By 'pragmatic' they meant that these professionals put an emphasis on practical solutions and on serving the individual needs of children with available resources. These authors also found clear expression of the educational ideal of individual care in the views of their respondents. This is an interesting study from several perspectives. First, its focus on professional views and the tensions revealed in these views has similarities to the earlier study of dilemmas (Norwich, 1993b). Second, though Croll and Moses make no reference to dilemmas of difference, their findings can be interpreted in these terms. Third, they do interpret their findings in terms of contemporary ideas about utopian thinking and the social and personal functions of such thinking.

They draw on Giddens's idea about 'utopian realism' (Giddens, 1994), which refers to a political proposal that has some utopian features but also corresponds to some observable trends. Croll and Moses see aspects of utopian realism in the inclusion views of their respondents. They also draw on Levitas's work where she distinguishes between hope and desire in utopian thinking (Levitas, 1990). Levitas argues that utopian ideals may be accompanied by hope that the idea may become a reality, but that the essential aspect of such thinking is the desire for a better world. In their interviews Croll and Moses found that many respondents desire an inclusive school system, but did not see it as realisable; they desired it but did not hope for it. However, there were some people, in their sample, a minority, who not only desired but also hoped for this inclusive ideal. When social ideals are called utopian, they are often being dismissed as unrealistic or at worse as dangerous (Levitas, 1990). Usually the mistrust of utopian ideals is over the methods that could be used to promote these ideals, where the ends are seen to justify the means. These fears relate to the promotion of totalitarian systems and the use of violence to pursue and maintain these systems. This point relates back to the discussion of plural values at the start of this chapter, and specifically the views of Isaiah Berlin, who criticises views that deny the potential conflict between values and those who are comfortable on the 'beds of dogma'. From the perspective of plural social values, totalitarian systems are those that deny potential conflicts of value as expressed in dilemmas, like dilemmas of difference.

This kind of critique of totalitarian systems might seem out of place and over-argued in terms of inclusive education ideals. However, though we are not considering totalitarianism on the scale of Hitler and Stalin, the principles are similar when applied to education. It could be argued that if 'full' inclusion is imposed – where literally all children in a locality have to go to the same schools and be in the same classrooms without any separate or specialist provision available – the desires and aspirations of many parents are likely to be denied and individual needs may not be fully met. Relevant to this analysis is the renewed critique of 'inclusive education' by Mary Warnock (2005) in the United Kingdom, who has questioned the concept of inclusion as all children 'under the same roof' and sees the need for some specialist provision for some children in separate settings.

In a recent paper Nilholm (2006) presents an argument about the relationship between special education, inclusion and democracy in which he recognises that the special education field is one where dilemmas are central. This is based on arguments developed by some of the authors discussed above. He also analyses inclusion as multi-dimensional, corresponding to levels in the education system. From this he presents his perspective as post-modern in the sense of not proposing one definitive and single kind of analysis. In so doing he indicates that 'the issue of *who should define the relevant perspective* becomes central' (Nilholm, 2006: p. 438, his italics) and that therefore a discussion about democracy is necessary prior to a notion of inclusion. He then considers different notions of democracy – representative, deliberative, law-governed and participatory – and proposes that:

> inclusion has to be arrived at in decision-making processes that are inclusive in nature.
>
> (p. 442)

More specifically this involves, as he argues, representative, deliberative and participatory forms of democracy. However, his argument does not connect the earlier recognition of the relevance of dilemmas to a wider analysis of political dilemmas in democracy of the kind discussed above (Dahl, 1982; Berlin, 1990). Facing hard choices about the balance between different values and resolving dilemmas of difference in education do not disappear by proposing inclusive or participatory decision-making processes, as Nilholm does.

Anita Ho in another recent US paper has identified a dilemma about labelling children as having a learning disability (Ho, 2004). Though she references Minow's 1990 book there is no reference to dilemmas of difference. Nevertheless, Ho is dealing with a version of the dilemma of difference in her recognition of the risks associated with identification in special education. In her analysis of practices in the USA and the United Kingdom, she notes that identification establishes eligibility to accommodations and to civil rights protections of these adaptations. However, Ho recognises that there are also negative aspects associated with stigma and devaluation that can lead to lower expectations for identified children. Her way out is to broaden the focus of analysis to how the general system deals with difference for all children. She argues that given the stigma traditionally attached to disabilities, it is important to recognise the dangers of 'pathologising differences' (p. 89) and to be aware of the 'disadvantaging potential of our educational and social structures' (pp. 89–90). In her view, the problems arise because:

> we either *ignore* differences or *stigmatise* those who are considered different.
>
> (p. 90, her italics)

Her proposed resolution to the dilemma of disability labels is to adopt the assumption that all children learn in unique ways and to apply this to how we design and manage our educational system. Second, while acknowledging that there may be neurological differences in some contexts, she argues against pathologising these differences. This resolution of the identification dilemma veers strongly towards the commonality option, in her terms 'refrain from pathologising academic difficulties as much as possible' (p. 90). But, this is an incomplete resolution as she does not say how far it is possible to refrain from identifying difficulties and disorders, to use a less negative sounding term than 'pathologising'. Instead she focuses on how the general system can implement 'flexible and customisable measures' (p. 91). She ignores the extent to which some children, even if far less than those currently designated as 'learning disabled' in the USA, might need some flexibility and customised provision, not available to other children. It is clear that this paper is very relevant to this study as it relates to one of the three dilemmas examined in this book, the identification dilemma.

Finally, I examine in this section a recent analysis of the dilemmas of difference, this time from a philosophical perspective (Terzi, 2007). Terzi's position, which is based on the capability approach of Amartya Sen (Sen, 1992), is that this approach 'takes the educational debate beyond the dilemma of difference in significant ways' (p. 1). The capability approach, as a framework for assessing inequality, proposes that equality/inequality be judged in terms of capabilities, rather than other factors, such as income, welfare, etc. Capabilities refer to real freedoms that people have to achieve their own well-being. From this it follows that a focus on capabilities requires an analysis of the interaction between individuals and their social circumstances. Terzi uses this interactionist assumption to argue against the false opposition between individual and social causes of disability, what are often called the medical versus the social model. In distinguishing between impairments (loss or lack of function) and disabilities (inability to perform some activity), she shows that disabilities are in relation to both impairments and the design of social arrangements. So, the capability approach focuses on what people can do or be (potential functioning), even if they choose not to use their freedoms. As Terzi points out, one of the benefits of the capability approach is that judgements about equality/inequality become a matter of capabilities, not about the causal origins of their disabilities. What matters is not the causes of the disabilities but that disabilities are limitations on relevant capabilities.

Although Terzi argues that the capability approach 'resolves the dilemma of difference by significantly addressing the tensions at its core' (p. 11), it is not made clear exactly how this is done. This approach does provide justifications for differential resources to those with disabilities, but how it relates to the implications of this differential allocation is not addressed. The dilemmas of difference are experienced more in the lived realities of separating some children, allocating differential provision and the significance attached to these arrangements. So, although the capability approach provides a useful perspective to the field of SEN/disability, this is at the level of principles and justifications and not about the actual design of educational provision and its consequences.

Ideological dilemmas in special needs education

In this final section of the chapter I summarise a study into ideological dilemmas, which I conducted in the early 1990s in England and the USA, that sets the scene for the international study reported in this book (Norwich, 1993b). In that study I explored the idea that key policy issues in special needs education took the form of ideological dilemmas. Using Billig's model of the dilemmatic nature of social thinking, discussed above, I aimed to explore how a group of educators in the USA and England saw various presented dilemmas and resolved them. As explained in the introductory chapter, my focus at that time was on dilemmas about differentiation and control. It was only after the study began that I came across Minow's (1985) chapter on dilemmas of difference as it applied to special education in the USA. In terms of policy and legislation at that time in the late 1980s and early 1990s, I analysed legislation in both countries to show tensions between principles of inclusion (then seen in terms of integration and in the USA, 'least restrictive environment') and differentiation in terms of a separate identification and provision (IEPs in the USA and Statements in the United Kingdom). In the US context, reference was made to the debate in the late 1980s about the concept of 'least restrictive environment', for example, with research showing parents' difficulties in choosing between segregated settings with more adequate services and integrated settings with less adequate services (National Disability Council, 1989). There was also US debate about the Regular Education Initiative (REI) which aimed to end the dual system of education and replace it by an integrated one (Will, 1986). It is interesting to note that one contribution to this debate argued against the REI as a flawed policy initiative (Kaufman, 1989), and advocated a model of policy formulation that involved considering options and recognising that policy decisions represent a trade-off with no final solutions – a dilemmatic approach.

This study was also presented as offering an alternative approach to the then current critical sociological perspective, as represented by Fulcher's comparative evaluation of special education policy in four countries – the USA, England, Australia and Scandinavia (Fulcher, 1989). Her theoretical approach assumed social actors pursuing their interests, making decisions in different arenas and deploying discourses to seek their objectives. In her perspective, policy was about the struggle over various objectives in which actors carried out discursive practices. Fulcher identified several discourses – professionalist, democractic, medical, charity, lay and rights discourses. Professional discourse related to medical, charity and lay discourses, while democratic discourse related to rights discourses. She identified in the US and UK systems at that time the use of a legal strategy in special education policy. Though US legislation reflected some rights discourse, the dominance of professional and medical discourses pervaded the operation of the legal procedures and the relationships between parents and professionals. In the United Kingdom she saw less democratic discourse with a strong emphasis on professional and medical discourses. However, what Fulcher did not consider was the dilemmatic nature of policy and practice issues, as I argued in the paper, and continue to contend in this book. It was assumed that social actors had ready-made discourses untroubled by contrary and opposing ideas and values. I was arguing for an approach which recognised the thinking and dilemmatic side of discourses and policy matters.

The aim of the study in the early 1990s was to investigate how educators responded to the possibility that there might be dilemmas in various areas of special education and how they might resolve the dilemmas if recognised. The focus was on the sense made of the negative consequences of alternatives to each dilemma and how they deliberated about the nature of these difficulties and ways of resolving them. Four areas were chosen in which different social values – equality, individuality and power-sharing – were relevant. These areas were:

i   What to learn – common curriculum dilemma – whether children with disabilities and difficulties would have the same learning content as other children or some different content.
ii   Whether to identify – identification dilemma – whether and how to identify children as needing special education provision.
iii Relative influence of parents and professionals – parent–professional dilemma – whether and how parents and professionals can share power or not relating to decisions about children with difficulties and disabilities.

iv   Where to learn – integration dilemma – whether and to what extent children with disabilities and difficulties would learn in regular classes or not.

Two groups of professionals from rural and urban areas of Pennsylvania, USA (n = 38) and Northampton, England (n = 43) were interviewed. In both areas, the 81 participants included teachers and senior teachers in ordinary/regular schools (primary and secondary) and in special schools, advisory teachers and support staff (psychologists, specialist teachers). Details of the interview methods will be discussed in Chapter 4.

Analysis indicated that most participants saw at least significant dilemmas in the three areas of identification, curriculum and location. In the USA, the identification dilemma was seen most frequently as a considerable dilemma and there were many more US than English participants who saw a significant curriculum dilemma. However, in both countries the presented parent–professional dilemma was not seen most frequently as a dilemma. As regards resolutions, most participants, who recognised the dilemma to some extent, also saw a significant resolution in all four areas. For the integration dilemma almost twice as many English participants saw a significant resolution as US participants. The reasons for recognising dilemmas were not analysed in this study. But the ways of resolving them were analysed and these were found to be similar across the two country groups, though with some country specific themes. This earlier study was taken as showing commonalities in the positions and judgements of a sample of professional educators in different national systems.

Concluding comments

The cross-national convergence in the 1993 study was taken to indicate that, despite policy and historical differences between the US and UK systems, there were common issues that reflect some shared social and political values. This fits with the overall position developed in this chapter that dilemmas of difference in the SEN/disability in education field reflect wider dilemmas of difference that apply to other aspects of difference and in other areas of society. These wider dilemmas of difference with other contemporary dilemmas, control versus autonomy and solidarity versus diversity dilemmas, make up what can be called progressive dilemmas, which can be seen to reflect a set of dilemmas of plural democracy.

Chapter 3

Policy and practice

Contexts in the three countries

> Only by knowing other realms of being, by real and vicarious travel, can one begin to gain distance on one's own daily existence, what is unique about it and what is shared with others.
>
> (Arnove, 2001: p. 501)

Introduction

This chapter sets the scene for the study of practitioners' and administrators' perspectives on the three dilemmas. It sets out recent historical, policy and legislative aspects in a way that relates issues to the dilemmas examined in the study.

USA

Overview and background

The US system has three administrative levels, Federal, State and School district. Though there has been a historic tendency for States to control education and for limited Federal education policy-making, central Federal policy-making has grown. There has also been a dynamic and uncertain relationship between the Federal and State levels of operation. As regards the education of children with SEN/disabilities, initial efforts to improve their educational opportunities were based in civil rights cases in the 1950s and 1960s which established rights to an education for all children. Since then legislation has been grounded in the equal protection clause of the US Constitution which influences Federal and State legislation. Individuals can seek to enforce their rights through State and Federal Courts and in this way policies and practice have been influenced by this interaction of legislation, court decisions, statutes and regulations. Several key Federal Court cases established a 'zero-reject' principle for special groups like those with disabilities by requiring public schools to provide them with 'free appropriate public education' (FAPE) (McLaughlin and Henderson, 2000). This led to the 1975 Education for All Handicapped Children Act (EAHCA, also known as PL 94-142) which was the precursor of the 1990 Individuals with Disabilities Education Act (IDEA) which has undergone further revisions in 1997 and more recently in 2004. There are two other Federal statutes that relate to special education under anti-discrimination legislation. One is Section 504 of the 1973 Vocational Rehabilitation Act, the other Title II of the Americans with Disability Act (ADA).

The overall proportion of all US students between the ages of 6 and 21 who have qualified for special education under the IDEA framework over the last ten years has been about 10 per cent in 1995–96 (US Department of Education, 1997) and 9 per cent in 2000–2001 (US Department of Education, 2002). Of the 13 categories in the system, four account for 86 per cent of those qualifying for special education – these are learning disability (about 50 per cent and which has increased three times over the 25 years till 2002), serious emotional disturbance, speech and language impairment and mental retardation (2001–2002 data). The US has a fairly detailed system of data collection about the operation of the IDEA that integrates statistics across the States. For example, placement of children under the IDEA framework is grouped into categories based on distance from regular classrooms. These proportions represent the national picture in 2000–2001 for these placement categories – less than 21 per cent of time outside regular classrooms (46.5 per cent of those in special education), between 21 per cent and 60 per cent outside regular classrooms (29.8 per cent), more than 60 per cent of time outside regular classrooms (19.5 per cent) and full time in separate provision in separate settings (4.2 per cent). For students in special schools or other separate settings that are non-residential, the proportion was 3 per cent in 2000, with State variations ranging from 0 per cent in Hawaii to 9.1 per cent in New Jersey. Also, almost half of those identified in the USA spend more than 80 per cent of lesson time in regular classrooms (US Department of Education, 2003).

Special education and disability statutory systems

The IDEA assures the educational rights of students with disabilities by a system that works through the Federal Department of Education, which requires State departments to develop plans of their special education services; these in turn set the framework for Districts, which operate the system closest to the schools. States that meet IDEA requirement receive Federal funds, which are then distributed to Districts. It was the intention that Federal funds cover 40 per cent of the State costs of special education, but estimates are that they only cover between 8–10 per cent of State costs (Katsiyannis et al., 2001). Services are now available for those between the ages of 3 and 21 years who meet two conditions, first, falling within one of 13 categories and two, being in need of special education or related services. The scope of the framework now includes infants and toddlers, if they are assessed as being at risk of experiencing developmental delay. The system requires the provision of free appropriate public education (FAPE) by means of an individual education plan (IEP). States are required to ensure 'full education opportunities', implying a full continuum of special education and related services and the team which decides on the IEP has to take into account that placements are in the 'least restrictive environment' (LRE).

Eligibility for special education depends on identifying a disability, which is often interpreted as involving a child deficiency that has been subject to criticism as an inappropriate medical model (Triano, 2000). This criticism is that the US practice has been at odds with research and practice which cannot easily distinguish between high incidence disabilities and low attainment arising from social and economic disadvantages. Learning difficulties or low attainment due to socio-economic factors is dealt with by another Federal framework, Title 1, the largest Federal school aid programme. However, the increased efforts to support school achievement, the standards agenda, to be discussed more fully below, has led to moves towards greater flexibility in how resources from different sources are used. The 1997 version of IDEA removed the requirement that special education resources not benefit incidentally those without disabilities, so encouraging some co-ordination of IDEA and Title 1 funds. These changes are relevant to the difficulties in distinguishing between high incidence disabilities and other high risk or low achieving students (McLaughlin and Henderson, 2000).

Though the basic model of the legislation has been retained from the original 1975 EAHCA, various changes were introduced with successive revisions. By the mid-1990s the initial intention of opening doors to all students with disabilities was considered by some as successful (Drasgow *et al.*, 2001). IDEA 1997 represented the most substantial changes to the legislation since the 1975 EAHCA, by stressing greater accountability for developing and implementing beneficial IEPs. Since 1975 there had been various problems with the IEP system, such as, inadequate teacher training about IEP development, mechanistic compliance with paperwork requirements, excessive demands on teachers' time, minimal co-ordination with general education as well as legal errors in the IEP process (Huefner, 2000). But, with the 1997 revisions, as Drasgow *et al.* (2001) have commented, 'appropriate education' now meant a quality education. IEPs now had to contain measurable annual goals and specify the methods by which the student would attain these.

What counts as the least restrictive environment has also been a continuing issue in US special education policy and legislation. There has been a tension between the IDEA requirement that the placement of students be decided in terms of individual needs and that a full continuum of placements be available to meet these needs, on the one hand, and for a regular education class to be the preferred placement, on the other (McLaughlin and Henderson, 2000). It is worth noting at this point, that this tension is related to the location dilemma that is examined in this study. How this tension has been resolved in some key court cases has led to several principles that have informed revisions of the IDEA about what LRE entails. As Howe and Welner (2002) explain, student placement in separate settings cannot now be justified by administrative convenience, but can only be in terms of the benefits for the individual student.

The other legislation that applies to educational provision for children with SEN/disabilities, is Section 504 of the 1973 Rehabilitation Act, which interestingly was passed before the 1975 EAHCA legislation, and the 1990 ADA. Section 504 applies to organisations that receive Federal funds, such as public funded schools, and ADA applies to most organisations. These aim to protect civil rights by preventing discrimination against people with disabilities. Section 504 stipulates that a person with a disability will not be 'excluded from participation in, denied the benefits of, or be subjected to discrimination under any program or activity receiving federal financial assistance' (29, USCA, sec.794). Organisations are required to make 'reasonable accommodations' to ensure that people with disabilities can access goods and services, under the ADA legislation. Where these statutes go beyond the IDEA framework is that they have a broader definition of disability, one not based on specific categories and so can include some children who might not meet the eligibility criteria under IDEA (Smith, 2000).

Other school changes

Two other significant changes in the US school system, school choice and standards agenda, have had a major impact on provision for students with special needs and disabilities. School choice principles have come to be increasingly accepted and implemented in the USA since the 1990s. They have emerged in a number of forms, eased enrolment areas, magnets, charter schools and the use of vouchers – all representing some aspects of a choice and diversity system of schooling. One of the criticisms of these developments has been that they have led to increasing stratification of schools and exclusions of students with special needs (Howe and Welner, 2002). These and other commentators have argued that these market driven changes have provided schools with incentives to exclude low scoring students, including those with special needs. Though the legislation for charter schools varies between States, this type of school involves exemptions from restrictions that govern traditional schools, though they have to abide by laws regarding safety, health and civil rights that include disability legislation. So, several States prohibit discrimination in admission on the basis of disability, others allow schools to select on the basis of a fit with the school's mission or that students with disabilities can place 'undue hardship' on the schools. These authors quote research, for example, showing that charter schools across the US have a lower proportion of students with disabilities compared to public schools.

The other related change in the USA has been the standards-based reform which has emerged from the 1980s with the call for rigorous academic standards. However, though the initial standards-based reforms referred to all students, there was a growing awareness that all did not mean literally all, it did not include those with disabilities and those with limited English proficiency (Thurlow, 2002). Nevertheless, there were strong calls from special educators for including students with disabilities in the standards and assessment systems. One argument was the historically low expectations held for students with disabilities and the resulting low level instruction they received, another was the lack of information about progress and achievement of these students (McDonnell et al., 1997). Federal initiatives promoted the standards agenda despite calls for local controls. These were evident in the IDEA 1997 revisions which required that students with disabilities have access to the general curriculum, participate in local assessment systems in aggregate and disaggregated versions, and that the IEP include relevant provisions for this participation as well as whether alternate assessment was required. Other legislation about elementary and secondary schools also required that States meet various standards-based conditions to receive Title 1 funding (for low attainment due to socio-economic factors). Such legislation was re-authorised as the No Child left Behind (NCLB) legislation of 2002.

NCLB has been criticised from a general education perspective in several ways, as not addressing the needs of education in a post-industrial society (Marshak, 2003) and as having professed aims that are contradicted by its actual provisions (Neill, 2003). Linn (2005) also identifies that some of the weaknesses of the NCLB system threaten its central goals: setting unrealistically high standards; having fixed targets in Adequate Yearly Progress (AYP), that do not take account of students' starting levels, rather than using growth or 'value added' measures; and unacceptable State variations in definitions of proficiency compared to national test standards.

In a National Research Council report on students with disabilities and the standards agenda, McDonnell et al. (1997) note that the diversity of students with disabilities (high incidence disabilities, which are sometimes hard to distinguish from those with low achievement, and low incidence disabilities) means that different students might participate to different degrees in the common aspects of the standards-based reforms. For a small percentage of these low incidence disabilities, mainly academic goals will not, they argue, be relevant to their life goals. Special education has also adopted goals that go beyond these academic goals, such as independent living, work place preparation, etc. These authors also question whether the content and performance levels embodied in some of the academic standards might take time away from time to teach what many might regard as more valuable skills. They concluded that three factors needed to be taken into account for each individual: (i) the relation of common content standards to desired post-school outcomes; (ii) the age of the student; and (iii) the extent to which teaching directed at academic standards takes time from other valuable goals. These factors are mentioned as they relate to the curriculum dilemma in this study.

It is clear that the standards agenda re-focused attention on curriculum issues for students with disabilities in the USA and that this change was regarded by many as long overdue (Pugach and Warger, 2000). Pugach and Warger have also noted that this move has redressed the priority attention paid to placement, due to a Civil rights orientation, towards a concern with what students with disabilities learn and their progress towards challenging standards. So after the IDEA 1997 legislation, the IEP could no longer be considered as the curriculum for students with disabilities. IDEA 1997 required that States organise for all learners to be part of State-wide accountability systems, so that students previously excluded would participate with accommodations or participate in alternative assessments arrangements (Ford *et al.*, 2001). Ysseldyke *et al.* (1997) estimated that between 1–2 per cent of students might need to have alternative assessment arrangements. More recently, McLaughlin *et al.* (2006) note that alternative or modified standards can include up to 3 per cent of the total student population (1 per cent for alternative standards and 2 per cent for modified standards).

Commentary on US system

Debates around the themes of inclusion are well developed in the USA. There has been criticism of the system of special education that has focused on identifying individuals' difficulties. This has questioned the value of the policy approach employed over the last three decades of providing a free appropriate public education at the cost of stigma (Triano, 2000). This kind of critique does not distinguish between a categorical system like IDEA or the general disability criterion, used in Section 504/ADA legislation, as both are seen as reflecting a medical deficit model and as involving a 'stigmatising and dehumanising labelling process' (p. 409). Critics like Triano call for a basic restructuring of the educational system where eligibility is based on need not deficit and where the system is responsive to the needs of all children with and without disabilities. How far such a system can do this without identifying conditions, where additional resourcing and different provision are required, is an important question. This question is about the consequences of individual identification, one of the dilemmas to be examined in this study. Others have taken this position further by suggesting that inclusion be a core value of the general system and that the focus of analysis shifts to general school-wide developments (Lipsky and Gartner, 1996; Sailor and Roger, 2005).

However, there have been some trenchant defences in the USA of a special education that does not merge its identity with a restructured general education. Kaufman *et al.* (2004), for example, have countered what they see as two extremes in conceptions about educating students with disabilities, denying disabilities exist, on the one hand, or accommodating them to an extent where there is no expectation of progress to realistic goals on the other. Their defence is based on exposing the negative aspects of the 'full' inclusion position, which they consider can promote an 'appearance of competence' rather than actual competence in students. These authors support the recognition of difference in a positive way in the name of justice and dignity and oppose the position that wishes to ignore and abandon differential approaches. It is clear that tensions about difference in special education provision continue to be debated and be reflected in policy and practice in the USA.

THE NETHERLANDS

Overview and background

Compared to many other European systems, the one in the Netherlands has been described as historically extensive and segregated. For example, by the mid-1990s the proportion of all children attending special schools full-time had doubled over 20 years to about 4 per cent (Pijl and Pijl, 1995). The system has been strongly differentiated; there were in the mid-1990s, for example, 14 different kinds of special schools (Reezigt and Pijl, 1998). Vislie (2003) examined the changes in the percentage of children in segregated provision across 14 countries, using OECD data between 1990–96; she grouped the degrees of segregated provision into five bands (< 1 per cent, 1–2 per cent, 2–3 per cent, 3–4 per cent and > 4 per cent). The Netherlands was one of four countries in 1990 with between 3–4 per cent in segregated provision, Belgium, France and Germany being the others. By 1996, France had decreased its proportion to the 2–3 per cent range, while the Netherlands and Germany had increased their proportion to the > 4 per cent range. As in other countries the majority of the identified children fall within the 'learning disabled' and 'mild mentally retarded' groups (LOM and MLK, to use the acronyms used in the Netherlands). Pijl and Van den Bos (2001) quote a figure of 70 per cent of all children in special education being in these groups. However, more recent national statistics for 2005 show a lower percentage of children of compulsory school age with SEN in segregated settings, 2.23 per cent (Netherlands Ministry of Education, 2006). However, this change reflects the removal of children with learning disabilities and mild mental retardation from the special education data. Children in segregated settings still constitute a majority of all children identified as having SEN (about 72 per cent for the 2005 statistics). The percentage of school children with SEN (in segregated and inclusive settings) was 3.14 per cent of all school children (Netherlands Ministry of Education, 2006).

This separatist system arises from the particular history of the Netherlands which has had a tradition of centralised policy legislation and decentralised administration and management of schools. The history of provision for children with special educational needs has been one of separate funding, regulations and teacher training. This separate funding stream created the incentives for referral to special schools. The constitution has played a key role in the development of this highly differentiated and decentralised system and the development of separate schools for different religious backgrounds. This system is the outcome of religious struggles at the beginning of the twentieth century, and as Reezigt and Pijl (1998) explain, these struggles are invoked whenever change is proposed. The constitution provides the right for people to found schools and provide teaching on religious, ideological or other educational beliefs. The result is that there are both publicly run and privately run schools (mainly Church run), with some 70 per cent of pupils attending privately run schools (Eurydice, 2004). This diversified system is also evident in the structure of the general school system. Primary schooling is between the ages of 5 and 12 years, while compulsory secondary education is differentiated into different pathways, a pre-university system (VWO) from 12–18 years, a senior general secondary system for 12–16 years (HAVO), a pre-vocational secondary system (VBO) leading to a vocational secondary system (MBO) and secondary special schools, from 12–20 years. Rodbard (1990) suggested that without this differentiated system of secondary schooling, the proportion in special schools might have been even higher.

There have been concerns and debates for some time about the growth of the special education system. Pijl and Van den Bos (2001) commented that there had been a growing group of policy-makers, educators and parents believing that segregation had gone too far. This reflects international moves and has been justified by parents in terms of wanting their children to socialise in ordinary schools and for their children with special educational needs to accompany their siblings who go to local schools. However, compared to other countries, especially the USA and United Kingdom, the other two countries in the study, parents in the Netherlands have not been prominent partners in the special needs/inclusive education debates. The statutory systems in the other two countries with opportunities for legal redresses are not available in the Netherlands. Nevertheless, there was an exception to this trend, the Association of Parents of Children with

Down Syndrome, which succeeded in influencing the education system. This organisation managed to persuade primary schools to accept children with Down Syndrome, even though these schools were not obliged legally to do so. From the late 1980s there was a rapid increase in the number of children with Down Syndrome in primary schools. So, by 1996–97 almost half of Down Syndrome pre-schoolers attended regular schools (Scheepstra *et al.*, 1999). Other parent groups have now also become more active in their pursuit of inclusion (European Agency for Development of Special Needs Education, 2004). It is notable that these moves towards more inclusive education in the Netherlands have not been in the context general disability rights, as in the USA and United Kingdom (Van Houten and Bellemakers, 2002).

Development of inclusive policies

Inclusion policies developed initially within the primary sector in the Netherlands. Various changes in the primary sector are relevant to this discussion. One was the merging of nursery schools (ages 4–6 years) with primary schools (6–12 years) into the 4–12 years system of today. Primary schools were charged with offering 'appropriate instruction to all children and to guarantee all children an uninterrupted schools career' (Reezigt and Pijl, 1998). This promoted the principles of 'adaptive instruction', which have been further developed and are still current in the Netherlands at present. Such adaptations to regular teaching were supposed to prevent learning problems and so reduce the number of children being referred to special schools.

However, as Reezigt and Pijl (1998) comment, adaptive teaching was not adopted generally nor was grade retention abandoned in primary schools. This led to policies which were geared more explicitly to building the capacity of primary schools to include children with special educational needs/disabilities. In a policy introduced in the early 1990s, the Government set out to have special needs children go to regular school with their peers – so the name for the policy became 'together to school again' or 'Weer Samen Naar School' or WSNS for short. The WSNS policy only focused on children with 'learning disabilities' and 'mild mental retardation' at primary level. As they constitute almost three-quarters of all children with special educational needs, this is a significant framework, especially as it established that they belonged to the primary sector. This inclusive policy was underpinned by a change in the funding system and the formation of regional clusters of special and regular schools. Clusters could involve between 15–20 regular schools collaborating with a couple of special schools. Extra funding was available for this. By 1995 there were just less than 300 regional clusters forming a network across the country in which these specific kinds of special schools were linked to ordinary schools. The

Government then changed the regulations for funding in 1995, so that half of the funds went directly to special provision and the other half to the school cluster. The result was that regions had to change their special educational provision

Under the WSNS policy the class teacher is responsible for assessing pupils who have 'learning disabilities' and 'mild educationally retardation.' The teacher can be supported by the school special needs co-ordinator or internal support co-ordinator (in Dutch, the 'interne begeleider') or support teachers from the regional school support service. A further step would be to refer the child to the regional assessment team. The inspectorate found that by 1997 about 75 per cent of schools had such co-ordinators and that teachers in this role also had opportunities to go to in-service training courses. These clusters and the co-ordinators were designed to provide conditions to support one of the other goals of the WSNS policy, to make regular schools more adaptive in their teaching approaches. It is clear that this innovation in primary schools was in opposition to the previous remedial teaching model of one-to-one withdrawal teaching. However, Pijl and Van den Bos (2001) found that few primary teachers used adaptive teaching practices, that co-ordinators had little available time for this role and that teachers wanted the support from remedial teachers to continue, while wanting the co-ordinators' support as well.

Following the introduction of the primary WSNS policy, it was extended in 1998 to secondary special schools in these mild educational disabilities areas. The effect was to restructure secondary special education into the general secondary education system. A support system was developed to ensure as many students as possible complete courses to get the VMBO vocational qualification. There is also a regional referral committee which makes decisions about eligibility for separate learning support or practical training (for those not expected even with considerable extra support to get their VMBO qualifications). This system came fully into operation in 2002.

Back-pack policy

The system for children with more significant special needs, those with sensory, physical and mental disabilities and those with behaviour problems has come under a different policy framework. Till 1996 these children received their special provision by full-time placement in special schools. From 1996 the Government outlined its plans to change the basis of funding from, what was called, a 'supply-oriented' system to a 'demand-oriented' system. Instead of funding children with special educational needs/disabilities by funding places in special schools, the funding came to be linked to the pupils themselves, wherever they were educated, at special or regular schools. Thus, the name back-pack came into use as the child can carry the resource wherever s/he is educated. What makes this a 'demand-oriented' system is that parents have a key role in stating their preferences about where to educate their children. As Hamstra (2000) commented, this policy of 'pupil bound financing' strengthens parental influence, stimulates more inclusion in regular schools and has the facilities following the child.

There were several aspects to this framework. One was the amalgamation of the different kinds of special schools into Regional Expertise Centres (REC), the other was the willingness of schools to accommodate children with special needs. Under the REC system, the ten different kinds of special schools, not covered by the WSNS framework, were re-organised into four RECs: (i) for blind/hard of sight; (ii) for deaf, hard of hearing and speech/language difficulties; (iii) for physically impaired, severely ill, multiple impaired and mentally impaired; and (iv) for severe psychiatric disorders. These Regional Centres were seen to have several advantages over more separate special schools. They support the development of professional knowledge and the interchange of expertise. They also have a broadened remit; in addition to teaching, they advise regular schools and are the base for 'indication' committees, which from 2003 decided about eligibility for additional funding. Previously, special schools admission boards used to make decision about eligibility without clear criteria. As part of the Government move to block further increases in special school numbers, the eligibility for additional resourcing were set out in more specific terms, largely based on those used in existing practice for admitting children into special schools (Pijl and Veneman, 2005). These authors found strong associations between the new and old eligibility criteria. But, up to 10 per cent of the cases would not be identified as eligible under the new tighter criteria. These authors explain that the Government decided to allocate on an open-ended funding system, to ensure that every child meeting the criteria receives the same resourcing. They also commented that if national Governments want sufficient funding for children with special needs (and not to have fixed total costs), with equal resourcing for similar needs and controls on numbers, then they would have to use tighter criteria and procedures nationally. They suggested that this leads to 'old psycho-medical indicators', which have negative effects of labelling and stigma. So, they point to the contradictory position of the back-pack policy, which while aiming to promote more inclusion, ends up with segregating consequences. This tension can be seen as an example of the identification dilemma to be examined in this study.

Although parents have an important say in stating a preference for a regular school rather than a special school through the back-pack policy, the regulations do not require regular schools to place children with special educational needs, even if parents request this. Schools need to show clearly that they are incapable of appropriate provision, if placement is denied in these circumstances (Pijl and Veneman, 2005). Soon after the introduction of the back-pack policy it was found that most schools were not ready to accept children with special educational needs either in terms of teaching capacity or required materials/facilities (Weber, 1997). In my school visits I found continuing evidence of ordinary schools setting entry criteria.

Almere experiment

The Ministry of Education supported the experiment in Almere in 1996 for a ten-year period to make inclusive education a priority in the city's primary schools. The plan was to teach children with sensory impairments, severe learning difficulties, physical impairments and those that were educable mentally retarded within regular schools. The goal was to realise high quality educational conditions to maximise the inclusion of children with special educational needs in regular primary schools. Schools were supported by an urban expertise centre and parents were to have a choice about the kind of special provision they preferred. Three models of inclusion were designed which reflect part of a continuum of special provision:

i   Child in group – child is fully included in a regular class, gets the same learning activities as others, but sometimes follows his/her own programme, with regular teacher teaching.
ii Group in school – child is in a special small class in a regular school, though they participate as much as possible with activities in the rest of the school. Special education teacher does the teaching.
iii Coupled to school – children with more significant/severe special educational needs, in the case of Almere, children with severe psychiatric disorders, go to a special school. However, these children participate with some activities in regular schools.

Hamstra (2000) studied aspects of this inclusion experiment in its early stages by examining aspects of the education experiences across 21 schools. Teachers and parents involved in the experiment were generally satisfied with the development, though there were some issues: concerns that some of these children did not have friends, teachers feeling unsupported and communication with parents being difficult at times.

During my visit to the Netherlands several professionals reported that the Government had recently announced (November 2005) that there were plans to close all special schools. For some people this was seen as the Minister of Education trying out some ideas to see what response they evoked, while for others, this was a more serious prospect. A senior national administrator believed that the Government's reported intention about the future of special schools was informed by the kind of provision which had been tried in Almere.

Comments on the Netherlands system

Though the Government had introduced a common national curriculum framework for schools in the Netherlands, there was no curriculum framework for special schools at the time of my visit. Nor did special schools take part in the national tests which were used in general schools. However, the general curriculum framework is more general and flexible than the English National Curriculum and it was evident that not all primary schools used the national tests. There were plans for a national curriculum framework for special schools, though there were some who took a more doubtful stance towards this development.

These differing perspectives on including children with special educational needs in a national curriculum framework are relevant to the curriculum dilemma examined in this study. These perspectives also reflect the separatism or differentiation in that system. Perhaps the historically and constitutionally based diversity in the school system makes it more 'normal' for children to go to different kinds of schools. This might be seen to moderate or reduce the negative labelling and stigma effects of going to a special school (Reezigt and Pijl, 1998).

Another explanation for the differentiated system in the Netherlands has been based on analyses of population density at a regional level and travelling distances to schools. Meijer (2000) has shown using European regional data, that there is a relationship across European Union countries between population density and the proportion of children going to special schools. This indicates that where population density is higher more children go to special schools. The relationship can be understood in terms of there being a need for more schools and there being more children with special educational needs where there are greater densities of population. Special schools are more likely to be established in such areas and travelling distances to them shorter than in low population areas. However, these demographic factors operate as conditions that can lead to separatist school systems, whether they do, depends on social policy decisions. This is where the school diversity that arises from historical and constitutional arrangements acts as a major influence on the system in the Netherlands.

ENGLAND

Overview and background

In discussing the English system of provision for children with special educational needs, it is important to distinguish between the four countries making up the United Kingdom. With the recent establishment of greater devolution of Government functions to Scotland and Wales, and education being a policy area where there are devolved powers, the systems have come recently to adopt different policies. This discussion focuses on the English system, though there will be some references to the Scottish system which has had a distinctive education tradition. Education has been administered historically by local education authorities (LEAs), within fairly general enabling national legislation. Since the late 1980s there has been increasing centralisation as Government adopted policies to increase school standards through the use of market-style strategies. As in the USA these changes to the general system have had a major impact on the course of special education in England.

Though national special educational policy goes back to the late nineteenth century when LEAs established special classes and schools, the key contemporary policy framework was introduced following the landmark Warnock Committee (DES, 1978). This committee introduced the concept of special educational needs, supported the principle of educating children with SEN in mainstream or ordinary schools and endorsed parental participation in decision-making about their children's SEN. These ideas were incorporated into the Education Act (1981) that established the legislative framework, which, despite various revisions in response to the changes in the general school system, still operates to the present time.

In the English system special educational needs is identified at three levels, which mark degrees of increasing need for additional or different provision. There are two school-based levels – *School Action* and *School Action Plus* – that are decided by professionals within schools (DfES, 2002). The school's SEN co-ordinator plays a key role in this process by responding to concerns about a child's inadequate progress in learning by designing an individual educational plan (IEP – to be distinguished from the US IEP which relates to the Statement in England). At the School Action Plus stage, outside support professionals, such as psychologists or specialised teachers, become involved in the design of the IEP. Where concerns persist, despite school-based special educational interventions, the Local Authority becomes involved in a multi-professional assessment to assess the child's special educational needs to decide if the LEA will determine the special provision. If the LEA decides to determine the provision, then the child will be issued with a Statement of SEN, which is a more detailed record of the child's individual educational needs, provision required and placement. In acting as a legal-style contract between the LEA and parents, the Statement is the English equivalent of the US IEP and has similar legal protections and rights for legal redress. In fact, the form of the UK statutory system was influenced by the preceding US EAHCA (1975).

In 2005, about 18 per cent of all children in England were recorded as having some degree of SEN (DfES, 2005). This includes about 3 per cent with Statements and 15 per cent with SEN without Statements (10 per cent at School Action and 5 per cent at School Action Plus). About 60 per cent of all children with Statements are in ordinary schools. The trends in recent years have also been notable – the proportion of children with Statements increased from about 2.5 per cent in 1994 to over 3 per cent in 2001 and then fell slightly to 3 per cent from 2002–4 and to 2.9 per cent in 2005. However, the proportion of children in special schools (all assumed to have Statements) fell more rapidly in the 1980s and still to some extent in the 1990s, from 1.83 per cent in 1983 to 1.3 per cent in 2001 (Norwich, 2002). This indicates that the increases in Statements since the mid-1990s were mainly in the ordinary schools. This is confirmed by data provided in the House of Commons Select Committee Report on SEN (House of Commons, 2006: p. 86). Since 2003 there have also been statistics in terms of 12 categories of SEN. These indicate that 86 per cent of all children with SEN at School Action Plus stage in 2005 were in the highest incidence categories – moderate learning difficulties (MLD – similar to EMR in the USA), specific learning difficulties (SpLD – similar to LD in the USA), speech, language and communication needs (SLCN) and social, emotional and behaviour difficulties (SEBD – similar to serious emotional disturbance in the USA). By contrast, only two of these four categories were high incidence for children with Statements (MLD and BESD). Autism and severe learning difficulties (SLD) had a higher incidence than specific learning difficulties and speech, language and communication needs. This suggests that the distinction between what is often called low versus high incidence disabilities/difficulties includes children with Statements and at School Action Plus.

SEN statutory system

The concept of SEN was introduced as a more positive and provision-oriented term to re-focus attention on required provision rather than concentrate on children's deficits. For many the Warnock Committee position was one of abandoning categories, and to this day there are those who consider that the English system is 'non-categorical and needs based' (p. 48, McClaughlin *et al.*, 2006; OECD, 2000). But the facts and analysis of them indicate that this is an over-simplification of the recent history of the system. The Warnock system is one which focuses on identifying individual educational needs in terms of required additional or different provision, but in order to specify these needs, a child has to be assessed as having (i) a 'learning difficulty' which (ii) calls for special education provision. Here is a two-part system, like the one used in the USA, not in terms of 13 categories of disability, but in terms of a general category of 'learning difficulty'. The Warnock position of abandoning categories was really about replacing more medically sounding categories like sub-normality, by softer more positive terms like moderate learning difficulties and by avoiding talk of handicap and disability by talking loosely about 'learning difficulties'.

Had the Warnock position been to broaden special educational needs beyond those with impairment and disabilities to include those who have additional needs due to mainly socio-economic, cultural or linguistic factors, then 'learning difficulties' would have been given this broader meaning. The OECD (2000) survey of the SEN classifications used this broader meaning in terms of the different areas that receive additional provision across different countries. Comparing the English with the OECD criteria shows the disability assumptions in the English concept of SEN. The Education Act (1981) is also clear that a child who has additional language learning needs is not to be counted as having a SEN. Also relevant are the later and recent comments of Mary Warnock about the remit of the Warnock Committee that it could not focus on difficulties arising mainly from socio-economic disadvantages (Warnock, 2005). Though the English system has not been up-front about impairment and disability in its explicit definition of SEN, it is clear that SEN has been regarded officially as about impairment and disability, as shown in Section 3 of the first SEN Code of Practice (DfE, 1994). The Warnock Committee position recognised a range of problems associated with traditional special education categories. Individual educational needs could not be read off from simple medically based categories. Other personal and environmental factors were relevant to assessing individual educational needs. Clear-cut boundaries between those with difficulties and disabilities and those without were also hard to draw. Categories were also associated with stigma and devaluation. This framework led to the circular and inadequately defined terms of the 1981 Education Act – in which SEN was defined in terms of learning difficulties which called for special educational provision.

The Warnock Committee and 1981 Act solution, by distancing the system from medical categories, by softening terms and by focusing on individual educational needs, held out the promise of replacing the individual deficit model. But, it did not deal with the question of eligibility for additional provision, a question that has not gone away and persists in the current problems experienced with the Statement system. Though the intention of the Statement of SEN was to protect provision, the unintended result was the huge increase in demand from parents and schools to identify SEN (see figures above for increases from 1994) and thus additional resources. LEAs were faced with considerable demands and an increase in litigation by parents that led to the setting up of the Tribunal system. There are tensions here between principles of parental partnership and parental rights to due process through legal redress. The Audit Commission – a Governmental agency concerned with efficiency in public services – returned to these problems after having identified them ten years before (Audit Commission, 2002a). It identified persistent problems with the Statement system as a way of allocating resources to children with severe and complex special needs. They highlighted the fact that responsibilities rest with LEAs, while most resources are held by schools, Statements can make potentially unlimited demands, but must be met within a finite budget, and parental expectations regarding their rights are raised within a process which can be bureaucratic, stressful and legalistic. Furthermore, there were variations between authorities in the issuing of statements, raising questions about definitions of level of need which 'triggers' a Statement, and reflecting the very different ways in which authorities resource SEN. Recent Government strategy has been to reduce reliance on Statements as a method for allocating resources by a variety of priorities: for example, delegating resources for early intervention and inclusive practices, improving information to parents on SEN arrangements and reducing the bureaucracy connected with SEN.

General school changes: their impact on inclusive developments

In the UK system there has been a conditional legal duty on LEAs to place children with SEN in ordinary schools, which goes back to developing practice in the 1970s and the endorsement of these moves by the Warnock Committee. In the original 1981 legislation there were four conditions: (i) that this was subject to parental wishes; (ii) that the child receives the special educational provision required by his/her learning difficulties; (iii) that placement was compatible with the efficient education of other children with whom educated; and (iv) the efficient use of resources. During the 1980s without extra Government resources to support these legal provisions, the initiative was up to LEAs to promote integration, as it was known then. Integration was not seen merely as placement, it was also conceptualised in terms of social integration and functional integration. It involved further development of SEN resourced units in ordinary schools and the development of whole school policies and practices to make accommodations for children with SEN at class and school level (Thomas and Feiler, 1988). As the figures set out above show, the most rapid decrease in the special school population was during the 1980s.

It was in the late 1980s that the Government introduced the Education Reform Act (1988) which had a major impact on SEN. This legislation altered radically the pattern of school governance, introduced market-style reforms into the system and established provision for raising school attainments through an assessment-oriented National Curriculum. This package of changes gave schools more management autonomy from LEAs in their budgets, which were based largely on pupil numbers, thus favouring popular schools. Schools were also allowed to opt out of LEA control completely by receiving their funding direct from Government – grant-maintained schools. Parents were given a greater say in their preference for schools and could exercise their preferences by using information about aggregated school attainments from the introduction of a system of national testing referenced to the new National Curriculum. In this way, school competition was introduced as the driver for raising school attainment. These changes evoked an ambivalent response from many working in the special educational needs field. Though a National Curriculum as an entitlement for all was something that aroused progressive hopes, its initial design and the accompanying assessment arrangements did not take account of those with SEN. The availability of test results in the form of school league tables also raised fears that children with SEN would be less appealing to schools keen to promote their league table position and popularity. It was anticipated that accepting children with SEN in ordinary schools who had lower attainments, or retaining them when they challenged the system either in behaviour terms or teaching time, would make them less appealing in the new competitive system.

As these changes came to be implemented, many of the fears came to be realised. The increasing demand for Statements through the 1990s was driven by ordinary schools which pushed for more additional provision for children who previously did not require a Statement. There was an increasing trend in permanent exclusions of children for behaviour problems with many of these children having already been identified as having SEN (Audit Commission, 2002b). The National Curriculum in its original design did not cater well for children whose learning was outside the range of their age peers. Many teachers in ordinary and special schools were not confident about adapting the National Curriculum out of fear that school inspections might be critical of these practices. And many with SEN were marginalised from the National Curriculum assessment arrangements. Following a successful lobby from voluntary and other organisations, the Government was persuaded to introduce a SEN Code of Practice (DfE, 1994), to promote whole school policies and practices for the wider group of those with SEN without Statements. The Code had an ambiguous status; its requirements had to be taken into account by schools, but did not have the force of law. Nevertheless, it did introduce procedures for identifying and providing individual plans for children identified as having SEN but without Statements. This was seen as one way of preventing the increasing school demand for LEAs to issue Statements, by requiring that schools develop their own internal graded systems of pre-Statement individual identification and planning (IEPs). However, these procedures were not connected with the implementation of the National Curriculum and ways of enabling curricula to be managed to meet diverse needs and this led partly to problems with writing and applying IEPs, especially in secondary schools. Though some of the hard edges of the market-style system of schooling were regulated by changes to the SEN Code, there have been continuing tensions experienced within schools and LEAs over the years between the raising standards and the inclusion agendas (Campbell, 2002; MacBeath et al., 2006).

Renewed inclusive commitments

From 1997 the new Labour Government renewed its policy commitment to inclusive education while aiming to present this as part of the standards agenda of seeking excellence for all (DfEE, 1997). The policy statement, however, still saw a future role for special schools and presented inclusion in conditional terms. The message in the Government Action Plan that followed was that excellence for all was compatible with more inclusion. What then followed were some significant changes and additions to the basic special educational legislation in the SEN and Disability Act (2001), known as SENDA. One notable change was in the conditions governing the LEA obligation to secure ordinary school placement for children with Statements. Two of the four conditions, that the child receives the special educational provision required by the learning difficulty and the efficient use of resources, were removed, leaving only two – about being in accordance with parental preferences and being compatible with the efficient education of others. This change was seen as a response to the pressures for legislative support for more inclusion. However, it could be and has also been seen as a way of removing a safeguard that ordinary school placement required specialist services for the child.

SENDA also introduced disability discrimination legislation into schools. Schools are required not to treat children with disability less favourably and for them to take reasonable steps to avoid putting these children at a substantial disadvantage compared to children without disabilities. But, being based on the concept of disability, it was unclear to what extent children with disabilities were also those with special educational needs. Disabilities were defined in the disability discrimination legislation as a 'physical and mental impairment that has a substantial and long-term adverse effect on the ability to carry out normal day-to-day activities'. The accepted position has been that most children with SEN would also be those with disabilities by this definition, but some with SEN do not have disabilities, while some with disabilities may not be identified with SEN. In England, children are often referred to as having 'SEN/disabilities'. LEAs were required to develop accessibility plans, showing how they were going to improve school access for disabled children and the Disability Rights Commission issued a Code of Practice on implementing SENDA in schools, which came into operation in 2003 (DRC, 2003). These duties have been strengthened more recently through the Disability Discrimination Act (2005).

Another key area where renewed inclusive commitments were evident concerned curriculum and assessment for children with SEN. Though all children were deemed by legislation in the mid-1990s to have the right to have access to the National Curriculum, there was no provision in the general curriculum structure or assessment arrangements for children with severe or significant SENs. It took over 13 years from the introduction of the National Curriculum to develop national adaptations of the curriculum framework for those with 'learning difficulties' (QCA, 2003). Not only did this provide adaptations of programmes across the range of National Curriculum subjects areas, but also a sequence of performance standards that could be used to assess learning progress below Level 1 of the general assessment scheme (P levels). Connected to this development was a revised version of the National Curriculum for England which set out schools' responsibility to provide a curriculum that meets the specific needs of individuals and groups of pupils. The statement provided examples of how this responsibility can be met. It sets out three principles that are essential for teachers and schools to follow when developing an inclusive curriculum: (i) setting suitable learning challenges; (ii) responding to pupils' diverse learning needs; and (iii) overcoming potential barriers to learning and assessment for individuals and groups of pupils.

What is notable about the Government's pursuit of inclusion is that it adopted a broader notion of inclusive education that not only included, but went beyond just those with SEN/disabilities. This was presented in terms of 'social inclusion', which focused on a wider group of children who were seen as vulnerable and 'at risk of social exclusion', such as children living in poverty, children from ethnic minorities, children in the care of social services ('looked after' by Local Authorities) and so on. Within this framework there have been major nationally funded initiatives in early intervention and prevention under the title of preventing social exclusion (for example, Education Action Zones, Sure Start, Children's Fund) that have gone beyond school as the base and could include children with SEN/disabilities. Within schools the development of the Primary Strategy, which extended the National Curriculum in numeracy and literacy for primary schools into guidelines for classroom teaching, was also based on a broadened notion of difficulties in learning that goes beyond just those with SEN. This has been developed in the 'three waves' model of intervention in the Primary Strategy, where Wave 1 is about the effective inclusion of all children in a daily and high quality teaching, Wave 2 is additional small-group interventions for children who can be expected to catch up with their peers as a result of the intervention and Wave 3 is specific targeted approaches for children identified as requiring SEN support (on School Action, School Action Plus or with a Statement of special educational needs) (DfES, 2003a). Consistent with the broader focus on vulnerable children, the Government has introduced significant changes in the organisation of local authority services for children, under what has been called the 'Every Child Matters' system (DfES, 2004). This integrates the various public services provided for children at local authority level in terms of an integrated set of outcomes (or what could be seen as needs) for every child. This new approach to the well-being of children and young people from birth to age

19 years focuses on these outcomes: (i) being healthy; (ii) staying safe; (iii) enjoying and achieving; (iv) making a positive contribution; and (v) achieving economic well-being. LEAs will be integrated into the new Children Services in local authorities and organisations involved with providing services to children – from hospitals and schools, to police and voluntary groups – will be teaming up in new ways, sharing information and working together towards these five outcomes. Associated with this development have been moves to having 'extended schools', which have broadened the school as the base for services to children, outside typical school hours. These developments are still at an early stage, but they will clearly impact significantly on how needs and provision for children with SEN/disabilities will be conceptualised, planned and put into practice.

Concluding comments

Although these recent national initiatives concerning social inclusion and integrated services show impressive commitment, there have been continuing problems associated with specific policies and practices about SEN/disabilities. For instance, Ofsted, the national inspectorate, has reported inflexibilities in the school system, inequalities in terms of quality and access to a broad range of provisions and slow progress towards more inclusive schooling (Ofsted, 2004). Prior to this report, the Audit Commission urged that SEN be regarded as a mainstream school issue (Audit Commission, 2002b).

There have been widespread calls for a basic national review of special educational needs and inclusive education (Audit Commission, 2002b; MacBeath *et al.* 2006; Warnock, 2005). This has centred round concerns about the nature and extent of inclusion, the usefulness of the concept of SEN and the future of Statements. However, policy-makers in the different parts of the United Kingdom have addressed these challenges in different ways, as shown in the recent changes to Scottish legislation and procedures. Under the new Education (Additional Support for Learning) Act 2004, which came into operation in November 2005, the Scottish SEN framework was replaced by a broader framework of 'additional support needs', which places duties on authorities to identify and address support needs arising from a wider range of factors, such as cognitive, social, emotional, linguistic, disability, family and care circumstances. The Record of Needs (the Scottish equivalent of the English Statement) has been replaced by a 'co-ordinated support plan' (CSP), which has similar legal and procedural aspects to Statements/Records, but applies only to children with long-term significant learning needs that require services outside school.

The House of Commons Select Committee on Education, which scrutinises Government education policy, has recently produced a SEN Report (House of Commons, 2006). One of its key conclusions was that the

Government had given a confused message about inclusion. On the one hand, most of its recent policies have been aimed at reducing the number of children educated in special schools, on the other, it has claimed that it does not take a view about the proportion of children in special schools (p. 5). The Government was urged to clarify its policy position about the field, to recognise that the Warnock SEN framework was no longer 'fit for purpose' (p. 6). It is clear that the basic issues that have re-surfaced in the English system involve questions about the identification of SEN, curriculum relevance and placement. This indicates the relevance of examining responses to dilemmas in these areas.

Chapter 4

Designing and doing the study

> Adaptive theory proposes that greater adequacy and validity should be understood as the best approximation to truth given the present state of knowledge and understanding. It is not a once-for-all notion ... it is revisable in terms of future research and theoretical developments.
>
> (Layder, 1998: p. 9)

Introduction, study aims and orientation

The primary aim of this study was to examine the positions of practitioners in specific school systems in England, the USA and the Netherlands to recognising and resolving dilemmas of difference in relation to special and inclusive education. There were two secondary aims, one was to compare these perspectives to the SEN/disability dilemmas with those from similar groups in the United Kingdom and the USA from the early 1990s, and the other, to examine perspectives about the possibility of related dilemmas or tensions about educational differentiation in other areas of difference, such as gender, social class, ethnic and cultural/religious differences. However, there has not been enough space in this book to present the findings relating to the second of these secondary aims.

The study is based on the assumption that there are hard decisions or dilemmas about difference and differentiation – whether or not to recognise and respond to learner differences. This is because there are positive and negative conceptions in our society about human differences and what we call differentiation in education. The negative perspective is that 'difference' reflects lower status, less value, perpetuating inequalities and poor quality provision and unfair treatment. The positive perspective is that 'difference' reflects the recognition of individuality and individual needs and interests. It is this tension between these conceptions of difference that leads us to confront dilemmas of difference. The dilemma is that both options, to recognise and respond or not to recognise and respond to difference, have negative risks. As discussed in Chapter 2, differences are addressed throughout education, not just in the field of disability and difficulties. So we would expect to find some expressions of the difference dilemmas in other areas and aspects of education. But, as we deal in special education with exceptional differences, we would expect to confront these general dilemmas in a more accentuated form here.

As argued in the 1993 study (Norwich, 1993b), it is possible to identify these difference dilemmas applying to the SEN/disability field in three areas:

i   whether and how to identify children with significant difficulties in learning as having SEN/disabilities or not – the identification dilemma;
ii   whether children with SEN/disabilities should learn the same common curriculum content as other children without SEN/disabilities or not – the curriculum dilemma; and
iii whether and to what extent children with more severe SEN/disabilities should learn in ordinary classrooms or not – location dilemma.

A similar research orientation was used in this study as in the study 13 years ago. This involved an exploratory semi-structured interview to generate both quantitative and qualitative data. The aim was to engage participants in explanations and justifications of their positions and perspectives and to see how they responded to suggested contrary positions, in what can be called an argumentative model. The methodological approach draws on adaptive theory (Layder, 1998 – see quote above).

Local and national settings

This study replicated key aspects of the 1993 study, but was also extended to include a third country, the Netherlands, for the reasons explained in Chapter 3. Given the nature of the study and the research resources involved (the author conducting all aspects of the study), it was decided to focus on one part or region of each country. In the USA, this was one State on the east coast, in the Netherlands this was in the north of the country and in England in the south-west region. These decisions were based on opportunity and access. However within these general areas of the countries, attempts were made to undertake the study in urban and rural settings and to involve participants from different levels and in different roles and school settings.

Table 4.1 below gives some background data on the two US school districts. This shows that the urban district, a large city school district, had a higher percentage of children identified as in special education than the State average, while the rural district, a farming and commuting area, had about the same percentage as the State average. The State average (13 per cent) was slightly higher than the US national figure of about 10 per cent (see Chapter 3). The urban district had more students with IEPs in separate

Table 4.1 Comparative data on two US school districts, 2004

	Urban district	Rural district	State average
Number of students with disabilities	14,900	3,700	111,600
Percentage of students with disabilities of general student enrolment	17	13	13
More than 60% of class time in separate settings	27	8	18
Percentage of students with disabilities by origin (% in general district population in brackets):			
African/American	87 (89)	4.7 (3.0)	40 (38)
White	12 (9)	93 (94)	51 (50)
Hispanic	1 (1.6)	2 (2.0)	6 (7)
Asian/Pacific islander	0.4 (0.6)	0.2 (0.3)	0.4 (0.4)
American Indian/Alaskan	0.3 (0.3)	1 (1.4)	2 (5)

Data source: State census data.

settings and the rural district had less than the State average. These data also show the predominantly African/American origins of students in the urban district, and white origin of those students in the rural district.

The urban English LEA, a city LEA, had a larger overall school population than the rural LEA, which consisted of some towns and farming areas. Table 4.2 shows that the rural LEA had a lower percentage of pupils with Statements than the national average, while the urban LEA had a higher percentage of pupils with Statements than the national average. A similar pattern is evident in the percentage of children with Statements in primary and secondary schools, the urban LEA above and rural LEA below the national average. The second part of Table 4.2 shows the pattern of placement of pupils with SEN across different kinds of provision. Both LEAs had a slightly greater percentage of pupils with Statements in full-time separate provision and a lower percentage in resourced or SE units in mainstream schools than the national average. For the percentage with Statements, the rural LEA had below national average levels of all pupils in separate provision full-time (0.89 per cent), while the urban area (1.41 per cent) had an above national average level (1.13 per cent). By comparison with the two districts in the USA, both LEAs had populations which were predominantly White British or White Other; both had low percentages of Black and Minority Ethnic populations, 1.38 per cent for the rural area and only very slightly higher at 1.65 per cent for the city area. (National Census data, 2001)

Data for the Netherlands rural school board show that this was a very small authority, being responsible for only about 2000 students. The board identified about 10 per cent of these students as in need of some special

Table 4.2 Comparative data on two English Local Education Authorities, 2006

	Total number of all pupils	% of all pupils with Statements	% of all pupils in primary schools		% of all pupils in secondary schools	
			School Action and School Action Plus	Statement	School Action and School Action Plus	Statement
Rural LEA	29,169	2.2	16.7	1.0	11.2	1.8
Urban LEA	39,931	3.4	19.4	1.7	13.9	2.3
National average		2.9	17.2	1.6	15.0	2.2

	Placement of pupils as % of pupils with Statements					Percentage of all pupils in full-time separate provision
	Resourced or SE unit in mainstream	Mainstream provision	Special school	Hospital school or pupil referral unit	Total in full-time separate provision	
Rural LEA	5.3	50.4	39.9	0.7	40.6	0.89
Urban LEA	7.3	50.6	38.9	2.7	41.6	1.41
National average	8.3	50.6	38.2	0.9	39.1	1.13

Data source: DfES Statistics, 2006.

Table 4.3 Breakdown of special education statistics for Netherlands rural school board, 2004

Number of students in rural board	about 2000
Number identified with needs for special education (including those with back-packs)	200 (10%)
Number with SEN back-packs in ordinary schools	50 (2.5%)
Number with SEN back-packs in special schools	5 (0.25%)

Data source: District education plan 2005.

education provision in ordinary schools. This included the 50 students with back-packs for their special needs in ordinary schools, about 2.5 per cent of all students. This board ran no special schools, but had five students in special schools in other areas, a quarter of a per cent of all students.

The data for the urban area in the Netherlands, in Table 4.4, show that 8.7 per cent of all children in the urban schools were in special schools or receiving services through the Expertise Centres. Of these, 2.3 per cent were in special schools, which is close to the national level of 2.2 per cent.

Table 4.4 Breakdown of special education statistics for Netherlands urban area, 2005–6

Number in primary schools	11,933
Number in secondary schools	12,990
Number receiving special education (special schools and through Expertise Centres)	2,381
Percentage receiving special education	8.7
Percentage in special schools	2.3
National percentage in special schools (2005)	2.2

Data source: OCSW, 2006.

Schools, administrative offices and participants

The research plan was to interview practising educators and administrators or advisers at each level in the system in each country across two authorities, districts or areas. The key contacts to gain permission to undertake the study at school level were senior administrative officers at US District or English Authority level. Securing permission in all three countries was not straightforward, though once given in the USA and England arrangements were easy. By contrast, in the Netherlands contacts were made directly to schools and services not through local administrators. This reflected a more diverse and loosely coupled system where headteachers and teachers had more control over participating in the study. This feature of the system made it much slower to gain permission to arrange interviews in the Netherlands and this explained the reduced number of participant interviews. Table 4.5 shows the number of visits to different kinds of schools and administrative offices to interview participants. This involved visits to national Departments of Education (Ministry in the Netherlands) in each of the countries. In the USA this also included visits to the State department, in England to the bases for those working at regional level. Where there were support service offices, for psychologists and specialist teachers, as in England and the Netherlands, these were visited too. The plan was to visit special schools for students/pupils with severe emotional and behaviour difficulties and with severe/complex learning difficulties/disabilities, as these represent two areas where research indicates that teachers in ordinary schools have some doubts about inclusion. Local contacts in the two areas in each of the three countries recommended schools. In the case of ordinary schools, these were often ones with special education resources or units attached or with an established internal SEN support system. All the indications were that I was directed to what my local contacts considered to be their 'best' provision. In all, 51 schools and offices were visited.

Table 4.6 shows the number of participants interviewed in the urban and rural areas and at national, state or regional levels. The plan was to interview 50 participants in each country from each of these levels. This was done

Table 4.5 The number of visits to different kinds of administrative, support offices and schools across the three countries

	USA	Netherlands	England	Total
National/State/Regional Departments/ Ministry of Education	3	1	4	8
District/Local Authority offices	2	2	2	6
Support service office	NA	2	2	4
Special schools/centres				
Severe/complex disability	4	2	2	8
Emotional/behaviour difficulties	2	2	3	7
Elementary/primary	4	3	2	9
Middle/junior high	3	NA	NA	3
High/secondary	3	1	2	6
Totals	21	13	17	51

NA = Not applicable.

Table 4.6 Breakdown of participants by area and level across the three countries

	USA		Netherlands		England		Totals	
Area/ level	No.	%	No.	%	No.	%	No.	%
Urban district/Authority/Board	23	46	24	75	22	44	69	52.3
Rural district/Authority/Board	19	38	4	12.5	21	42	44	33.3
State/regional/national	8	16	4	12.5	7	14	19	13.4
Totals	50	100	32	100	50	100	132	100

for the USA and England, but for the Netherlands it was only possible to interview four participants in the rural area.

Table 4.7 shows that the plan to cover the range of roles was successfully implemented. The total number of participants was 132.

Designing the data generation methods

It was decided after careful consideration to use an exploratory semi-structured interview method to generate the data for several reasons. This approach had been used successfully in the 1993 study. Using a similar approach this time would also assist in comparing the results. However, other options about presentation and responding had been examined. There were two options about presentation that were considered. One was to use a particular case presentation of the dilemmas, instead of presenting the dilemmas, as in the 1993 study, as general sets of options and their negative consequences. An example of this particular approach was used by

Table 4.7 Breakdown of participants by role across the three countries

Roles	USA No.	%	Netherlands No.	%	England No.	%	Total No.	%
SE resource teachers/ SE supervisors in regular school/ SEN co-ordinators	9	18	4	12.5	8	16	21	15.9
Senior teachers, regular school	2	4	3	9.4	4	8	9	6.8
Class teachers, regular school	5	10	2	6.3	3	6	10	7.6
Senior teachers, special school/centre	5	10	4	12.5	7	14	16	12.1
Class teachers, special school	7	14	5	15.5	7	14	19	14.4
Resource teachers, special school/centre	4	8	3	9.4	2	4	9	6.8
Counsellors/psychologists/ therapists	7	14	3	9.4	6	12	16	12.1
Teaching assistants	1	2	–	–	3	6	4	3.0
School district/LEA/Board administrators	2	4	4	12.5	3	6	9	6.8
Administrators/advisers in State/ National SE department	8	16	4	12.5	7	14	19	14.4
Totals	50	100	32	100	50	100	132	100

Kohlberg in his well-known study of children's moral reasoning (Kohlberg, 1984). An advantage of the vignette method was that hard choices could be illustrated in particular terms, but the disadvantages were seen to outweigh this advantage. Particular cases might not be transferable across the different countries. An advantage of the general presentation was that participants could make sense of the dilemmas in terms of their particular situations, though this required that the interviewing encouraged an engagement with the presented general dilemma. This factor proved crucial in deciding to use a general presentation as in the 1993 study. Options about participants' response mode were also considered. Instead of leaving it open to participants to structure their own responses to the presented dilemmas, response options could be provided for participants to choose their explanations and justifications. This approach would have also enabled the use of a questionnaire and possibly a larger sample of participants. However, the crucial disadvantage with this method was that it gave little flexibility to participants to present their own interpretations, explanations and justifications. So it was decided that participants would structure their own responses and use a semi-structured interview method as in the 1993 study. As in that earlier study this put much emphasis on the methods of interviewing, in particular to engage participants in considering various perspectives that differed from their own perspectives. This style of argumentative interviewing pursued participants' responses by asking for reasons for not accepting different perspectives and positions.

Figure 4.1 sets out the provided dilemma statements. Some of the wording in the dilemma statements was altered from the 1993 study. Now that the term 'disability' is more current in the United Kingdom, as it is in the other two countries, it was decided to adopt the phrasing 'disabilities needing special education'. In the location dilemma the reference is to 'moderate and severe disabilities' and this was explained in interviews as compared with mild disabilities or what is sometimes called 'high incidence' areas. These are not precise terms, but participants could understand enough to make their own sense of this end of the range of SEN/disability. As in the 1993 study, these dilemmas could have been presented with more than one outcome for each option. However, this would have complicated the participants' evaluation of the dilemmas. In any case, it was possible to examine whether they identified other negative and positive outcomes other than the negative ones presented. The dilemma areas were also in the same sequence as in the earlier study.

Participants were provided with a booklet which set out the dilemmas in written form. In the Netherlands, where all the interviews were conducted in English, participants were provided with a Dutch and English version of the dilemmas. Following each dilemma statement in the booklets, partici-pants were provided with two rating scales for them to give their rating of

---

Identification:
- If children experiencing difficulties in learning are identified and labelled as having a disability (needing special education), then they are likely to be treated as different, devalued and stigmatised.
- If children experiencing difficulties in learning are NOT identified as having a disability (needing special education), then it is less likely additional educational resources will be identified and ensured for them.

Curriculum:
- If children identified as having a disability (needing special education) are offered the same learning experiences as other children, they are likely to be denied the opportunity to have learning experiences relevant to their individual needs.
- If children identified as having a disability (needing special education) are NOT offered the same learning experiences as other children, then they are likely to be treated as a separate lower status group and be denied equal opportunities.

Location:
- If children with moderate and severe disabilities (needing special education) are taught in general classrooms, then they are less likely to have access to scarce and specialist services and facilities.
- If children with moderate and severe disabilities (needing special education) are NOT taught in general classrooms, then they are more likely to feel excluded and not be accepted by other children.

Figure 4.1 Formulation of three dilemmas.

their degree of recognition of the dilemma and degree of resolution, only if they had recognised it – see Figure 4.2.

Interviewing procedures and ethical issues

Interviews took between 45 and 60 minutes and were conducted on an individual basis, except on two occasions when there were more involved (in one case, two teachers and in another four State administrators). This was done because of the pressure of time. All participants consented to the interviews on the basis of an explanation of the purposes of the study and what would happen to the interviews. Confidentiality and anonymity were assured. It was explained that this meant that there would be no reference to themselves as individuals, their service or school or their authority/district. They were promised a report on the findings before any publications about the study. These conditions have all been met. Participants also consented to tape recordings, except in three cases in the USA where handwritten notes of their responses were taken during the interviews.

At the start of the interviews participants were shown the first page of the booklet which set out the form of the dilemmas – see Figure 4.3. This was used to explain what was meant by a dilemma in the study and the interview.

---

1. To what extent do these statements represent a dilemma for you?

Choose one of the answers:

| Cannot decide | Not at all | Marginal extent | Significant extent | Considerable extent |

2. If you see a dilemma, how would you resolve the dilemma?

Choose one of the answers:

| Cannot decide | Not at all | Marginal extent | Significant extent | Considerable extent |

Figure 4.2 Dilemma recognition and resolution rating scales.

Dilemmas:

Involve decision situations where there are options (1 and 2) and each has negative consequences or risks;

If I do 1, then there is a risk of a negative consequence

If I do 2, then there is also a risk of a negative consequence

---

Figure 4.3 Account presented about the nature of dilemmas.

The booklet was used to provide some structure and sequence for the interviews, though there was much opportunity to be flexible as well. Participants also explained at the start of the interviews the various aspects about their work settings and the background to their local and national systems. The interviewing style also enabled discussion and interchange to take place to allow for other matters to arise and be examined. One emergent aspect that arose during the resolution to the location dilemma was the future of special schools.

How participants dealt with the presented dilemmas

A small minority of participants across the three countries reported that they could not decide about their response to one of the dilemmas. The frequencies for this are reported in Chapters 5–7. Some other participants wanted to give different responses to what they saw as different aspects. All of these participants were content to split their response in terms of two different aspects, whether it was in terms of the kind of school or the degree of severity of SEN/disabilities. The flexibility of the semi-structured interview method made this possible. Details about this kind of split response are also reported in Chapters 5–7.

The recording and transcribing of the interviews in full also made it possible to examine some of the different ways in which participants responded to the dilemmas in addition to the content of their responses. During the qualitative data analysis it was possible to code those interactions that revealed some of these ways. There is no space to provide excerpts to illustrate this analysis of the 13 distinct ways of responding, which were identified in terms of the general theme 'ways of dealing with dilemma presentation' across the three countries. For example, when some participants were asked if they saw a dilemma they responded by 'quickly giving a resolution'.

Another fairly common response was to relate the general formulation of the presented dilemmas to a familiar concrete situation. These responses led to the interviewer trying to re-focus on the question. Related to this 'concrete way' of dealing with the dilemmas were responses that raised a 'different issue'. Several participants also responded by trying to make sense of the presented dilemmas by thinking aloud. This deliberating process also eventuated in some participants 'clarifying and then changing their position during interview'. It is notable that very few participants questioned the wording of the dilemma statements.

Analysing the data

Dilemma recognition and resolution ratings were transferred from the interview transcripts to SPSS data files and from these analysed in terms of their distributions and some simple bi-variate relationships. The qualitative data, which constituted about 600,000 words or about 1,200 pages of single-spaced transcribed interview text across the three countries, were analysed at several levels using the NVIVO programme. Figure 4.4 below shows the design and process of this analysis. The numbers in each box of the figure show the order in which analysis took place. For each country's set of transcriptions, the data were analysed in terms of six areas, made up of three dilemma areas × two (recognition and resolution) responses. The US interviews were the first to be analysed in terms of 1st level themes, using a grounded style of comparing responses in each of the six areas to identify distinct themes which applied across the responses of the participants. In terms of Drisko's approaches to qualitative data analysis, the 1st level was an editing approach, which emphasises the interpretation of meanings in the text in a grounded theory style (Drisko, 2000). Table 4.8 shows the number of distinct 1st level themes that were identified for the six areas across the three countries.

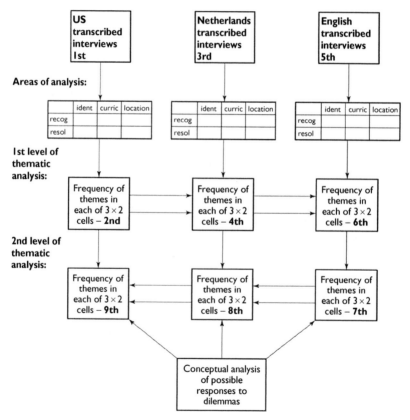

Figure 4.4 Design and process of qualitative data analysis (numbering from 1st to 9th represents steps in the sequence of analyses).

Table 4.8 Frequencies of 1st level themes across the three countries

		Identification	*Curriculum*	*Location*
Recognition	USA	38	31	54
themes	England	49	48	75
	Netherlands	37	39	52
Resolution	USA	30	29	47
themes	England	39	41	68
	Netherlands	30	32	49

In generating 1st level themes for the second step, the Netherlands data, themes that were generated for the US data were used when they fitted. Otherwise, new themes were generated. Similarly, themes for the English data, drew on themes generated for the US and Netherlands analyses where they fitted, otherwise new ones were generated. Table 4.8 shows that the numbers of themes across the six areas was similar for the US and Netherlands data, but consistently more themes were used for the English data. This could be due to the much greater length of the English transcriptions (279,000 words) than the US (175,000 words) and Netherlands (144,000 words) transcripts.

The 1st level coding of the data then made it possible to derive the frequencies with which these themes were used in the six areas across the three countries. This was done by setting up SPSS data files for each of the six areas across each country (18 files) to cross-reference the themes used by each of the participants. From these data files it was possible to identify the overall frequency of use of the 1st level themes and the frequency of use of themes for different levels of dilemma recognition and resolution.

Given the extensive range of distinct themes used to explain and justify recognition and resolutions of these dilemmas, it was decided to develop a 2nd level of thematic analysis. The aim was to identify commonalities across the 1st level themes within each area, which would also relate to a conceptual analysis of the kinds of responses expected for these dilemmas. So, the themes were generated, on the one hand, by using a grounded style of comparing 1st level themes, and on the other hand, by relating these emergent themes to the conceptual analysis. In terms of Drisko's approaches, this 2nd level of thematic analysis was a template approach, which uses themes derived from top down (conceptual analysis) and bottom up influences (emergent 1st level themes) (Drisko, 2000).

Four broad alternative responses can be identified to a dilemma in the form of the one used in this study (see Figure 4.5). One alternative is that the hard choice is recognised and experienced, called 'tension'. Another assumes that there is still some tension but a choice has been made through some balancing, called 'resolved tension'. The third alternative questions

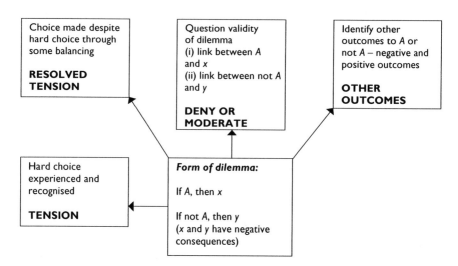

Figure 4.5 Map of conceptual analysis of different responses to a dilemma (in the form presented in study) for use in the 2nd level themes.

the validity of the dilemma by questioning the link between the option and negative outcome. This can be done for one or both options, though doubt about either one is enough to 'deny or moderate the dilemma'. The fourth alternative presents other outcomes for either option, which could be more negative outcomes or some positive ones, called 'other outcomes'. The 2nd level thematic analysis undertaken integrated this conceptual analysis with the emergent analysis of the 1st level recognition themes. Table 4.9 shows the 2nd level themes across the three dilemmas which were used across the 1st level themes in all three countries.

The theoretical input into the derivation of the 2nd level themes for resolving the dilemmas also followed from dilemmatic assumptions. First, it was assumed that there would be some recognition of the persistence of issues in the resolutions. Second, it was assumed that some resolutions would take the form of either balancing or trading off between options or giving priority to certain options. Table 4.9 shows for all three dilemmas that there was a 'continuing issues' 2nd level theme and that there were instances of balancing between and prioritising options.

Concluding comments

Reliability of 1st and 2nd level coding was checked by an independent coder and found to be at a satisfactory level (80 per cent and above). Because of space limits these details will be reported in a journal publication. The following three chapters will each focus on one of the dilemmas in terms of the quantitative and qualitative data analyses described above. These chapters contain examples of excerpts from the interviews to illustrate 1st level themes. These excerpts were selected from the NVIVO database of themes. The selections were in terms of excerpts which best illustrated the theme, but space limits meant keeping excerpts to illustrate the themes to a minimum.

Table 4.9 Breakdown of 2nd level themes for recognition and resolution of dilemmas across the three countries

	Identification dilemma	*Curriculum dilemma*	*Location dilemma*
Recognition	Tensions	Tensions	Tension
	Resolved tensions	Resolved tension	Resolved tension
	Other positive consequences	Other positive consequences	Moderate/deny reduced specialist provision
	Other negative consequences	Other negative consequences	Moderate/deny feel excluded
	Negative consequences by other means	Moderate relevance/ individual needs consequence	Positive aspects inclusion
	Moderate or deny devaluation consequences	Moderate lower status consequence	Positive aspects separation
	Moderate or deny resources consequences	Wider than SEN tensions	Depends
	Depends	Depends	Comments
	Comments	Comments	
Resolution	Continuing issue	Continuing issue	Continuing issue
	Reduce special education identification	Balance common/ different aspects	Balance included/ separate provision
	Change attitude to disability/SEN	Priority to individual relevance	Student and parent participation
	National/local developments	Priority to common aspects	Accept separate specialist provision
	Go beyond negative labels	Promote positive aspects of difference	Limits to inclusion
	Choice	Enhance staffing/ resources	Promote positive contacts, attitudes, reduce feelings of exclusion
	Communication	System development	Enhance flexible specialist services/ staffing in regular schools
	Comments	Participation Comments Depends	Systemic/national changes Comments

Chapter 5

Identification dilemma

and so before you start labelling kids you want to have an intervention that's really robust.

(US Federal administrator)

a lot of people in the normal education can't see beyond the label; I think at special school people work with these children, they see who they are.

(Netherlands special school teacher)

whilst there's still some people outside who are still using derogatory terms about people with disabilities, you are going to be up against it, so it will not be resolved totally, without any doubt.

(English special school teacher)

Introduction

The first of the chapters about the findings will be about responses to the identification dilemma. This dilemma is about using a label such as special educational needs or disability in relation to individual children who experience difficulties in learning. The identification dilemma took the following form:

- If children experiencing difficulties in learning are identified and labelled as having a disability (needing special education), then they are likely to be treated as different, devalued and stigmatised.
- If children experiencing difficulties in learning are NOT identified as having a disability (needing special education), then it is less likely additional educational resources will be identified and ensured for them.

The chapter includes the recognition and resolution ratings, thematic analyses and selected excerpts from what the participants explained in interview across the three country groups.

Identification recognition ratings

Table 5.1 shows that the most frequent recognition rating by US participants was 'marginal' (34 per cent) compared to 'significant' for the Netherlands group (38 per cent). English participants had two ratings as most frequent, 'not at all' and 'significant', both at 26 per cent. However, this difference missed statistical significance at the 0.05 level, using a chi-square test (chi-squared = 17.6, df = 10, p = 0.06).

Taken overall this table shows that a majority of participants in each country recognised the identification dilemma to some extent (marginal, significant or considerable ratings – 68 per cent for the US, 72 per cent for the Netherlands and 56 per cent for the English participants). The corresponding figures indicate that a minority of the country participants recognised no identification dilemma – 20 per cent in the US group, 16 per cent in the Netherlands and 26 per cent in the English. This needs to be set in the context that only one participant (a US one) was uncertain about adopting a rating position and that a minority in each country found it useful to split their responses in terms of a distinction between two aspects – what is called a split response in Table 5.1.

Split identification recognition responses

Participants in each country split recognition responses to distinguish between some aspect where they saw no dilemma (such as severe disabilities, special schools or themselves) and another aspect where they usually saw a significant dilemma (such as moderate disabilities, ordinary schools or other professionals). There were fewer split responses to this dilemma by the US and Netherlands participants than by the English participants and little overlap in the aspects distinguished.

Identification resolution ratings

Table 5.2 shows the extent to which participants considered that the identification dilemma could be resolved. The most frequent resolution rating was 'significant' across all three participants groups – 38 per cent for the US, 48 per cent for the Netherlands and 32 per cent for the English participants. This consistency is reflected in the non-significant association between resolution ratings across the three countries, using a chi-square analysis (chi-squared = 8.3, df = 10, p = 0.60). Overall Table 5.2 shows that with the exception of three US participants all believed that there could be some degree of resolution (marginal, significant or considerable). However, there were more English participants who were uncertain about their resolution or who split their resolution responses than for US or Netherlands participants – for uncertain responses 5 versus 3 and 0, and for split responses

Table 5.1 Breakdown of identification recognition ratings across the three countries

	USA	Netherlands	England
Not at all	10 (20%)	5 (16%)	**13 (26%)**
Marginal	**17 (34%)**	2 (6%)	7 (14%)
Marginal/significant	0	0	2 (4%)
Significant	11 (22%)	**12 (38%)**	11 (22%)
Significant/considerable	2 (4%)	1 (3%)	0
Considerable	4 (8%)	8 (25%)	8 (16%)
Uncertain	1 (2%)	0	0
Split responses	5 (10%)	4 (13%)	9 (18%)
Breakdown of pairs of ratings	Not at all + significant 1	Not at all + marginal 1	Not at all + marginal 1
	Not at all + considerable 1	Not at all + significant 2	Not at all + significant 6
	Not at all + marginal 1	Not at all + considerable 1	Not at all + significant 2
	Marginal + significant 2		
Totals	50 (100%)	32 (100%)	50 (100%)

Notes
Bold represents most frequent ratings.
Uncertain – participants were reluctant to indicate a degree.
Split responses – participants interpreted issue by responding in two distinct ways.

Table 5.2 Breakdown of identification resolution ratings across the three countries

	USA	Netherlands	England
Not at all	3 (6%–8%)	0	0
Marginal	11 (22–28%)	9 (28–33%)	4 (8–11%)
Marginal/significant	2 (4%) }	1 (3%) }	2 (4%) }
Significant	**15 (30–38%)**	**13 (41–48%)**	**12 (24–32%)**
Significant/considerable	1 (2%)	12 (38%) }	5 (10–19%) }
Considerable	2 (4%) }	0	2 (4%) }
Uncertain	3 (6%–8%)	1 (3–4%)	3 (6%)
Split responses	5 (10–13%)	4 (13–15%)	5 (10–14%)
			11 (22–30%)
Breakdown of pairs of ratings	N/a + marginal — 1 Considerable + uncertain — 1 **Significant + uncertain — 2** Marginal + significant — 1	N/a + marginal — 1 Significant + significant — 1 **N/a + significant — 2**	N/a + not at all — 4 N/a + marginal — 1 **N/a + significant** N/a + uncertain — 1 Marginal + significant — 2 Significant + significant — 2
Those recognising dilemma	40 (80%)	27 (84%)	37 (74%)
Those not recognising dilemma	10 (20%)	5 (16%)	13 (26%)
Totals	50 (100%)	32 (100%)	50 (100%)

Notes

Figures in brackets: first figure, percentage out of all participants; second figure, percentage out of those who recognised the dilemma.

Bold represents most frequent rating.

Uncertain: participants were reluctant to indicate a degree.

Split responses: participants interpreted issue by responding in different way.

N/a: not applicable – when dilemma not recognised, resolution question is not applicable.

11 versus 5 and 4 for English versus US or Netherlands participants, respectively.

It is also notable that for those splitting their responses, resolution levels were mostly at a significant level – 3/5 US, 3/4 Netherlands and 8/11 English participants – which corresponded with the most frequent resolution level for the majority of participants who did not split their response to the identification dilemma.

Recognition and resolution ratings by professional role

With the study participants in each country holding a wide variety of roles across the system it was necessary to reduce the range of recorded roles from ten (see Chapter 4 for details) to four broad areas – administration (including local, regional, State or national administrators), support professionals (school/educational psychologists, counsellors, therapists, advisory teachers), regular school professionals (senior and class teachers and resource/SEN coordinators) and special school professionals (senior and class and resource teachers).

For the US participants it was found that the most frequent recognition level for the identification dilemma was 'marginal' for support professionals, regular and special school professionals, in line with the most frequent overall marginal rating for all US participants (see Table 5.3). This contrasts with the finding for the administrative group where the most frequent recognition level was 'not at all'. No statistical analyses of the asso-

Table 5.3 Breakdown of most frequent recognition and resolution ratings by role

		USA	Netherlands	England
Recognition	Administrators	Not at all	Considerable	Significant
	Support professionals	Marginal + significant	Significant	Significant
	Regular school professionals	Marginal	Significant	Not at all
	Special school professionals	Marginal	Considerable	Not at all
	Overall	**Marginal**	**Significant**	**Not at all + significant**
Resolution	Administrators	Significant	Significant	Significant + split
	Support professionals	Marginal	Significant	Uncertain
	Regular school professionals	Significant	Marginal	Significant
	Special school professionals	Marginal + significant	Significant	Split
	Overall	**Significant**	**Significant**	**Significant**

ciations between role and recognition and resolution levels were conducted because sample sizes were too small. For the breakdown of resolution ratings by broad role area, it was found that the most frequent ratings for administrators and regular school professionals was 'significant' and for special school professionals, 'significant and marginal'. This is consistent with the most frequent overall significant resolution rating for all US participants. By contrast the most frequent resolution rating for support professionals was 'marginal'. The 'marginal' modal rating for special school and support professionals is in line with the second most frequent resolution rating (marginal).

For the Netherlands participants the most frequent recognition level was 'significant' for support and regular school professionals, This is consistent with the most frequent overall recognition level for Netherlands participants. However, the most frequent recognition rating for administrators and special school professionals was 'considerable'. For the breakdown of resolution ratings it was found that the most frequent rating was 'significant' for administrators, support professionals and special school professionals. This was in line with the most frequent overall rating, but contrasted with the most frequent resolution being 'marginal' for the ordinary school professionals.

For the English participants it was found that the most frequent recognition level for administrators and support professionals was 'significant'. For the other two broad groups, ordinary and special school professionals it was 'not at all'. The administrators and support professionals, those outside schools, tended to see a significant identification dilemma, while school professionals, in both special and ordinary schools, tended to see no dilemma. For resolution ratings, only ordinary school professionals and administrators had the same level as the overall most frequent rating (significant). However, administrators also had the same frequency of split responses and the most frequent rating for special school professionals was for split responses. For support professionals the most frequent resolution rating was 'uncertain'. This breakdown of English resolution ratings shows a notable proportion of English participants who split their responses to this dilemma or were uncertain about its resolution.

Qualitative accounts of the recognition of identification dilemma

As explained in Chapter 4, the explanations for recognising the dilemmas were analysed at two levels. The number of distinct 1st level themes across the three countries ranged from 37 to 49, while most participants used between two and three themes to explain their position, with some participants using up to six and nine themes.

Table 5.4 shows the nine common 2nd level themes which were used to

Table 5.4 Comparison of all 1st and 2nd level themes for recognising identification dilemma across the three countries

	USA	Netherlands	England
Tensions	N=33(66%)[a]	N=23(72%)	N=32(64%)
	*Tension experienced 7[b]	*Tension experienced 6	*Tension experienced 13
	*Students try to avoid stigma 7	*Students try to avoid stigma 1	*Students try to avoid stigma 2
	*Over-identification problem 2	*Over-identification problem 1	*Over-identification problem 4
	*Double jeopardy 1	*Double jeopardy 1	
		*SEN label as negative 7	*SEN label as negative 2
		*Label can lead to stigma 3	*SEN label can lead to stigma 8
		*Some parents experience stigma 4	*Some parents experience stigma 5
	Negative evaluation of additional help 7	Schools use labelling to get resources 2	Teenagers are sensitive to different treatment 6
	Most stigma mild disabilities 3	Students experience stigma in peer relationships 2	Parents do not want label 4
	Stigma for families 3	Scary for parents to have label 1	Reduced individual identification is still needed 2
	Implicit stigma 3	Tension for regular schools letting go' 1	Label of any kind leads to devaluation 1
	Stigma associated with ability grouping 2	Parents complain about students' behaviour problems 1	Disability label is problem 1
	Implicit tension 1	Negative labelling by going to special school 1	Hard to identify without negative label 1
	In-class support increases stigma 1	Wider community stigma 1	
	Most stigma behaviour problems 1		
	Stigma if at school after usual leaving time 1		
	Stigma if special education for long period 1		
	Stigma prevents earlier intervention 1		
Resolved tensions	N=9(18%)	N=5(16%)	N=12(24%)
	*Need outweighs stigma 8	*Need outweighs stigma 5	*Need outweighs stigma 12
	Weigh risk versus benefits 1		

Other positive consequences	N=0	N=8(25%) *Identification is required for positive outcomes 4 Need for objective identification 3 Labels useful for pupils 2 Labels useful to peers 2	N=10(20%) *Identification is required for positive outcomes 10 Labels support understanding and sensitivity 1 Well-explained labels are positive 1
Other negative consequences	N=2(4%) *Teacher denies responsibility by labelling 2	N=4(13%) *Teachers/schools deny responsibility 4	N=3(6%) *Teacher denies responsibility by labelling 2 Labelling can lower expectations 1
Negative consequences by other means	N=2(4%) *Stigma exists without labels 2	N=0	N=3(6%) *Stigma exists without labels 3
Moderate/deny devaluation consequences	34(68%) *Positive action has been taken 13 *Stigma has reduced 13 *Disability positive image 12 *Label does not lead to devaluation 8 *Parents want label 5 *Most students do not care about label 2	N=16(50%) *Positive actions 6 *Stigma has reduced 3 *Disability more positive image 3 *Label does not lead to devaluation 1 *Some parents want label; some not 4 *Most students do not care about label 2	N=27(54%) *Positive action has been taken 5 *Stigma has reduced 5 *Disability positive image 2 *Label does not lead to devaluation 11 *Parents want label 6 *Most students do not care about label 2

Table 5.4 (Continued)

	USA	Netherlands	England
	*Reduced degree identification 3 *Stigma less in junior years 3 *Less stigma within special school 3 In-class support reduces stigma 10 Student unaware of stigma 3 Student unaware in special education 3 Older students cope with labelling 1 Students separate classes also join in 1	*Reduced degree of identification 1 Parents mostly positive about labelling 2 Reduce stigma by placing in regular school 2 Less student stigma in smaller groups 1	*Stigma less with younger children 3 *Less stigma within special school 4 Can identify needs without labelling 11 All have different needs, treat as individuals 4 Treated as different does not necessarily lead to devaluation 3 Stigma issues worked through 1 Very few parents do not want label 1 Ignore labels 1 Parents do not see stigma 1
Moderate/deny resource consequences	N=11(22%) *Alternative non-SE services 8 *How alternatives to SE work 5	N=2(6%) *Alternative non-SE provision 1 *Some parents want additional resources without labels 1	6(12%) *Alternative non-SE services 1 *How alternatives to SE work 3 *Do not need label for resources 2
Depends	N=5(10%) *Depends on many factors 3 *Stigma depends on school 3	N=2(6%) *Stigma depends on many factors 1 *Depends on perspective 1	N=12(24%) *Stigma depends on many factors 1 *Depends on how inclusive school 7 *Depends on perspective 5 Depends on where in country Depends on child seeing benefits 1

Comments	N=2(4%)	N=6(19%)	N=7(14%)
	Self-limiting purpose of special education provision 2	Parental reasons for labelling and not labelling 5 Voluntary organisations want to over-label 1 Some parents are shocked then accept label 1	Focus on old thinking in special education 2 Stigma is in wider society 2 Focus on wider vulnerable group 1 Parents views do vary 1 Some parent are shocked then accept label 1 Some cannot see beyond labels 1 Reduced Statements means reduced resources 1

Notes

a N: number of participants using 2nd level theme (% of all participants – in bold if more than 30%).

b * Indicates similar 1st level themes used in two or three of the countries (numbers after 1st level themes represent frequency of use of this theme).

analyse the 1st level themes for each country group. The table also indicates which 1st level themes were common across two and three countries (indicated by an asterisk). Second level themes which were used by more than 30 per cent of the participants are in bold.

'Tensions' was the most frequently used theme (by about two-thirds or more of participants in each country). The second most frequently used 2nd level theme 'moderate/deny devaluation consequence' was used by about half of the Netherlands and English participants, but by about two-thirds of the US participants (68 per cent). In fact, the US participants used this moderate/deny theme slightly more than the tensions theme (66 per cent).

The other moderate/deny 2nd level theme – 'moderate/deny resource consequence' – was used more frequently by US than Netherlands or English participants (22 per cent versus 6 per cent and 12 per cent, respectively). This finding can be linked to the previous finding that the US participants had a consistently lower modal recognition rating than the Netherlands or English participants (marginal versus significant and significant/not at all, see Table 5.1 above). It is these two moderate/deny consequences themes which reflect the participants' direct questioning of the negative consequences presented in the identification dilemma. Another 2nd level theme – 'resolved tensions' – reflects a recognition of tensions between needed provision and stigma, but weighs the two in favour of needed provision. Almost a quarter of English participants (24 per cent) used this theme compared to fewer US and Netherlands participants (18 per cent and 16 per cent, respectively). The greater use of this theme by English participants can be linked to one of the two most frequent recognition ratings – 'not at all' (26 per cent of participants each).

Second level theme 'tensions'

Table 5.4 shows that there were three 1st level themes, under this 2nd level theme, which were used by participants in each of the countries. These included some of the more frequently used 1st level themes, such as 'tension experienced', 'students try to avoid stigma' and 'over-identification problem'. One theme was common to only the US and Netherlands groups, 'double jeopardy', while three were common to the Netherlands and English groups, 'SEN label as negative', 'label can lead to stigma' and 'some parents experience stigma'.

The following excerpts illustrate the 1st level theme 'tensions experienced':

'tensions experienced'

> where the students are receiving the services you don't want them to be emotionally, you know, experience emotional turmoil from their peers

or educators because they're labelling them as different. However if you don't identify them then they may not get the resources and the instructions they need to make the progress that they are capable of.

(US class teacher, regular school, rural district)

The tension is that if you don't identify them as learning disabled or dyslexic or whatever then the way of looking at the pupils by teachers can be misread. If, for example, you see a student with dyslexia and you don't know if it's dyslexia, you can think 'read harder, do more your best,' etc, and it denies the problem that the child has. On the other hand, if the teacher knows that it's dyslexia 'oh it's dyslexia, I don't have to do anything about it because he cannot read,' and so it's a kind of withdrawal from support, you can get additional resources, but knowing what kind of problem it is or identifying, ADHD is a very beautiful example of it 'It's ADHD so oh any behaviour he expresses it's ADHD, it's not the child, it's ADHD,' and not a child with ADHD.

(Netherlands psychologist, urban area)

Because I think the first one, I feel that if, particularly in a comprehensive school where there are several different teachers teaching the students I do feel that if we identify their difficulties then we are raising awareness and understanding about the difficulty and that, to me, can only be good at the end of the day, however you do run the risk that some staff will treat them less favourably or stigmatise them or whatever. I think it is a significant dilemma. Sometimes when you give them a label you actually kind of create the problem as it were.

(English SEN coordinator, rural area)

The following are excerpts of the second 1st level theme common to each country group, 'student try to avoid stigma':

'student try to avoid stigma'

Oh they know they are (in special ed) but they don't term it special ed either, I mean if you say to them 'I'm having an IEP meeting for you today,' they're like 'What's an IEP?'

(US special education teacher, regular school, rural district)

then it's a secret, they're happy to accept it with you privately but they don't want it publicly announced. Maybe twenty percent or fifteen percent.

(Netherlands, SEN resource teacher, secondary ordinary school)

Absolutely, you know there are certain children that are Statemented that would, despite the fact that they have a teaching assistant assigned to them full time, would insist that it was for the rest of the class, somebody for the whole class, and there are times when she would work with somebody else to avoid that so . . . So yes I mean there's a certain dilemma.

(English teacher, special unit for emotional/behaviour
difficulties, rural area)

There was also some recognition of an 'over-identification problem' across the three groups, but to less a degree:

'over-identification problem'

> And there are pathologies but I don't acknowledge that they are to that extent to which are identified in America . . . they're over identified, yes.
>
> (US Federal administrator)

> I mean I think that the difficulty is the diagnosis, if you actually say . . . I mean you know I've done the interviews a million times over, I teach lots of EBD kids and I think 'yeah but you actually don't, what you deal with is kids with slightly challenging behaviour,' I'm talking about, I think there's a difference between challenging behaviour and EBD, there's a mile of difference.
>
> (English head of behaviour unit, rural area)

One participant in each of the US and Netherlands groups used the theme 'double jeopardy' which indicates that the negative consequences operate both ways – stigma and inadequate services. Here are two excerpts to illustrate this theme:

'double jeopardy'

> once the child is identified as having special education needs they are, they're stigmatised, and many times it sticks and they still don't fix the services.
>
> (US Federal Department administrator)

> Yes because if a child is labelled as having a disability it's also quite frequently thrown in to the hands of teachers who have not been trained to deal with this type of children. So it's not to the child's own advantage. It's not just that they're, as you say, likely to be treated as different, but they're given a label without appropriate help so there's no advantage at all sometimes for those children.
>
> (Netherlands senior teacher, secondary school, urban area)

There were three 1st level themes which were used by Netherlands and English participants. Two were similar, 'SEN label as negative' and 'label can lead to stigma'. Taken together there were ten participants in each group who used these labels. The following are excerpts reflecting these 1st level themes:

'SE label as negative'

> . . . he knows he's labelled and for him or her it could be a very big problem, and parents also have problems with putting a label on their child, so there you have a big tension . . .
>
> (Netherlands advisory teacher, special school)

'label can lead to stigma'

> The possibility, if you label a child with a learning problem the possibility is that they get stigmatised.
>
> (Netherlands class teacher, primary school, urban area)

> I think we're quite a tangible society and therefore as soon as we identify difficulties in learning we tend to short hand that in to a label rather than doing what we should be doing perhaps, looking at needs, and then show which programmes, which interventions should follow. We tend to short hand that in to dyspraxia, dyslexia, these umbrella label terms which actually don't describe the individual need of the child at all. From that short hand they then go into being different, devalued, and stigmatised and we're not careful enough with our language to avoid that.
>
> (English senior psychologist, rural area)

The third 1st level theme, used by both Netherlands and English participants, was 'some parents experience stigma':

'some parents experience stigma'

> There's a stigma for parents, often parents are very reluctant for their children to be referred here and that's not to do with reputation, that's simply to do with wanting their kids to be normal and for parents normal means mainstream school.
>
> (English head of rural behaviour unit)

> A couple of years ago we had a mother saying 'well I don't want the child to know that he's . . . ' I forget what it was, some form of autism, 'I don't want the school to know,' but then we said 'ok' then you have,

leave the responsibility with the school to try and find out again, and why not do a short cut so that we know how to handle it – reason was to try to avoid being stigmatised.

(Netherlands class teacher, urban regular high school)

As Table 5.4 shows most of the other 1st level themes that were country specific were about stigma and devaluation. For the US participants, 10 of the 11 specific themes were on this theme. Here is an excerpt of the most frequently used (11) of these 1st level themes:

'negative evaluation of additional provision'

If a child has an IEP and is receiving special education, they (teachers) sometimes do form certain ideas in their mind that they're going to have to give that child more attention. Sometimes more experienced teachers can be like 'no I don't want any special ed kids in my room,' so there's sometimes a problem . . .

(US School district administrator, urban area)

For the Netherlands participants four of the six specific themes were also about stigma and devaluation. Here is an excerpt of the theme 'students experience stigma in peer relationships':

'students experience stigma in peer relationships'

They tease each other about going to a stupid school. And that's also the reason why we don't have our name on our sweater, you know or their work. It's neutral, so that you know they can show their marks and show what they have been doing and nobody can see.

(Netherlands class teacher, urban special school)

For the English participants five of the six specific themes were about stigma and devaluation.

Second level theme 'moderate/deny devaluation consequences'

Table 5.4 shows that the other more frequently used 2nd level theme had six 1st level themes which were used in each of the three countries, though they were used more frequently in the US than the other two groups. Here are examples of these themes:

'disability positive image'

> they're so welcome here and they feel so accepted here, it's just like any other child.
>
> (US counsellor in rural district high school)

> if I hear parents talk about it it's not in a negative way, it's more like 'oh my child is dyslexic so I can get extra help and she has more time for tests,' things like that, so it's thought of in a more positive way I think instead of a negative way.
>
> (Netherlands national administrator)

> I think that people who are involved with so called special children are much more likely to have a liberated view than people that haven't had close contact, and people are different, let's not pretend that there aren't differences and different needs.
>
> (English special school class teacher, urban area)

'stigma has reduced'

> Yeah exactly and it's become such a part of education that I think there's less and less stigma, yeah it's become very common, and we try to approach it ... more positively where we are providing support rather than 'oh I can't do it'.
>
> (US regular class teacher, urban district)

> I think it's getting better, it's getting better for sure, and I think the stigma with physical problems or hearing problem disabilities and mental disabilities, that's less stigma I think, we are used to it and ok there is a mental problem. But I think with autistic children there is no understanding for these children, there is a stigma of strangeness and I think that stigma in Holland is getting, yeah it's getting better because of the media.
>
> (Netherlands SE advisory teacher, urban area)

> I think the notion of stigma is less prevalent in schools really, I think most children, for example, are largely unaware that they've got a label and those labels are used discreetly. For example there's a surprising number of students in secondary are unaware that they actually have a statement and their entitlement as a result of that. I guess that in my opinion it seems to have moved on.
>
> (English psychologist, urban area)

'positive action'

> you tend to want to intervene and we do tend to be advocates for our kids and like to think of ourselves as not being prejudicial if a child is identified.
>
> (US Federal Department administrator)

> I don't know what happens in other schools – here we have a lot of handicapped children, the children from our school find it normal, in almost every classroom there has been a handicapped child for several years already, so the children of our school think it's normal.
>
> (Netherlands SEN teacher, primary ordinary school, urban area)

> We have spent a long time working with parents, working with their understanding, working with children throughout the school, and we do that through circle times and a whole school ethos that has been built up for a large number of years, and I've been here now eleven years, and so it really, children accept, and the way we view labelling and identification, they accept that in a way they're special and unique.
>
> (English SEN advisory teacher, urban area)

Three other 1st level themes were used across each country, 'label does not lead to devaluation', 'parents want labels' and 'most students do not care about labels'. The first of these, 'label does not lead to devaluation', was used only by one Netherlands participant, but by more US (8) and English (11) participants. Examples of this theme are as follows:

'label does not lead to devaluation'

> they're not stigmatised, they're not devalued. We are aware of the fact that they have problems and we do all we can to make sure that their educational needs are met.
>
> (US senior teacher, regular school, urban district)

> Ok if children do have difficulties in learning and it is recognised that they have difficulties in learning and they do have a label of disability, I don't feel that they are treated as different, devalued, or stigmatised, they are treated as individual children, and because they're treated as individual children, because they are labelled if you like, they will receive the additional needs that are appropriate for them to enable them to learn in school.
>
> (English local administrator, urban area)

The 1st level theme 'parents want a label' was also used across all three countries:

'parents want a label'

> some parents are like 'I still want to keep the child on an IEP or labelled just so that it will help them get in to a college or it will help them get . . .'. I've already gone to a few . . . , when I'm in a meeting and say 'your student not longer requires services, no longer qualifies for services,' the parent fights and says 'well I want them on'.
>
> (US SE teacher, regular high school, rural area)

> I don't think there is a best way, that's the problem. I think some people and some parents can cope really well with the labelling, and even they are happy with the labelling because they can talk, tell the neighbours 'my child has to go to a special school because he has a problem, you can't see it but he has a problem' so in some ways it might be an advantage for them as well.
>
> (Netherlands class teacher, special school, urban area)

> I think it's a difficulty, I think in my role of being in charge of transition from primary to secondary school, obviously I find that a lot of parents want the label for their children, particularly if they are causing real concern in the primary schools from the behavioural point of view, because they feel that if they were labelled as somebody with autism, Aspergers. It would help and it would take some of that pressure away from them, it would help with the provision, but there would also be an explanation for it. We've got a student here at the moment who is in year eight and she's never been officially diagnosed as autistic, but it's alarm bells ringing for her autistic strain, you know, and mum really would like her, in a way, to have that label, and we would like her to have that label.
>
> (English senior teacher, regular school, urban area)

The 1st level theme 'most students do not care about labels' was only used by a couple of participants in each country:

'most students do not care about labels'

> I don't think too many people actually care too much, I mean there's some kids, it's more within their own thinking than in others thinking. I don't think personally that the majority are bothered by it.
>
> (US regular class teacher, high school, rural area)

But most children think 'well I have autism but no problem'.
(Netherlands class teacher, special school, urban area)

It is notable that for the US participants there were six others, in addition to the two who used the above 'not care about labels' 1st level theme, who explained that 'students were unaware of stigma' or 'student was unaware that they were in special', making eight participants overall. No Netherlands or English participants used these latter themes. This greater US reference to students/children not being aware or caring was reinforced by the emergent theme in the analysis: 'awareness of being separate, different or stigmatised'. While 12 of the US participants referred to students with severe intellectual disabilities as probably not being aware, only two Netherlands and five English participants did.

Only US and English participants questioned the extent of the devaluation consequences in the presented dilemma by reference to less stigma in early or more junior years and by being in special schools. The latter 1st level theme was used only by special school professionals:

'less stigma within special schools'

I mean this is from my student teaching experience I remember the students getting a little harassed because they were in special education whereas here they don't because everybody is in the same boat.
(US class teacher, special school, urban area)

In a special ed school I mean you're looking at the whole spectrum of children that have got a statement, their needs have been identified and therefore the children are treated as individuals within the school anyway and supported in that respect.
(English class teacher, special school, urban area)

Of the 1st level themes, making up the 2nd level 'moderate/deny devaluation consequences' theme, that were specific to the US participants, 'in-class support reduces stigma' was most frequently used (10). There were fewer 1st level themes specific to Netherlands participants, 'parents mostly positive about labelling' (2), 'reduce stigma by placing in regular schools' (2) and 'less stigma in smaller groups' (1). The most frequent 1st level theme used specifically by English participants was 'can identify without labelling' (11). Other specific English 1st level themes focused on individuality.

Second level theme 'moderate/deny resources consequences'

The other way in which participants could question the identification dilemma was to address the resource consequences statement. This was done much less often than questioning the devaluation consequence – 22 per cent of US, 6 per cent of Netherlands and 12 per cent of English participants only. There were three 1st level themes which made up this 2nd level theme and they were used in two or more of the country groups. Though the 1st level theme 'alternatives to special education services' was used mostly by US participants (8), it was also used by one Netherlands and one English participant. 'How alternatives to special education work' was used by more English participants (3) and by US participants (5).

Here are examples of these 1st level themes:

'alternatives to special education services'

> in the new authorisation you'll see early intervening services which are supposedly to get at those students who maybe don't need to be identified and can get resources other ways.
> (US State Education Department administrator)

'how alternatives to special education work'

> We usually get resources, if we need help we can get resources anyway . . . on the 504 they can get resources. . . . one parent might go for the 504 and say 'this is ok, I want this for my child but I do not want them labelled as special ed'.
> (US class teacher, regular school, rural district)

This teacher is referring to the section 504 system of the 1973 Rehabilitation Act and the Americans with Disability Act 1990, which gives parents some protection for their children (see Chapter 3).

> in the three tier intervention models.....all children get really robust pedagogy happening at level one . . . and before you start labelling kids you want to have an intervention that's really robust. . . . And, when you're doing that you're going to have about seventy five to eighty percent of the kids reading and making progress and doing milestones. ' . . . and it's not a wait to fail model so that those additional resources are coming more quickly. I think that there's an assumption that once a kid has moved to special ed they'll have one to one or lower class ratio and while some of those concepts are useful, they can get in the way of thinking about what robust instruction and opportunities . . ..
> (US Federal Department administrator)

> Well in the last few years there's definitely been a focus on greater delegation to schools in order to ensure that the needs are being met proactively at an earlier stage rather than having to go down the identification

and statementing route, and that's definitely a positive way forward in my view. Those needs are and should be met at a much earlier stage, you're not going down the bureaucratic process and those authorities who have handled that sensitively and effectively and have taken their partner agencies as stakeholders on board, are actually seeing that they have gained the trust of parents and professionals, but it does have to be handled very, very sensitively.

(English national/regional administrator)

Second level theme 'resolved tensions'

This 2nd level theme reflects some recognition of a tension that is seen as resolved to some extent. It was used by between 16 and 24 per cent of participants across the three countries, mostly by English (24 per cent), then by US (18 per cent) and least by Netherlands participants (16 per cent). There was only one 1st level theme 'need outweighs stigma' across all groups, with an extra one for the US group. One US participant used the 1st level theme 'weigh risk versus benefits' a slightly more general explanation. Here are examples of the 'need outweighs stigma' theme across the three countries:

'need outweighs stigma'

yes there is that possibility but I think the advantages outweigh the disadvantages. I think the advantage, you know, the specialised education and the supports that we provide for those children outweigh that, the labelling.

(US special school teacher, rural district)

Yes I think it's an issue but I think the most important thing is in the Netherlands and in my experience, it's important that they are labelled because if they are not labelled they do not get the extra support and the means they need. So in one way or another it's not, maybe it's not really a dilemma because you need the labelling to get the means, the support you need.

(Netherlands national administrator)

No, not particularly, it's a risk worth taking. It's a risk worth taking because of the way the world works, you know, if there is a need let's have it identified to try and get the resources because without identification you can forget it.

(English senior teacher, secondary regular school, urban area)

Other second level themes

Another more frequently used theme, but only by Netherlands (25 per cent) and English participants (20 per cent) was 'other positive consequences'. This theme picked out positive consequences of identification: the understanding, sensitivity and the usefulness of identification and labels. Netherlands participants used these 1st level themes – 'identification required for positive outcomes' (4), 'need for objective identification' (3), labels useful for pupils' (2) and 'labels useful for peers' (2). English participants mostly used the 1st level theme 'identification required for positive outcomes' (10) and one each used 'labels support understanding and sensitivity' and 'well-explained labels are positive'. Here are examples of the most frequently used 1st level theme 'identification is required for positive outcomes':

'identification is required for positive outcomes'

> I think that in most cases it's very important to identify a child because the teacher knows then what is the problem . . . they are different and you have to treat them differently and then you know how to handle these children. I work a lot with autistic children and I think it's very, very important for teachers to know, to identify, and that really the problem is not the parents fault or something like that, it's a disability.
>
> (Netherlands SEN advisory teacher, urban area)

> Because I think the first one, I feel that if, particularly in a comprehensive school where there are several different teachers teaching the students, I do feel that if we identify their difficulties then we are raising awareness and understanding about the difficulty and that, to me, can only be good at the end of the day.
>
> (English SEN co-ordinator, secondary school, rural area)

Two other 2nd level themes, about negative consequences, 'other negative consequences' and 'negative consequences by other means', were used infrequently across each country group. Between 4 and 13 per cent of participants across the three countries saw another negative consequence of identification and labelling in addition to stigma and devaluation, namely, 'teachers denying responsibility by labelling'. But, only one English participant saw labelling as lowering expectations. Here are examples of the 'denying responsibility' theme:

'denying responsibility'

> but often lessons are not really differentiated for the different learning styles and abilities so you have to identify them as having a need and

often after that happens you will find that a regular educator would prefer that the IEP student socialise or get more instruction from a special educator than themselves.

(US special education supervisor, middle regular school, urban area)

Not really the other children, not the other children, but the school, the school will say 'no we cannot take this child because it needs special care and we don't give that,' when I think 'well this child could go to that school with a little bit more help, it could be in this school,' and the school says 'no because he has this label, we don't take it.' that's why I have a problem with these labels.

(Netherlands class teacher, regular primary school, urban area)

Even fewer participants (4–6 per cent), and no Netherlands ones, saw 'negative consequences by others means'. The 1st level theme 'stigma exists without labels' was the only one making up this 2nd level theme.

'stigma exists without labels'

if you're talking about the students that I deal with, you know they're going to be identified and stigmatised just because of the way they are, I mean their disabilities are so severe that they wouldn't be able to function in the regular school without special services.

(US special school teacher, rural area)

I think if they weren't labelled and identified officially it would be still be very clear anyway, so they would then also, they would still get that difference. If they're just in a mainstream classroom it will be evident to the other pupils and to the teachers whether they've been identified or not and so they're going to get called names, it doesn't matter that they've been identified and put in a separate unit, I think they get the stick anyway.

(English senior teacher, special school, rural area)

It is notable that the two US and three English participants who used this theme all worked with children with severe/profound intellectual disabilities.

Second level themes used to explain different recognition positions

Table 5.5 shows the breakdown of the use of the 2nd level themes by US recognition level. Bearing in mind that most participants in each country group used two to three 1st level themes and the range was between two

Table 5.5 Second level themes used by US participants to explain position to identification dilemma

US 2nd level themes	Recognition level						
	Not at all	Marginal	Signifi-cant	Consider-able	Split response	Uncertain	Total
	N = 10	N = 17	N = 11	N = 5	N = 5	N = 2	N = 50
Tensions	7	7	10	5	3	1	33
Resolved tensions	0	4	2	1	2	0	9
Other positive consequences	0	0	0	0	0	0	0
Other negative consequences	0	0	0	1	1	0	2
Negative consequences by other means	0	0	2	0	0	0	2
Moderate/deny devaluation consequences	10	13	6	1	4	0	34
Moderate/deny resources consequences	4	5	1	1	0	0	11
Depends	1	2	2	0	0	0	5
Comments	0	2	0	0	0	0	2

Note
Top two frequencies in rows in bold, if >1.

and seven themes per participants, we would expect participants to use a mix of 2nd level themes. We would also expect participants with higher recognition levels to use the 'tensions' theme more. The analysis shows that 10/11 with significant recognition used this theme while all five with considerable recognition did. Lower proportions with no or marginal recognition used it, 7/10 and 7/17, respectively. Another expectation would be that the use of 'moderate/deny devaluation consequence' would be greater with less recognition of this dilemma. All ten participants who did not recognise this dilemma used this theme, while 13/17 with marginal recognition did. Those with higher recognition used it less – 6/11 with significant and 1/5 with considerable recognition. 'Resolved tensions', which reflects some resolution of a tension, was most frequently used by those with marginal recognition levels. Sample sizes were too small for statistical testing.

The analysis in Table 5.6 shows a similar pattern of use of 2nd level themes with recognition level for the Netherlands participants. 'Tensions' was used more by those with significant and considerable recognition level (9/12 and 7/9, respectively). Those with lower recognition used this theme less – not recognise 3/5 and marginal recognition 1/5. Similarly, the

Table 5.6 Second level themes used by Netherlands participants to explain position to identification dilemma

Netherlands 2nd level themes	Recognition level					
	Not at all	Marginal	Significant	Consider-able	Split response	Total
	N = 5	N = 2	N = 12	N = 9	N = 4	N = 32
Tensions	3	1	**9**	**7**	3	23
Resolved tensions	**4**	1	1	0	0	9
Other positive consequences	2	0	4	2	0	12
Other negative consequences	0	0	2	1	1	6
Negative consequences by other means	0	0	0	0	0	0
Moderate/deny devaluation consequences	**4**	1	**6**	1	4	16
Moderate/deny resources consequences	0	0	2	0	0	2
Depends	0	0	0	2	0	2
Comments	1	0	3	1	1	6

Note
Top two frequencies in rows in bold, if >1.

'moderate/deny devaluation consequences' theme was used more by those not recognising the dilemma (4/5) and less by those with higher recognition (6/12) and considerable (1/5). While the 'resolved tensions' theme was mostly used by US participants with marginal recognition, for Netherlands participants it was mostly used by those not recognising the dilemma.

A similar pattern of association between theme use and recognition levels was found for English participants – see Table 5.7. More English participants used the 'tensions' themes with significant and considerable recognition – 13/13 and 6/8, respectively – while a lower proportion used this theme with marginal or no recognition of the dilemma – 5/7 and 3/13, respectively. For the 'resolved tensions' theme, as with Netherlands participants, the highest use was by those not recognising the dilemma (6/13). For the 'moderate/deny devaluation consequences' most use was by those with lower recognition–not recognise (12/13) and marginal (5/7). Lower use was made by those with greater recognition – significant recognition (3/13) and considerable recognition (2/8).

Table 5.7 Second level themes used by English participants to explain position to identification dilemma

English 2nd level themes	Recognition level					Total
	Not at all	Marginal	Significant	Consider-able	Split response	
	N = 13	N = 7	N = 13	N = 8	N = 9	N = 50
Tensions	3	5	**13**	**6**	5	32
Resolved tensions	**6**	**3**	2	0	1	12
Other positive consequences	**3**	1	**3**	2	1	10
Other negative consequences	1	0	0	1	1	3
Negative consequences by other means	1	0	0	0	2	3
Moderate/deny devaluation consequences	**12**	**5**	3	2	**5**	27
Moderate/deny resources consequences	**3**	1	1	0	1	6
Depends	0	1	3	2	**6**	12
Comments	**2**	0	0	**2**	**3**	7

Note
Top two frequencies in rows in bold, if >1.

Qualitative accounts of the resolution of identification dilemma

The number of distinct 1st level themes across the three countries ranged from 29 to 39, with most participants using between two and three themes to explain their position, and some participants using up to five and seven themes.

Table 5.8 shows the eight common 2nd level resolution themes which were used to analyse the 1st level themes for each country group. The 2nd level theme 'national/local developments' was used most frequently across the three countries. 'Change attitude to SEN/disability' was used more frequently (> 30 per cent) by Netherlands and English participants, but not US participants. Netherlands participants only used the 2nd level themes 'continuing issues' and 'communication' more frequently, while English participants used 'go beyond negative labels' more frequently. As Table 5.2 above showed, the most frequent resolution rating in each country was 'significant' for those recognising the dilemma. However, more Netherlands than US or English participants used significant resolution (48 per cent

Table 5.8 Comparison of 1st level themes for resolving identification dilemma across the three countries

	USA	Netherlands	England
Continuing issues	N = 10(20%)[a] *Unsure of resolution 7[b] *Residual stigma 2 Issues arising 1	N = 10(31%) *Residual tension, hard to resolve 9 Limits to what special schools can do 1 Stigma issues fade slowly 1	N = 11 (22%) *Residual – continuing tension 6 *Residual stigma 6 More difficult to resolve in regular settings 1 Identify and manage risks 1
Reduce special education identification	N = 9(18%) *Use alternative provision 8 *Reduce identification 2	N = 1(3%) *Use alternative provision 1 *Reduce identification 1	N = 6 (12%) *Use alternative provision 2 *Reduce identification 5 Individual identification for minority with complex needs 2
Change attitude to SEN/disability	N = 12(24%) *Show potential for progress 1 *Positive image disability 4 *Mixing with regular students 5 *Respect and acceptance from peers 4 Students see each others work 1	N = 12(38%) *Show potential for progress 7 *Positive image disability 8 *Focus on positive strategies 1 Potential to transfer regular school 1 Show disabled people not so different 2 Increased teacher contact/experience with SEN students 1	N = 21 (42%) *Show potential for progress 7 *Positive image disability 6 *Mixing with regular students 3 *Respect and acceptance from peers and others 2 *Focus on positive strategies 2 Focus on achievement and progress 5 Open special provision to non-disabled 2 Positive image for special unit/school 1

National/local developments	N = 22(44%)	N = 11(34%)	N = 26(52%)
	*Training 8 *Develop an inclusive approach 4 *Improve general education 2 *Need more disability in community 4 *Aware of tension re identification 1 *Positive school ethos/practices 3 More teacher collaboration 4 Use of some mixed ability classes 3 Universal design 1 Provide provision needed 2 More staffing 1	*Training 4 *Develop an inclusive approach 3 *Improve general education 1 *Develop positive school ethos/practices 4 National inclusive education system 2 Special schools build confidence and relationships with peers 1 Develop motivation for inclusion 1 In-class and withdrawal support 1 More special provision in regular schools 1	*Training and education 12 *Develop an inclusive approach 10 *Improve general education 5 *Need more disability in community 3 *Become aware of tension 2 Plan and resource holistically 3 Flexible resource patterns 3 Additional help for SEN and others 3 Change national standards agenda 2 Improve monitoring, so know what works 1
Go beyond negative labels	N = 8(16%)	N = 5(16%)	N = 15(30%)
	*Treat as individuals 4 *Show sensitivity about labelling 4	*Treat as individuals 5 *Focus on provision needed, not labels 2 *Use language of need 1 Analyse in terms of processes, not diagnostic labels 1 More accurate diagnosis 1	*Treat as individuals 4 *Focus on provision needed, not labels 4 *Use language of need 2 *Show sensitivity about labelling 3 Avoid language of disability 2 Minimal labelling approach 2 Promote more positive meaning of labels 2

Table 5.8 (Continued)

	USA	Netherlands	England
Choice	N = 1 (2%)	N = 0	N = 2 (4%)
	*Students choose additional provision 1		*Students and parents choose additional provision 2
Communication	N = 8(16%)	**N = 11(34%)**	N = 13(26%)
	*Open positive communication parents 2	*Open positive communication parents 11	*Open positive communication with parents 7
	*Positive communication to students 6		*Positive and open communication with students 7
		Listen and respond to parents 1	Parental support group 1
			Convergent perspectives of parents and professionals 1
Comments	N = 5(10%)	N = 4(13%)	N = 4 (8%)
	Receiving support can stigmatise 1	Parents address tension 2	Inclusive approach is a long haul 4
	Depends on many factors 1	Parents advocate for children 1	
	Confused resolution 1	Some regular schools reject students with emotional/behaviour difficulties 1	

Notes
a N: number of participants using 2nd level theme (% of all participants – in bold if more than 30%).
b * Indicates similar 1st level themes used in two or three of the countries (numbers after 1st level themes represent frequency of use of this theme).

versus 38 per cent and 32 per cent, respectively). This difference can be linked to the finding in Table 5.8 that Netherlands participants used four of the more frequent 2nd level themes (> 30 per cent) compared to three for English and one for US participants.

Second level theme: 'national/local developments'

Three 1st level themes making up this most frequently used 2nd level theme, were used in each of the three country groups, 'training', 'develop an inclusive approach' and 'improve general education'. They were also amongst the more frequently used 1st level themes making up the 2nd level theme.

Here are some examples of these themes:

'develop an inclusive approach'

> I am a firm believer in inclusion – children want to be in the mainstream. They live in communities with other children. Children also make allowances for their peers as do colleagues for their colleagues. Inclusion makes it possible to have less public labelling and to be more accepting.
>
> (US senior teacher, special school, urban district)

> Well in two ways I would think, you have to connect regular and special anyhow because it's a common responsibility, if you separate responsibility you always will meet the dilemma you've formulated. If you share responsibility in principle that dilemma is resolved.
>
> (Netherlands national administrator)

> well for me it's a significant extent because I can see how some young people are being included in mainstream schools. Actually the young people with them in the classrooms actually . . . an awful lot and . . . my own children who have been in classes with children with considerable disabilities have a very tolerant attitude towards them and a greater understanding as well of the issues. I know that when I was at school disabled children went to a completely different school and I never really got to know them very well and therefore didn't understand the issues that they were facing.
>
> (English psychologist, urban area)

'improve general education'

> I think you resolve it by making general education much, much, much better.
>
> (US Federal Department administrator)

We do that with several methods, one is effective education, classroom organisation is very important, another one is a programme for behaviour, another is cooperative learning and cooperative teaching.

(Netherlands local authority administrator, urban area)

To me it's about culture and ethos of the school, accepting the children that it has and having a basic ethos of meeting needs and that the basic level of entitlement is increased for certain children but that it is accepted that that's part and parcel of the whole schools culture and attitude.

(English local administrator, rural area)

Two other 1st level themes were used only by US and English participants, 'need more disability in community' and 'aware of tension re identification'. Here are examples of these:

'need more disability in community'

our communities need to be much more diverse in terms of disability and they don't seem to be. I mean I went many years, when I never worked with a person with a disability until about twelve years ago

(US Federal Department administrator)

'aware of tension re identification'/'become aware of tension'

I think it's a significant dilemma that has an evolutionary solution, so it changes slowly but it will only change if you focus on it as a dilemma and the reasons why it's a dilemma and how you can make it less of a dilemma.

(English national administrator)

Another 1st level theme was used only by US and Netherlands participants:

'develop positive school ethos/practices'

... it's the policy of the school and the staff and I think you have to support schools in that and teachers in that. The culture of the school, the way teachers look at children, the way they are trying to give children a real, a good place in their classes and they let them be a part of the group and that kind of thing, it's the culture of the school, of the class, I think you have to show people, teachers, how they can do that and to show them good examples of how it's possible to do that kind of thing.

(Netherlands national administrator)

The more frequently used 1st level themes, making up the 2nd level theme ' national/local developments', that were specific to US participants were 'more teacher collaboration' (4) and 'use of some mixed ability classes' (3).

First level themes, making up this 2nd level theme, that were specific to Netherlands participants reflected contrary resolutions, for example, having 'national inclusive education system' and 'develop motivation for inclusion' versus 'special schools build confidence and relationships with peers'. Here is an example of the 'national inclusive education system' theme:

'national inclusive education system'

> Well they should be organised in one system under one authority, that's very important, and the well known categorising of pupils should disappear. Categorising is typical results of a system that is selecting, screening pupils all the time, and at the same time it's picking up the children who fall out and offering them help and support. Do you want to help every child to get the opportunity to show what he can do, or are you selecting for aims and goals that go beyond the school? That's what I mean, yes, every child will get a place and it will get what it needs, and I know about the organisational problems, but they are solvable.
>
> (Netherlands national administrator)

The most frequent 1st level themes that were specific to English participants, were 'plan and resource holistically', 'flexible resource patterns' and 'additional help for SEN and others'. Here is an example of the former:

'plan and resource holistically'

> our thinking increasingly is around 'how do we plan holistically for children?' rather than seeing it as a resource tension or dilemma. It's a case of what works and if we're thinking in a mainstream context to start with. They're one group of vulnerable children and in so far as you can target or focus your planning in terms of that sort of diversity, one can reduce the amount of individual identification.
>
> (English national administrator)

Second level theme: 'change attitude to SEN/disability'

The second most frequently used 2nd level theme was 'change attitude to SEN/disability'. Around two in five of the Netherlands and English participants used 1st level themes making up this 2nd level theme. This contrasts with only one in four US participants who used this theme. The 1st level themes, 'show potential for progress' and ' positive image disability', that made up this 2nd level theme, were used in each country group. Here are examples of these themes:

'show potential for progress'

> so you have to look at them as individuals and see exactly what they need in a setting to try to bring out something that has not been brought out in them.
>
> (US class teacher, special school, urban area)

> Mainly because, mainly if a child has a label, you have to see what are the options, not what they cannot do. Not what you cannot do with the children, but what you can do with the children. If you have a mark on a child you can more easily say 'this is what the child can do and this is what the child cannot do', so it's ok for you as a teacher that the goals you set with other children, you cannot reach, because teachers are feeling guilty because they cannot reach the goals with that particular child.
>
> (Netherlands head teacher, regular primary school, urban area)

'positive image disability'

> There's nothing wrong with being different, being different should not necessarily mean that someone is devalued, I need to wear glasses to drive but nobody devalues me because of that, that's a disability but I don't need to let it be a handicap, and there's a difference between having a disability and allowing it to negatively impact your life and I think it's up to those of us who are in education and in clinical positions to help students who are identified to not have a lessening of self esteem, not to be devalued by others.
>
> (US psychologist, secondary school, urban area)

> Well I guess that would be a society problem wouldn't it? Because people need to actually accept that nine out of ten of us have difficulties in one area or another and if there wasn't a stigma . . . you know that dates back to years gone by, doesn't it? That is a mental health issue.
>
> (English head of emotional and behavioural unit, secondary school, urban area)

'Focus on positive strategies' was a 1st level theme used by Netherlands and English participants only:

'Focus on positive strategies'

> It's not the label, it's not what the student has, whatever syndrome it is or whatever, it's what strategies we are going to use. So it isn't the label that's important, it's the strategies that we put in place at the end of the day, which are.
>
> (English SEN co-ordinator, secondary school, rural area)

Here are examples of the two 1st level themes used only by US and English participants: 'mixing with regular students' and 'respect and acceptance from peers':

'mixing with regular students'

> Well I would start a dialogue, if I'm on the campus, and this is what we're trying to do, smaller learning communities. I think that the regular education students can then see our students as not so different as themselves. I remember when we had a May day out here on our school grounds and they were invited, this hasn't happened in the last few years, but that school was invited and they are not so different.
>
> (US teaching assistant, special school, urban area)

'respect and acceptance from peers'

> then they will kind of accept them and I think there would be less tension and they will be thought of more. Well it will be kind of normal to have a spectrum of people and to include them.
>
> (English class teacher, special school, rural area)

Second level theme: 'communication'

The 'communication' 2nd level theme was used most by Netherlands participants (34 per cent), but less by English participants (26 per cent) and US participants (16 per cent). The 1st level theme 'open positive communication with parents' was used in each country group, though it was used more frequently by Netherlands and English participants. Here are examples of this theme:

'open positive communication with parents'

> When I have a conversation with the parents I try to explain what's the benefit for the child, what is it that the child needs and how can we give it to him or her.
>
> (Netherlands class teacher, regular primary school, rural area)

...saying 'we are identifying needs here or differences here in order to be able to get better, provide better services if you like, to provide a better education for all of our children and that's the reason for us...' – we are trying to get those arguments across in a positive way and reassuring people that it isn't designed to stigmatise, it's designed to make sure that children get the right support to make progress.

(English national administrator)

Here are examples of the 1st level theme 'positive communication with students', which was used only by US and English participants:

'positive communication with students'

I think that pointing out their positives and their strengths and saying that 'no, you know, you're not weak in everything, look at what you can do, yes you may have difficulty with this...' and sometimes I point out what my difficulties are, weaknesses are, to them, so they see it's not just them that has a weakness.

(US special education teacher, regular school, rural district)

Being very positive, making sure that the children are aware, presenting self targets, getting children involved in their own targets for their learning, listening, actively listening to both children, parents, and teachers.

(English advisory teacher, urban area)

There was only one 1st level theme specific to the Netherlands, 'listen and respond to parents' which was a more specific version of the more frequently used theme 'open and positive communication with parents'. There were two 1st level themes that were specific to English participants, 'have parental support group' and 'convergent perspectives of parents and professionals'.

Second level theme: 'go beyond negative labels'

This 2nd level theme, 'go beyond negative labels', was used more by English participants (30 per cent) than US or Netherlands participants (16 per cent each). Only one 1st level theme was used in each country group, 'treat as individuals', which was one of the more frequently used themes. Here are examples of this theme:

'treat as individuals'

You have to look at the children, if you say 'he is an autistic, so accept he is autistic so we can treat him as an autistic', but no, this isn't the approach. This is a child and you have to treat him in terms of what he needs and not only because he is autistic, no, as a whole child.

(Netherlands class teacher, special school, urban area)

you say 'well all children are different', and you look at them as individuals and they might be very gifted and highly talented and need stretching and so you adjust what you do to account for that and that's no different or it's part of adjusting for a disability or a special educational need. I would think so and it's a trendy, well it's certainly in the policy of personalisation and so on. You expect that to be a product of that if we were truly personalising education, learning for each individual child.

(English national administrator)

The 1st level themes 'focus on provision needed not labels' and 'use the language of need' were used only by Netherlands and English participants, while the 1st level theme 'show sensitivity about labelling' was used only by US and English participants. Here are examples of these themes:

'focus on provision needed not labels'

Yeah, because in one way or another we have to know that. With the example of dyslexia, we have to know that it is dyslexia, we can focus on the underlying processes and we need to know it, but we have to be aware that it's a very severe problem and that's why we label with dyslexia, so we need the label but the label is not the solution.

(Netherlands psychologist, urban area)

'use the language of need'

I'm talking about the child and what he needs. You focus positively on what the child needs. You've got to use language that is positive and constructive.

(Netherlands psychologist, urban area)

'show sensitivity about labelling'

No you don't call it being in special ed and if a student asks me 'why do I come?' you know, you talk about, well I would say to them 'well how do you feel when you're in the classroom?' and have them identify the areas where they need help and let them see that I'm there to help them get through the trouble spots.

(US special education teacher, regular school, rural district)

There were no US specific 1st level themes under this 2nd level theme. There were two Netherlands specific 1st level themes, 'analyse in terms of processes, not diagnostic labels' and 'more accurate diagnosis' (each used once). There were three 1st level themes specific to English participants, 'avoid language of disability', 'minimal labelling approach' and promote more positive meaning of labels' (each twice).

Second level theme: 'continuing issues'

This 'continuing issues' theme was used more by Netherlands participants (31 per cent) than US (20 per cent) or English (22 per cent) participants. Its use indicates that between 20 and 30 per cent of the participants recognised that despite their suggested resolutions, some of the tensions persisted. The most frequent US 1st level theme was 'unsure of resolution' and this had links to the most frequently used Netherlands and English 1st level theme – 'residual tension, hard to resolve'. Here are examples of these themes:

'unsure of resolution'

> I'm not sure that we can, that we have a lot of control.
> > (US class teacher, middle school, rural area)

'residual tension, hard to resolve'

> . . . you don't get away from the tension, but you can help them understand why you do this and ease it.
> > (Netherlands resource advisory teacher, special school)

> . . . but until they are thriving, the labels play an important role, so I think there is kind of an ongoing tension between what's the right level of labelling to ensure that things move forward, but without driving us in to a kind of cul-de-sac of ever more differential diagnosis which doesn't necessarily actually do any more than provide them with labels. I think that that will always be there, partly because of the human need to put things in to boxes for their own safety and for the purposes of communication so I don't think you can ever get away from it.
> > (English national/regional administrator)

One 1st level theme 'residual stigma' was used by US and English participants only:

'residual stigma'

> as I have indicated before, there are those who might not be fully

catered for within this universal design set of principles and for them there might still be some stigma.

(US Federal administrator)

There was only one US specific 1st theme, 'issues arising', two Netherlands specific themes, 'limits to what special schools can do' and 'stigma issues fade slowly', and two English specific themes, 'more difficult to resolve in regular settings' and 'identify and manage risks'.

Second level themes: 'reduce special education identification' and 'choice'

It is notable that these two 2nd level themes were amongst the least used themes. The 'reduce special education identification' theme was used more by US (18 per cent) and English (12 per cent) participants than Netherlands ones (3 per cent). The two 1st level themes, making up this 2nd level theme, that were used across the three countries were 'use alternative provision' and 'reduce identification'. Here are examples of these themes:

'use alternative provision'

I think that every case needs to be looked at individually, certainly if some students truly are learning disabled, I think other times we can put some other resources into place such as our instructional support team who can provide support for the students, so I think each case needs to be looked at individually and just determine what is best for that child.
(US special education teacher, regular school, rural district)

Some children are targeted for something additional but they do not have to come in to the special education system. They don't jump through any major bureaucratic hoops if you like, and absolutely shouldn't, and I would expect hoops to be necessary for only a very small fraction of children with additional needs.
(English psychologist, rural area)

'reduce identification'

. . . in the process where we do not need to label students so I think first of all investigating what we have available at the general education level to see what we can do. But if it ends up that we are moving towards special education then looking at how providing those services can be the least intrusive so if that is providing those services in the general education classroom if that's appropriate for a student so it's less intrusive for them.
(US advisory teacher, rural area)

sometimes it's possible to give the teacher self reflection methods. So long as it is working like that, you don't need the identification to handle the problem

(Netherlands advisory teacher, rural area)

There was only one 1st level theme that was specific to a country group, 'individual identification for minority with complex needs', which was specific to two English participants.

As regards 'choice' as a 2nd level resolution theme, no Netherlands participants used it, while only one US and two English participants did. The one 1st level theme making up this 2nd level theme was 'students choose additional provision' (US theme) and 'students and parents choose additional provision' (English theme).

Second level themes used to explain different resolution positions

One expectation from the dilemmatic model as regards resolutions is that participants who recognise 'continuing issues' will have lower resolution levels. This was found for the Netherlands, where most users of the 'continuing issues' theme held marginal resolution levels (8/10), but not for the US nor English groups (see Tables 5.9, 5.10 and 5.11). For the US and English participants, the 'continuing issues' theme was used across the different resolution levels.

Table 5.9, about US participants, also shows no differences between marginal and significant levels in the use of the most frequent themes. However, more use of the 2nd level theme 'go beyond negative labels' was associated with significant and considerable positions (6/18) than marginal positions (1/11). Table 5.11 shows a similar pattern of 2nd level theme use for English participants. Only for the less frequently used 2nd level theme 'reduce SE identification' was there a difference between marginal versus significant, considerable and split positions. (Split resolutions used mainly significant resolutions.) None of the four English participants with marginal positions used this theme, while all seven who did had either significant, considerable or a split resolution position.

Table 5.9 Second level themes used by US participants to explain resolution of identification dilemma

US 2nd level themes	Resolution level						Total
	Not at all	Marginal	Signifi-cant	Consider-able	Uncertain	Split response	
	N = 3	N = 11	N = 15	N = 3	N = 3	N = 5	N = 40
Continuing issues	2	**3**	**4**	0	0	1	10
Reduce SE identification	0	**3**	**5**	0	0	1	9
Change attitude to SEN/disability	0	3	3	3	3	0	12
National/local developments	0	**6**	**8**	2	1	5	22
Go beyond negative labels	0	1	**4**	2	0	1	8
Choice	1	0	0	0	0	0	1
Communication	0	**3**	**4**	0	1	0	8
Comments	1	**2**	1	0	0	1	5

Note
Top two frequencies in rows in bold, if > 1.

Table 5.10 Second level themes used by Netherlands participants to explain resolution of identification dilemma

Netherlands 2nd level themes	Resolution level					Total
	Not at all	Marginal	Significant	Consider-able	Split response	
	N = 0	N = 9	N = 13	N = 1	N = 4	N = 27
Continuing issues	0	**8**	**2**	0	0	10
Reduce SE identification	0	0	1	0	0	1
Change attitude to SEN/disability	0	**6**	**5**	0	1	12
National/local developments	0	**3**	**6**	1	1	11
Go beyond negative labels	0	**2**	**2**	1	0	5
Communication	0	**4**	**5**	0	2	11
Comments	0	**3**	1	0	0	4

Note
Top two frequencies in rows in bold, if >1.

Table 5.11 Second level themes used by English participants to explain resolution of identification dilemma

English 2nd level themes	Resolution level						
	Not at all N = 0	Marginal N = 4	Signifi- cant N = 12	Consider- able N = 5	Uncertain N = 5	Split response N = 11	Total N = 37
Continuing issues	0	3	**9**	3	4	**7**	26
Reduce SE identification	0	0	**3**	1	0	**3**	7
Change attitude to SEN/disability	0	3	4	**5**	3	**6**	21
National/local developments	0	3	**9**	3	4	**7**	26
Go beyond negative labels	0	2	**6**	2	2	**3**	15
Choice	0	0	**2**	0	0	0	2
Communication	0	3	**5**	0	2	**3**	13
Comments	0	0	**3**	0	0	1	4

Note
Top two frequencies in rows in bold, if >1.

Chapter 6

Curriculum dilemma

It is a catch 22, we want to give them opportunities and also meet their needs. If you choose one or the other, neither is good by itself. In a special ed classroom like at this school, the IEP focuses on skills and there is a tension between the IEP and the curriculum.

(US senior teacher, special school, urban district)

In one way we want to give children all the same, but you can't give the same to all children. But they are part of the community, so they have to do things together in the community and sometimes it's a problem, yes.

(Netherlands head teacher, primary school, rural area)

I think the dilemma comes from having to try to do something that's a national requirement and trying to cater for the children's needs at the same time. We used to feel almost embarrassed that they needed hydrotherapy or speech and language, but we used to try and slot it in somewhere in the day around the curriculum and we've gone away from that. I hope we've gone away from that and we say 'if that's what the child needs then that's what they must have'.

(English senior teacher, special school, urban area)

Introduction

This chapter considers the curriculum dilemma which is about the consequences of having or not having a common curriculum for all children. As explained in Chapter 4, the dilemma took the following form:

- If children identified as having a disability (needing special education) are offered the same learning experiences as other children, they are likely to be denied the opportunity to have learning experiences relevant to their individual needs.
- If children identified as having a disability (needing special education) are NOT offered the same learning experiences as other children, then

they are likely to be treated as a separate lower status group and be denied equal opportunities.

As in the previous chapter this one includes analysis of the recognition and resolution ratings, thematic analyses and selected excerpts from what participants explained during the interviews across the three country groups.

Curriculum recognition ratings

Table 6.1 shows that the most frequent curriculum recognition rating as 'significant' for each country group. This consistency across the three countries is reflected in analysis of the non-significant association in the cross-tabulation of country by rating (chi-squared = 9.5, df = 10, p = 0.50). Taken overall the table also shows that the majority of participants in each country recognised the curriculum dilemma to some extent (marginal, significant or considerable extent) – 68 per cent for US, 72 per cent for Netherlands and 70 per cent for English participants. The corresponding figures indicate a minority not recognising the curriculum dilemma – 16 per cent for US, 13 per cent for Netherlands and 12 per cent for English participants. These results need to be set in the context that only four participants, all English, reported being uncertain about their response and a minority split their responses (see below). For those who split their response the most frequent ratings for the two aspects was 'not at all + significant' across all three country groups.

The reasons for splitting responses to this dilemma, as for the identification one, was to distinguish between some aspect where the dilemma was recognised not at all or marginally and another aspect where it was recognised significantly or considerably. Participants distinguished between these different aspects in the three country groups: policy versus practice (USA and Netherlands), self versus others and mild versus severe disabilities (all three groups) and special versus regular/ordinary settings (Netherlands and England).

Curriculum resolution ratings

Table 6.2 shows that the most frequent resolution rating was 'significant' for Netherlands (43 per cent) and English (34 per cent) participants, but only 'marginal' for US participants (31 per cent). This difference missed statistical significance (at the 0.05 level) in a test of the association between resolution by country group, using chi-square analysis (chi-squared = 17.2, df = 11, p = 0.06).

This table also shows that with the exception of four US participants and one English participant all others considered there to be some degree of resolution (marginal, significant or considerable). However, there was a

Table 6.1 Breakdown of curriculum dilemma recognition ratings across the three countries

	USA	Netherlands	England
Not at all	8 (16%)	4 (13%)	6 (12%)
Marginal	6 (12%)	5 (16%)	10 (20%)
Marginal/significant	**22 (44%)**	**15 (47%)**	**23 (46%)**
Significant	6 (12%)	3 (9%)	2 (4%)
Significant/considerable	0		4 (8%)
Considerable	8 (16%)	5 (16%)	5 (10%)
Uncertain	0	5 (16%)	4 (8%)
Split responses	8 (16%)		
Breakdown of pairs of ratings	**7**	**2**	**4**

Breakdown of pairs of ratings

USA:
- Not at all + significant } 0, 22 (44%)
- Not at all + considerable } 0, 6 (12%)
- 1

Netherlands:
- 3 (9%)
- Not at all + significant } 12 (38%)
- Not at all + considerable } 1 (3%)
- Marginal + significant } 2 (6%)
- Marginal + considerable — 0
- 1, 1, 1

England:
- Not at all + significant } 0, 23 (46%)
- Significant + considerable } 0, 2 (4%)
- 1

| Totals | 50 (100%) | 32 (100%) | 50 (100%) |

Notes
Bold represents most frequent ratings.
Uncertain – participants were reluctant to indicate a degree.
Split responses – participants interpreted issue by responding in different ways.

Table 6.2 Breakdown of curriculum dilemma resolution ratings across the three countries

	USA	Netherlands	England
Not at all	0	0	1 (2%)
Marginal	11 (22%) }	9 (26–32%)	13 (26–30%)
Marginal/significant		3 (9%) }	0 }
Significant	**13 (26–31%)**	9 (26%) **12 (35–43%)**	15 (30%) **15 (30–34%)**
Considerable	11 (22–26%)	1 (3–4%)	1 (2%)
Uncertain	3 (6–7%)	1 (3–4%)	9 (18–20%)
Split responses	3 (6–7%)	5 (16–18%)	5 (10–11%)
Breakdown of pairs of ratings	8 N/a + significant	**2** N/a + significant **2** Marginal + significant 2 Marginal + significant 1 significant	— N/a + not at all — N/a + marginal — N/a + significant — Marginal + marginal — Missing + marginal
Those recognising dilemma	42 (84%)	28 (87%)	44 (88%)
Those not recognising dilemma	8 (16%)	4 (13%)	6 (12%)
Totals	50 (100%)	32 (100%)	50 (100%)

Notes
Figures in brackets: first figure, percentage out of all participants; second figure, percentage out of those who recognised the dilemma.
Bold represents most frequent rating.
Uncertain: participants were reluctant to indicate a degree.
Split responses: participants interpreted issue by responding in different way.
N/a: not applicable – when dilemma not recognised, resolution question is not applicable.

higher proportion of English participants compared to US and Netherlands ones who were uncertain about a resolution rating – 20 per cent compared to 7 per cent and 4 per cent respectively.

Recognition and resolution ratings by professional roles

As with the analysis of identification ratings by role of participants, it was necessary to reduce the range of roles to four broad ones. Table 6.3 shows the most frequent ratings for these different roles across the three countries. As with the identification dilemma no statistical analysis was conducted for sample size reasons. Nevertheless, it can be seen that for US participants the most frequent recognition rating across three of the roles was 'significant', which was in line with the overall US recognition rating. For administrators the most frequent response was to split the dilemma into two aspects. For the aspect where they recognised a dilemma, their most frequent recognition was also 'significant'.

For the US resolution ratings only two of the four broad roles had 'marginal' as the most frequent rating (support and special school professionals). Support professionals also had 'significant' as the most frequent rating as did regular school professionals. Administrators had split response

Table 6.3 Breakdown of most frequent recognition and resolution ratings by role

		USA	Netherlands	England
Recognition	Administrators	Split (significant)	Significant	Significant
	Support professionals	Significant	Marginal	Marginal + significant
	Regular school professionals	Significant	Significant	Significant
	Special school professionals	Significant	Significant	Significant
	Overall	**Significant**	**Significant**	**Significant**
Resolution	Administrators	Split (significant)	Significant	Significant + split (marginal)
	Support professionals	Marginal + significant	Significant	Uncertain
	Regular school professionals	Significant	Marginal + significant	Significant
	Special school professionals	Marginal	Marginal	Split (marginal)
	Overall	**Marginal**	**Significant**	**Significant**

Note
Brackets after split response – most frequent recognition and resolution ratings for aspect of dilemma.

as their most frequent response, with 'significant' as the most frequent rating where they recognised a dilemma.

Table 6.3 also shows that for three of the four broad Netherlands roles the most frequent recognition level was 'significant', in line with the overall most frequent rating. Only for support professionals was the most frequent recognition lower, at a marginal level. Similarly, for Netherlands resolution levels, three of the four roles had 'significant' as the most frequent rating, in line with the overall ratings. However, regular school professionals also had 'marginal' as the most frequent rating (with 'significant'), while special school professionals had 'marginal' as the only most frequent resolution rating.

This table also shows that for English participants all four broad roles had 'significant' as the most frequent recognition level, in line with the overall most frequent rating. But, English support professionals also had 'marginal' as their most frequent recognition level. For English resolution ratings, the overall most frequent rating was found only for two of the four broad roles, administrators and regular school professionals. However, English administrators also had split responses as their most frequent response, as did special school professionals, with marginal resolutions being the most frequent resolution ratings for the aspects where they recognised a dilemma. It is also notable that English support professionals had 'uncertain' as their most frequent resolution response.

Qualitative accounts of the recognition of the curriculum dilemma

The number of distinct 1st level themes in the three countries ranged from 30 to 49, with most themes arising from the English participants. Most participants used between two and three themes to explain their position, with some participants using up to five and six themes.

Table 6.4 shows that the most frequent 2nd level theme in each country group were 'tensions' and 'resolved tensions' at similar levels with more than 60 per cent of participants using them. None of the other 2nd level themes were used by more than 30 per cent of participants in any of the country groups. Only one of the two 2nd level themes that questioned the validity of the dilemma, 'moderate/deny lower status consequences', was used in each country group. However, only 14 per cent of English participants, 10 per cent of US and 6 per cent of Netherlands participants used this 2nd level theme. No participants used the other 2nd level theme that questioned whether providing similar experiences denied relevant opportunities, 'moderate/deny relevance to individual needs consequences'. Similarly low proportions used the 'other negative consequences' and 'other positive consequences' 2nd level themes, only 6 per cent for positive consequences and 4 per cent for negative consequences by English participants and none

Table 6.4 Comparison of 1st level themes for recognising curriculum dilemma across the three countries

	USA	Netherlands	England
Tensions	N = 36(72%)[a]	N = 24(75%)	N = 33(66%)
	*Current tensions 13[b]	*Current tensions 13	*Current tensions 25
	*Academic curriculum not meet needs 16	*Academic curriculum not meet needs 2	*Academic curriculum not meet needs 5
	*Problems in implementing differentiated programmes/teaching 9	*Problems in implementing differentiated programmes/teaching 4	*Problems in implementing differentiated programmes/teaching 2
	*Some curriculum areas left out 1	*Some curriculum areas left out 2	*Some curriculum areas left out 5
	*Expectations too low 2	*Expectations too low 4	
	*Problem in using same standards and tests 7	*Problems in using same tests 1	
	*Parental concern about alternative curriculum/tests 3		*Parental concern about reduced curriculum 1
		*Same experiences for all inappropriate 1	*Same experiences for all inappropriate 2
	Unrealistic expectations 4	Therapies use up curriculum time 1	School wants to maximise GCSEs 1
	One size fits all diploma a problem 3	Sometimes query relevance of common curriculum 1	Cost of alternative vocational curriculum 1
	Some unwilling to differentiate 2	Hard choice between academic and vocational routes 1	National Curriculum over-prescriptive 5
	Standards disaffection tension 1	Pressure for common curriculum from parents 1	Tension if crude common curriculum 1
	Students aware/query different work 8	Problems in designing special school national curriculum 1	Entitled to same common curriculum 1
	Students accept programme not meet needs 1	In emotional/behaviour difficulties in special schools, only some children use regular curriculum 1	KS3 NC not all appropriate 1
	Simplifying curriculum is dumbing down 1		Curriculum disadvantage of small special school/unit 3
	Fall between regular and alternative curriculum 2		
	Outdated notions of curriculum 1		

Table 6.4 (Continued)

	USA	Netherlands	England
Resolved tensions	**N = 30(60%)**	**N = 23(72%)**	**N = 37(74%)**
	*Meet individual needs and experience general curriculum 3	*Meet individual needs and experience general curriculum 5	*Meet individual needs and experience general curriculum 7
	*Curriculum benefits of special school/class 2	*Curriculum benefits of special schools 2	*Curriculum benefits of special schools/ unit 1
	*Use alternative curriculum/ assessment to meet needs 7	*Use alternative curriculum to meet needs 2	*Use alternative curriculum to meet needs 3
	*Same areas at appropriate level and way 12	*Same areas at appropriate level and way 5	
	*Differentiating general curriculum for younger children easier 1	*Differentiated general curriculum for young children easier 1	
		*Maximise common curriculum 10	*Maximise common curriculum 7
		*Priority to what is relevant 3	*Priority to what is relevant 8
		*Individual relevance more important than common aspects 1	*Individual relevance more important than common aspects 2
	*Modifying general curriculum for all 11		*Modifying general curriculum for all 8
	Relevant programmes but not apart 1	Formal national adaptation 1	KS3–4 vocational/life skill, differentiated curriculum 4
	All participate in social activities 1	Curriculum adapted to specific SEN areas 1	Same curriculum areas, differentiated teaching approach 8
	Additional classes for all 1	Curriculum based on difference 2	Offer broad curriculum to see what can do 1
		Provide extra help 2	Range of activities labelled as curriculum area 3
		Therapy during lessons; make up afterwards 2	Core and what is personally relevant 1
		Have realistic expectations 2	Give opportunity, if not learn, alternative programme 1
		Move towards common curriculum 2	Post-16 use life skills programme 1
		Curriculum based on learning potential 2	
		Use flexible teaching approaches 1	
		Well trained and coping teachers 1	

Moderate/deny lower status consequences	N = 5(10%) *Modified curriculum not lower status 4 *Students and parents accept alternative curriculum/assessment 2	N = 2(6%) *Modified curriculum not lower status 1 *Students and parents accept alternative curriculum/assessment 1	N = 7(14%) *Modified curriculum not lower status/ stigmatised 5 *Parents accept/want alternative/ different curriculum 4 Peer modelling and teaching adaptations 1 Different experience but same learning path 1 Differentiated teaching approach 3 More curriculum programme flexibility allowed 2 Well planned differentiated curriculum not tokenism 3 For some need to focus core areas 2
Wider than SEN tensions	N = 0	N = 1(3%) *Wider issue than SEN one 1	N = 6(12%) *Wider issue than SEN 5 Lower ability groups lower status 1
Other positive consequences	N = 0	N = 0	N = 3(6%) Social learning priority over different experience 1 Flexible use of National Curriculum framework, interesting programme 2

Table 6.4 (Continued)

	USA	Netherlands	England
Other negative consequences	N = 0	N = 0	N = 2 (4%) Limited focus on literacy/ numeracy reduces enjoyment 1 Query that different programme enhances education aims 1
Depends	N = 1(2%) Depends on quality of general differentiation 1	N = 1(3%) Depends on several factors 1	N = 2(4%) Depends on breadth of common curriculum 1 Depends on area of SEN 1
Comments	N = 5(10%) Testing affecting curriculum 3 Unsure reason 2	N = 3(9%) Special schools believe they are treating children 1 Students aware of learning difficulties 1 Special school curriculum too narrow 1	N = 3(6%) Students disappointed about not reaching GCSE level 1 Hierarchy of different certification 1 Curriculum pressures more in regular schools 1
Moderate/deny relevance to individual needs consequences	N = 0	N = 0	N = 0

Notes

a N: number of participants using 2nd level theme (% of all participants – in bold if more than 30%).

b * Indicates similar 1st level themes used in two or three of the countries (numbers after 1st level themes represent frequency of use of this theme).

by Netherlands and US participants. More English participants also used the 2nd level theme 'wider than SEN tension' (6) than Netherlands (1) and US participants (0). Between 2 and 10 per cent of participants used the 2nd level themes 'depends' and 'comments'.

Second level themes: 'tensions'

About half the 1st level themes, making up the 2nd level theme 'tensions', were shared across one or more of the countries and these tended to be the more frequently used 1st level themes. Four 1st level themes were used by participants in each country: 'current tensions', 'academic curriculum not meet needs', 'problems in implementing differentiated programmes/teaching' and 'some curriculum areas left out'. The most frequently used 1st level theme making up the 2nd level theme 'tensions' was 'current tensions'. Examples of this 1st level theme are set out below:

'current tensions'

Is there a tension between No Child Left Behind and IDEA?, this comes down to an issue that's being played out right now and I'm sure people will talk to you about the two percent, one percent issue.
(US Administrator, Federal Department)

Equal opportunities is, it's hard to make a definition and what you actually want is that the child in the future can do as well as possible in his work, in his living, in his spare time And there is a possibility that if children are not in this school, then they are missing something and we discuss it and we say to parents 'well if you really want to have individual lessons for your child then you should choose the special school because there are less children in the room, more teachers in it, but then you miss on the other side, the other things from the regular school'.
(Netherlands advisory teacher, urban area).

It's a specialist language school, in terms of the government . . . But there are children within the school and for those children sometimes they're dis-applying them from what is an opportunity there for everybody else in the school and I think that's the right thing to do. A lot of them would have struggled with learning those languages, but actually I mean what they do there is they don't stop it completely, they link it in to something like the business studies and they do Spanish within some business studies. So they're not getting no access to it but it's tailored in, perhaps in a more appropriate way to make it more relevant, more practical, you know, and I wouldn't want them to be not having access to languages at all. I mean children in schools with severe learning difficulties, for example, are learning languages, so we can't be saying that 'ok this is a mainstream school and we can't let, we're not going to tailor the curriculum to be for you and you're not going to do it at all'. So I mean it's those sort of dilemmas.

(English psychologist, urban area)

Another common 1st level theme was 'academic curriculum not meet needs', but it was used more frequently by US (16) than Netherlands (2) or English participants (5). Examples of this theme are:

'academic curriculum not meet needs'

No Child Left Behind requires that all children be exposed to regular curriculum. I understand this and by the same token if a child has an IEP and been through assessments by psychologists and social workers, and their difficulties in functioning in a regular setting has been documented e.g. oppositional, on medications attaining at below age level. I believe that the regular teachers do not have time to do the IEP and do their regular thing too.

(US resource teacher, special school, urban district)

That is an issue but what comes to mind for me is the number of disaffected youngsters in key stage four and that is a growing concern and an issue, no matter how much you allow those youngsters to access the present curriculum, it isn't the answer for them and what, are we doing them any favours by actually focusing in on this curriculum.

(English national administrator/adviser)

The third 1st level theme used in each country group was 'problems in implementing differentiated programmes/teaching', but again these were used more by US participants (9) than Netherlands (4) or English participants (2).

'problems in implementing differentiated programmes/teaching'

Because even though we receive . . . the teachers receive the training to do the differentiated teaching, all of our teachers aren't as skilled as we would like them to be.

(US senior teacher, special school, urban area)

We have some children with a label who get more money from the government to help them, to make plans, individual plans for that particular child. The problems, the difficulty is that you have a group of children who you are teaching the normal curriculum and you have some children in the classroom who are doing parts of the curriculum. And that's a challenge for the teachers, using different instruction and having the children all the time in their classrooms, so we're, the policy in our school is the children are getting help in the classroom, not outside the classroom.

(Netherlands senior teacher, primary school, urban area)

Here are examples of the fourth 1st level theme 'some curriculum areas left out' which was used across the three countries:

'some curriculum areas left out'

I think like in math I think there are some things I don't cover because I don't think my kids need, I think in math they need more . . . addition, subtraction, multiplication, division.

(US resource teacher, middle school, rural area)

Two 1st level themes were used by US and Netherlands participants, 'expectations too low' and 'problem in using same tests', though the latter one was used more by US (7) than Netherlands participants (1):

'problems in using the same general standards and tests'

I have had children who have been non-readers and worked with them one to one but they were given the same assessments as other reading children. There are two worlds. Decisions are made by people who are not in the real world.

(US resource teacher, special school, urban district)

'expectations too low'

The curriculum in the special school is adjusted to the level of the students. It's not challenging enough I think because the progress they make is not the progress that a child makes in a regular school.

(Netherlands psychologist, urban area)

Other similar 1st level themes about parental views on alternative or reduced curriculum were used more by US than English participants.

'parental concern about alternative curriculum/tests'

Where it became an issue today is the parent being afraid that the student would be treated as a lower status group, not the child, because they're smaller and not being given equal opportunity because they wanted no pull out services for the student, they wanted everything in the classroom.

(US advisory teacher, rural area)

'parental concern about reduced curriculum'

I've had a parent who didn't want their child to go out of the class because they actually felt that that was withdrawing them from the rest of the curriculum. So for instance if we were doing geography and they were going off to do some literacy work, they felt that they should have the balanced curriculum rather than the additional support, but that's only one in ten years of school experience.

(English senior teacher, primary school, rural area)

Finally, another 1st level theme, 'same experiences for all inappropriate' was used by Netherlands and English participants. Here is an example of this theme:

'same experiences for all inappropriate'

Because you can't give all the children the same experience because they are, they have, they can't learn all things.

(Netherlands senior teacher, special school, urban area)

Several of the 1st level themes that were specific to US participants were about the current US standards agenda, for example, the specific frequently used 1st level theme, 'unrealistic expectations':

'unrealistic expectations'

I also think that all learning doesn't have to hinge on, as you're sitting at a desk, so that's a big dilemma. You know, I have parents, I had a parent today cry, I've had a lot of parents this year crying about 'what is my kid going to do? Why does my kid have to take this class and do, you know find the hypotenuse of a triangle when they're just going to work?' and these are the parents crying so you can imagine what the students are going under, that's a big problem.

(US resource teacher, high school, rural area)

First level themes specific to the Netherlands participants were mostly about issues concerned with designing and using a common curriculum. By contrast 1st level themes specific to English participants were focused on standards, finance and an over-prescriptive National Curriculum. The most frequently used specific English 1st level theme was 'national curriculum over-prescriptive':

'national curriculum over-prescriptive'

> I would certainly maintain that over the last ten years there has been an unrealistic expectation of the common entitlement linked to an age which actually doesn't help anybody very much. Yes, there is a tension because we've created it through the structure of the curriculum that we impose on schools.
>
> (English national administrator)

Second level theme: 'resolved tensions'

As explained with the identification dilemma, this 2nd level theme reflects some recognition of a tension that is seen as resolved to some extent. When applied to the recognition of the curriculum dilemma it was used approximately as frequently as the 'tensions' theme. Between about one-third and two-thirds of the 1st level themes, making up this 2nd level theme, were used across each country group.

Three 1st level themes were used in each country group, 'meet individual needs and experience general curriculum', 'curriculum benefits of special schools/unit' and 'use alternative curriculum to meet needs'. The first of these 1st level themes assumes a balance between individual relevance and common experiences, while the second two adopt a resolution based more on relevance. Examples of these themes follow:

'meet individual needs and experience general curriculum'

> that our special education students are never denied access to the experience with the general curriculum or any other opportunity and that their individual needs are specifically addressed in the IEP's.... because the way they adapt them it has to do both, meet the individual needs and the curriculum, it has to, and it's done in such a way that it does.
>
> (US special education supervisor, high school, urban area)

> I myself think that the common curriculum is the basis from where you can work and I always say to the schools that you have to start with the same education, the same curriculum as the other children and you have to do the right observation and see where your child with special needs cannot follow it any more and at that moment you can see what those small steps are to get to a higher level.
>
> (Netherlands advisory teacher, urban area)

'curriculum benefits of special schools/unit'

> We try to give them that in our school but there are some things which I think are important but we cannot offer it. Like cooking, doing the wash. Special schools can offer them that but we can't, but we think there are a lot of things that are very important for our handicapped children, we try to teach them as much as possible and when the point nears, we say we can't offer no more. We try, together with the parents, to look for a school where they can learn the things we didn't teach them.
>
> (Netherlands SEN resource teacher, primary school, urban area)

> We feel that we're talking about pupils who have been failed by the system, they sense they've failed themselves but they've been failed by the system by twenty-five, twenty-six hours of academic work sitting behind a desk. This hasn't worked for the people who are here. So we have to develop our timetable so that only fifteen per cent of their time, in some cases thirty or forty per cent, we'll have a concrete academic programme. And, the rest of the time is to build skills that they have been lacking, team skills, individual skills, looking at things that they've never had the opportunity to do before.
>
> (English senior teacher, behaviour unit, rural area)

'use alternative curriculum to meet needs'

> so they work towards their IEP goals which are the state goals, ok. So the state has to identify that everybody doesn't come under one umbrella, that these kids have what they call the alternate assessment and this is how they address it. And that's on their IEP, the goals the teachers are addressing.
>
> (US senior teacher, middle school, urban area)

> It's appropriate to have different goals. I think where a child is, it doesn't matter. They have to be offered what they can handle and for one child it's less, not very much, and for another it's very much and you should offer it all.
>
> (Netherlands class teacher, primary school, urban area)

The two 1st level themes which were used by US and Netherlands participants, 'same areas at appropriate level/way' and 'differentiating curriculum for younger children easier' both refer to a balance between commonality and individuality, though for the second theme only for younger children. The 'same areas at appropriate level/way' theme was the most frequently one used by Netherlands participants. Here are examples of these themes:

'same areas at appropriate level/way'

> I believe that they should be offered the common curriculum but in a modified way. They don't need all of the extra fluff, they need the basics that they're going to need to know, the basic facts, the main ideas, especially in science and social studies, I think they can handle the regular curriculum as long as they have a study guide to help them, you know I firmly believe that they should be offered the same.
>
> (US resource teacher, elementary school, rural area)

> . . . and for autistic children, it's hard to pick up instruction and all that kind of thing but you can do that in your class, so they get more instruction, maybe they get the same curriculum, but taught in another way
>
> (Netherlands advisory teacher, urban area)

'differentiating curriculum for younger children easier'

> Well on my level it's not difficult, my curriculum isn't difficult, we are so hands on, you know. Whether they are a special ed student or not at my level differentiating, coming up with a different way to learn for any child is very, it's much more simple. I can see that as the curriculum gets more difficult it becomes more difficult.
>
> (US class teacher, elementary school, rural area)

> Yes I think there is a particular tension, it's to do with, in our schools, the age of the children. I think it's not, for the younger ones it's not. As they get older you have to make a choice about curriculum because otherwise the child doesn't have any good experience at all.
>
> (Netherlands advisory teacher, rural area)

Another 1st level theme used by US and English participants, 'modify general curriculum for all students', was one of the most frequently used themes in both country groups. This theme involves taking account of the individual needs of all learners, not just those with SEN/disabilities. Here are examples of this theme:

'modify general curriculum for all students'

> I think this school does a nice job of making sure students are in a classroom where they fit in academically, ability wise, and even personality wise, through the tracking and just, the guidance counsellors understand too, you know – 'if this teacher is this way, here I have some students, they're going to need to be in here'.
>
> (US special education teacher, high school, rural district)

I don't actually, not in the way that I work with these two situations. I use the national curriculum as my guide but then I, within that, have to make it relevant to the children that I teach in terms of their communication issues, I have to make it accessible, and so I feel sometimes I can interpret it but I, to me this is what my job is, that I take a requirement and I take individual children and I blend as best I can.

(English class teacher, special school, urban area)

There were three 1st level themes which were used by Netherlands and English participants, 'maximise common curriculum', 'priority to what is relevant' and 'individual relevance more important than common aspects'. The first of the themes recognises the balancing, while the other two themes put greater weight on relevance. 'Maximise common curriculum' was one of the more frequently used in these country groups, as was 'priority to relevance' for the English participants. Here are examples of these themes:

'maximise common curriculum'

Well what you want to achieve is that the children are able to follow the curriculum that is as close to their peers as possible, but you equally have to have in mind what works because if these children aren't able to follow a particular lesson and structure, then they may need an alternative form of that lesson geared to them. And if it's so different within that particular learning setting that they can't make progress, then we need to think again about whether that learning setting is right or whether it can be adapted further. But equally you've got to be wary about a diet of our basic skills that actually denies children the range of experiences.

(English national administrator)

'priority to what is relevant'

I think the possibilities of the child are more important, that's more important and you have to, that's part of, that's where you're starting and then you have to do your best to teach the child as much as possible. That's part of the dilemma, that a lot of teachers in schools are thinking 'well this child is . . ., it never will learn anything and so we don't offer it.'

(Netherlands national administrator/adviser)

'individual relevance more important than common aspects'

Well it's not so much of a tension from my point of view because they can't get access to the broad and balanced without having done the individual bit. So you've got to give them that, there isn't a tension, there's no question in my mind. Common requirements are important, but not as important . . . you've got to, say with communication, you've got to support children and help them with the development of their communication skills before they could even look or listen. That's just at the very basic level here.

(English senior teacher, special school, rural area)

There were fewer 1st level themes that were specific to US participants (3) than specific to Netherlands (10) and English participants (11). It is notable, that with a few exceptions, most of these country specific 1st level themes were used less frequently than the shared themes.

Balance in use of 'resolved tensions' 2nd level theme

The 1st level themes, making up this 2nd level theme, were also analysed in terms of the emphasis given to commonality versus differentiation/relevance. These themes were sorted into three categories: (i) emphasis on commonality; (ii) emphasis on differentiation/relevance; and (iii) balance between commonality and differentiation/relevance. Table 6.5 shows the frequency of these 1st level themes for different emphases on commonality–differentiation across the three countries.

The 1st level themes reflecting an emphasis on commonality were used least frequently across the three countries, though they were used more by Netherlands (18 per cent) than US (2 per cent) or English participants (10 per cent). The 1st level themes reflecting a balance between commonality and differentiation/relevance were most frequently used across the three countries, though least by Netherlands participants. This analysis shows that the Netherlands participants used the emphasis on commonality and emphasis on differentiation/relevance themes more than the US or English participants and the balance between commonality and differentiation/relevance theme less (chi-squared = 9.9, df = 4, p = 0.04).

Table 6.5 Breakdown of frequency of use of 'resolved tensions' 1st level themes

	USA	Netherlands	England	Total
Emphasis on differentiation/relevance	9	14	19	42
	21%	37%	28%	29%
Emphasis on commonality	1	7	7	15
	2%	18%	10%	10%
Balance between commonality	32	17	41	90
and differentiation/relevance	76%	45%	61%	61%
Total	42	38	41	147

Second level themes: moderating or denying consequences

It is notable that no participants in any of the country groups used 1st level themes that questioned the negative consequence of providing the same curriculum experiences in terms of denying relevant opportunities. However, some participants in each group, although a minority, did question the negative consequence of providing some differentiated curriculum experiences. There were two 1st level themes which were used in each country group, 'modified curriculum not lower status/stigmatised' and 'parents accept/want alternative/different curriculum'. The first theme denies the consequence while the second questions it by claiming that parents want differentiation. Both themes were used more frequently by US and English than Netherlands participants. Here are examples of these themes:

'modified curriculum not lower status/stigmatised'

> they (students) are not really concerned about it, I think they are more concerned about 'do you understand what I'm going through? Do you understand what makes me tick? Do you understand how I process things?' They know that there's a difference but I think they're more interested in 'are you understanding of what I need you to do in order to be successful?'
>
> (US class teacher, special school, urban area)

> Well if they were only offered the same then that would be a huge dilemma – I don't see that they get treated as lower status people because they've got something different. To me it gives you the same status as everybody else. It's catering for what you need actually, gives you a higher status I think. What's the point of trying to teach someone ancient history or something if they really aren't understanding it, that's just patronising.
>
> (English senior teacher, special school, urban area)

'parents/students accept or want alternative/different curriculum/assessment'

> Many do not realise that the certificate is not a diploma. Parents seem to be satisfied with the certificate.
>
> (US resource teacher, special school, urban area)

> However there are some children whose parents are more sort of attuned and want to focus more on the life skills and experiences that

those children need in order to survive once they leave the school. That is an issue that cannot be undermined because for some youngsters access to the curriculum in a highly differentiated form is a necessity.

(English national administrator)

Second level themes: other areas

There were few references to other positive or negative consequences than those referred to directly in the presented dilemmas. Only three English participants referred to some positive consequences of a common curriculum, that it meant learning together and the national curriculum framework is useful for the development of interesting programmes. Only two English participants saw negative consequences in the narrowness that can arise from a focus mainly on core curriculum areas. Again, it was mainly English participants (5) who saw the issues in this dilemma as applicable beyond the SEN field. Here is an example of this 'wider than SEN' 1st level theme:

So that, so it isn't actually to do with special needs in a way, it's a wider structural issue. And learning experiences, I would say that children should have as much as possible similar experiences, except of course they don't and each school is different. I would say a child who needs . . . should have differentiated programmes or experiences within that learning experience.

(English senior psychologist, rural area)

Second level themes used to explain different recognition positions

Table 6.6 below shows the breakdown of the US 2nd level curriculum recognition themes by recognition level. This shows that US participants use both the 'tensions' and 'resolved tensions' themes to explain their recognition levels. However, there is a tendency for more of those with lower recognition levels to use the 'resolved tensions' theme: 8/8 (not recognise), 4/6 (marginal), 8/22 (significant) and 2/6 (considerable recognition). Similarly, there is a tendency for more of those with higher recognition levels to use the 'tensions' theme: 2/8 (not recognise), 4/6 (marginal), 17/22 (significant) and 5/6 (considerable recognition). Two of the eight who did not recognise this dilemma also used the 'moderate/deny low status consequences' 2nd level theme.

Table 6.7 shows that both the 'tensions' and 'resolved tensions' 2nd level themes were used across the different Netherlands recognition levels. Only 1/4 of those not recognising the curriculum dilemma used 'tensions' themes, while 3/4 used 'resolved tensions' themes. For those recognising a marginal dilemma, 4/5 participants used 'resolved tensions' themes, while all of them

Table 6.6 Second level themes used by US participants to explain position to curriculum dilemma

US 2nd level themes	Recognition level					
	Not at all	Marginal	Signifi- cant	Consider- able	Split response	Total
	N = 8	N = 6	N = 22	N = 6	N = 8	N = 50
Tensions	2	4	**17**	5	7	35
Resolved tensions	**8**	4	8	2	**8**	30
Other positive consequences	0	0	0	0	0	0
Other negative consequences	0	0	0	0	0	0
Moderate/deny relevance to individual need consequences	0	0	0	0	0	0
Moderate/deny low status consequences	2	1	1	1	0	5
Wider than SEN	0	0	0	0	0	0
Depends	0	0	0	0	1	1
Comments	1	1	3	0	0	5

Note
Most frequent use in rows in bold, if >1.

Table 6.7 Second level themes used by Netherlands participants to explain position to curriculum dilemma

Netherlands 2nd level themes	Recognition level					
	Not at all	Marginal	Signifi- cant	Consider- able	Split response	Total
	N = 4	N = 5	N = 15	N = 3	N = 5	N = 32
Tensions	1	**5**	14	2	3	25
Resolved tensions	3	4	**10**	2	**4**	23
Other positive consequences	0	0	0	0	0	0
Other negative consequences	0	0	0	0	0	0
Moderate/deny relevance to individual need consequences	0	0	0	0	0	0
Moderate/deny low status consequences	1	0	1	0	0	2
Wider than SEN	0	1	0	0	0	0
Depends	0	0	1	0	0	1
Comments	1	0	1	0	0	2

Note
Most frequent use in rows in bold, if >1.

used 'tension' themes. For participants who recognised a significant or considerable curriculum dilemma, more used the 'tensions' (16/18) than the 'resolved tensions' theme (12/18). This shows a similar pattern of theme use by recognition level as in the US group.

Table 6.8 Second level themes used by English participants to explain position to curriculum dilemma

English 2nd level themes	Recognition level						Total
	Not at all	Marginal	Signifi-cant	Consider-able	Uncertain	Split response	
	N = 6	N = 10	N = 23	N = 2	N = 4	N = 5	N = 50
Tensions	2	**5**	**19**	1	1	**5**	33
Resolved tensions	5	**8**	**13**	2	3	**5**	36
Other positive consequences	0	1	0	0	0	2	3
Other negative consequences	0	1	1	0	0	0	2
Moderate/deny relevance to individual need consequences	0	0	0	0	0	0	0
Moderate/deny low status consequences	1	2	2	0	2	0	7
Wider than SEN	0	3	3	0	0	0	6
Depends	1	0	1	0	0	0	2
Comments	0	0	3	0	0	0	3

Note
Most frequent use in rows in bold, if > 1.

Table 6.8 shows a similar pattern of association between the use of the 2nd level themes 'tensions' and 'resolved tensions' for English participants. 'Resolved tension' themes were used most by those with lower recognition levels: 5/6 (not recognise), 8/10 (marginal) and 13/23 (significant recognition) – numbers for considerable recognition are small. 'Tensions' themes were used most by those with higher recognition levels: 2/6 (not recognise), 5/10 (marginal) and 19/23 (significant recognition). Though there were seven participants who used the 'moderate/deny low status consequence' 2nd level theme, it was used across the recognition levels.

Qualitative accounts of the resolutions of the curriculum dilemma

The number of distinct 1st level curriculum resolution themes across the three countries ranged from 29 to 41, with most participants using between two and three themes each to explain their position, with some participants using up to five and eight themes.

Table 6.9 shows that of the ten 2nd level themes used to analyse the 1st level themes two were used by more than 30 per cent of participants across

Table 6.9 Comparison of 1st level themes for resolving curriculum dilemma across the three countries

	USA	Netherlands	England
Balance common/ different aspects	N = 18(36%)[a]	N = 17(53%)	N = 26(52%)
	*Modify general curriculum to meet individual needs 9[b]	*Modify general curriculum to individual needs 7	*Modify general curriculum to individual needs 10
	*Changes to instruction, same objectives 5	*Changes to instruction, same objectives 2	*Changes to instruction, same objectives 4
	*Same general area, differentiated programme 4		*Same general area, different programmes 8
		*Mid-way, individual needs and cover general areas 7	*Mid-way, meet individual needs and cover general areas 10
	Mix regular and alternative curriculum 5	National curriculum for special schools 1 Broad targets in national SE curriculum 2 National SE curriculum depends on SEN area 1 Same curriculum areas; geared person relevance 1 Severe EBD, link curriculum to mental health programmes 1	Educate in different not alternative way 1 Same programme but different certificate 1 Reduce what is missed of common curriculum 1 Catch up programme justifies withdrawal 1
Curriculum and teaching flexibility	N = 16(32%)	N = 14(44%)	N = 20(40%)
	*Collaboration SE and regular teachers 3	*Collaboration SE and regular teachers 1	
	*Tension as creative 1	*Tension as creative 1	
	*Different curriculum for severe disabilities 5		*Different curriculum for severe disability 2
	*Extra time for learning 1		*Provide extra time for learning 1
		*Emphasis on life skills 2	*Emphasis on life skills, personal, social education 3

	Appropriate support for learning 3 More than one type diploma 2 More flexibility for teachers 3	Flexible adaptive class teaching for all 6 Use peer collaborative learning 1 More flexible curriculum in regular schools 3 Special school gives greater flexibility and coverage 2 Person-centred teaching approaches 1 Support progress in small steps 1	More flexibility for curriculum framework 8 Move from National Curriculum as older to life skills 2 Use of work-related programmes 1 Way of teaching important 4 Move from National Curriculum at transition from foundation stage 1 Special teaching equipment and modes critical 1 Curriculum flexibility formally recognised 1 Link across curriculum 1 Broad curriculum, not just literacy and numeracy 2 Take account of emotional/social aspects 1
Continuing issues	N=6(12%) *Hard to resolve 6	**N=11(34%)** *Hard to resolve 8 *Some common areas left out 5	**N=18(36%)** *Hard to resolve, continuing issue 15 *Accept some get less 1 Adaptations harder in secondary schools 2
Priority to individual relevance	N=6(12%) *Work from individual needs 1 *Need realistic expectations 5	N=9(28%) *Work from individual needs 5 *Need realistic expectations about abilities 4 Provide relevant opportunities 2 For EBD students, focus on positive feelings 1	N=13(26%) *Work from individual needs 12 *Need realistic expectations 2 More comfortable within capabilities 1

Table 6.9 (Continued)

	USA	Netherlands	England
Enhanced staffing/ resources	N = 8(16%)	N = 3(9%)	N = 9(18%)
	*Better trained teachers 5	*Better trained teachers 3	*Better trained teachers and assistants 7
	*More resources 1		*More resources 4
	Teachers not all skilled 2		Curriculum depends on teacher skills available 1
	Commitment to field 1		More curriculum support, build capacity 2
	Improve subject knowledge of special education teacher 2		
Systems development	N = 8(16%)	N = 4(13%)	N = 3(6%)
	*Differentiation as management issue 1		*Differentiation as management issue 2
	Policy change 6	Use additional resources for smaller classes 1	Change to national assessment, accountability system 1
	System needs to crash 1	Need change of attitude 2	
	Avoid short term fashions 1	Raise learning expectations 1	
	Need to supplement State curriculum 1	Curriculum focus on socialisation, knowledge follows 1	
	Mixing benefits all students 1		
Priority to common aspects	N = 1(2%)	N = 3(9%)	N = 6(12%)
		*More emphasis common aspects 1	*Basic core common 5
	Age appropriate materials 1	Focus on learning rather than behaviour 2	Common learning principles 1

Promote positive aspects of difference	N = 1 (2%) Instill own worth 1	N = 5(10%) Equal worth to different kinds of achievement 3 Meeting needs of all is equal opportunities 1 Vocational programmes not seen as ower status 2
Participation in decisions	N = 0	N = 1(3%) Involve parents in curriculum decisions 1	N = 1(2%) Give child some choice, even of subjects 1
Depends	N = 0	N = 0	N = 1(2%) 1% of 2nd level themes depends on area SEN 1

Notes
a N: number of participants using 2nd level theme (% of all participants – in bold if more than 30%).
b * Indicates similar 1st level themes used in two or three of the countries (numbers after 1st level themes represent frequency of use of this theme).

each country, 'balance common/different aspects' and 'curriculum and teaching flexibility'. The former was the most frequently used 2nd level theme, with Netherlands (53 per cent) and English (52 per cent) participants using it more than US participants (36 per cent). A third 2nd level theme, 'continuing issues' was also used more by Netherlands and English participants than by US participants. More participants across the three countries also used the 'priority to individual relevance' 2nd level theme than the 'priority to common aspects' theme. However, more Netherlands (28 per cent) and English (26 per cent) participants used the 'priority to individual relevance' theme than US ones (12 per cent).

Second level theme: 'balance common/different aspects'

Two 1st level themes, making up this most frequently used 2nd level theme, were used across the country groups, 'modify general curriculum to meet individual needs' and 'changes to instruction, same objectives'. Both themes were amongst the more frequently used 1st level themes. Here are some examples of these themes:

'modify general curriculum to meet individual needs'

> I think that my preference is modifying curriculum, I think that all kids can learn, I think that all kids benefit from being in general education, I've seen kids that have fairly significant impairments, in general education do they get everything? No, but they're getting many more exposures to things than what I would twenty years ago when we were having self contained classes all day long with no mixing.
>
> (US district administrator, rural district)

> You have to make your own shape and adaptations for the child. He can do things with the other children, but adapt it to his level. So you change a little bit what they are doing, for example in mathematics – the other children do this or that and he does it a little bit different.
>
> (Netherlands resource teacher, primary school, urban)

'change to instruction, same objectives'

> the lessons should be the same as for the non-disabled but use strategies/techniques that fit the disability, not watering down the programme. We need to change the way of delivering. This involves a lot of planning and work. Getting the teachers to plan appropriately is an issue. To get them to the same experience as normal children takes a lot of work, when someone has worked 10+ years and they do not want

to change. It is different for younger teachers. Teaching in this context continues to be an intense and demanding job.

(US senior teacher, special school, urban area)

I mean I think it does take it quite a way in that you can modify bits of the curriculum, you can teach things in different ways, it's fairly broadly described isn't it? Not only just in terms of the levels but in terms of the knowledge and understanding and skills and so on. You can tailor things quite well to very different needs and very different levels. It takes a bit of imagination and a bit of working out.

(English national/regional administrator)

The 1st level theme 'same general areas, different programmes' was also used more frequently by US and English participants. Here are examples of this theme:

'same general areas, different programmes'

I think that they should get some parts of the curriculum but it should be manipulated in a way that it's really different for them but they're getting the same bases and basics as everyone else is.

(US class teacher, special school, urban area)

Well that's what's happening here, but in one of their Ofsted reports it said 'you're a secondary school, you should have a science lab', ... so when the new school was built that had to go in. I mean if they are used they might be used for filling test tubes full of water, you won't be looking at chemistry, you know, it's pretty basic science.

(English senior teacher, special school, rural area)

The 1st level theme 'mid-way–meet individual needs and cover general areas' was also used more frequently by Netherlands and English participants. Here are examples of this theme:

'mid-way–meet individual needs and cover general areas'

I think we should look, it's too general, you should look at the child. If the child is able to understand and to do something with those abilities you should give as much of this normal curriculum. But you have all kinds of types and so you should look at the child.

(Netherlands resource teacher, special school, urban area)

Well actually I don't know the answer to that, I think I suppose that really it's a balance isn't it really about how much we need to give them and to some, and looking at it and saying 'well they need to be able to do this but we've got to have a certain level, we've got to work to a certain level for life skills to be able to function', and that sort of thing.

(English advisory teacher, urban area)

There was only one 1st level theme that was specific to US participants and four specific to English participants, which covered a range of themes. However, there were five 1st level themes specific to the Netherlands group, some of which related to developing a national curriculum framework for special education.

Second level theme: 'curriculum and teaching flexibility'

Four 1st level themes, making up this 2nd level theme, were used across the country groups. Two of these 1st level themes were used only by US and Netherlands participants, 'collaboration special education and regular teachers' and 'tension as creative'. Here are examples of the themes:

'collaboration special education and regular teachers'

> teachers collaborate to provide instruction, of how they involve parents and how they think of assessment and learning opportunities as they design programmes and as they work together.
>
> (US administrator, Federal Department)

'tension as creative'

> so it's my job to make that experience in one way relevant and be creative to make that work for a child.
>
> (Netherlands class teacher, primary school, urban area)

Two 1st level themes, 'different curriculum for severe disabilities' and 'extra time for learning', were used only by US and English participants. Here are examples of these themes:

'different curriculum for severe disabilities'

> Yes, we feel like we could have done that much better with things that would be more relevant to the children, what they're really going to need when they go out in to the world of work or even living in a group home, we used to really be able to concentrate more on job skills, home skills . . . and maybe instead of the Diary of Anne Frank we could use a story about getting ready for a job, what things do you need to do in the morning before you go to work. And you could sequence those activi-

ties rather than sequence the events in the story of Anne Frank, something like that.

(US special class teacher, regular school, rural district)

'extra time for learning'

I think the only way around that is to provide extra support in terms of hours for youngsters that, you know. An extended time table, maybe they need to stay in school an hour longer at the end of the day or maybe come in an hour earlier in the morning, because I don't think substituting their mainstream curriculum with their individual needs being met is the way to do it because then I think they miss out on a lot of opportunities. But they also miss out on a lot of stuff that they can actually do and actually enjoy without the pressure of, you know 'I can't do this'.

(English class teacher, special school, urban area)

One 1st level theme 'emphasis on life skills' was used only by Netherlands and English participants. Here is an example of this theme:

'emphasis on life skills'

Actually that is what all people do, they learn those kind of things that give them more life skills coming from their own interests. So you have to look at what is this child interested in. What motivates this child? And then they can learn, and if it is the normal curriculum of course you have to offer them that.

(Netherlands advisory teacher, urban area)

There were fewer 1st level themes that were specific to US participants (3) and to Netherlands participants (6) than specific to English participants (10). Several of the English themes referred explicitly to the need for more flexibility over the National Curriculum framework.

Second level theme: 'continuing issues'

The 'continuing issues' was used by more than 30 per cent of Netherlands and English participants, and less by US ones (12 per cent). As with the identification dilemma resolution, its use indicates that for these participants there is an explicit recognition that despite the suggested resolutions, some tensions are seen to persist. The most frequently used 1st level theme making up this 2nd level theme across the three country groups was 'hard to resolve'. Here are examples of this theme:

'hard to resolve'

> in one way we accept it, you can't do everything with these children, you do the best you can and then you have to make . . . and we look at every child – this does not fully resolve the problem.
>
> (Netherlands head teacher, regular primary school, rural area)

> It's pretty hard, in an ideal world one would give them what they need, but again what the parents want, what the school wants (. . .) it's a hard one to resolve.
>
> (English psychologist, urban area)

There was also one 1st level theme which was similar between Netherlands and English participants, 'some common areas left out' (Netherlands) and 'accept some get less' (English).

Second level theme: 'priority to individual relevance'

It is notable that this 2nd level theme was used more frequently across the three countries than the other 2nd level theme 'priority to common aspects'. Though the 2nd level theme, 'priority to individual relevance', was not used at the 30 per cent level in any of the three country groups, it almost reached this level for Netherlands (28 per cent) and English participants (26 per cent). Two of the more frequently used 1st level themes were used in all three country groups, 'work from individual needs' and 'need realistic expectations'. Here are examples of these themes:

'work from individual needs'

> I think the solution, the way I would do it is to make the IEP, what's in the plan for this child? What I'm trying to say is that it's different for each child, whether he has to have additional instruction outside the classroom or the goal of the IEP is participation (so it's driven by) the child's needs and the goals of the lesson. And, although the goals of the lesson are far beyond the level of the child, he could benefit from it so the decision is to keep him in the classroom instead of a separate curriculum or additional instruction outside the classroom.
>
> (Netherlands psychologist, urban area)

> And obviously we've got children, fourteen-year-olds who can't read and that's a serious issue that we have to address so we've got to spend more time on that but, well because we have to, you know, the education system will not allow you to progress if you can't read.
>
> (English class teacher, behaviour unit, rural area)

'need realistic expectations'

> I completely understand the federal government's idea that we have to raise standards but ok you're raising standards, but we're still working with the same kids. How, the hardest part of our job is how do we get them from here to up here and when you're looking at, like I said, if the support isn't there, if the kid doesn't want to do it, then we're not going to get them there.
>
> All I know is that if they're expecting us to continue to raise test scores, raise standards, raise this, raise that, I see that and I say 'ok that's fine', but then I look at society and I say, and again this is just my experience with the kids I work with, but less parent involvement, less importance attached to school, it doesn't match . . . So ok where is the home training coming from? Where does the importance of education come into this?
>
> (US behaviour resource teacher, high school, rural area)

> An autistic person can be taught a limited amount about imagery and its meaning, so for that person it will be sufficient to cope and enabling him to do other types of tasks, but within his range. I can't expect a blind man to see can I? Nor can I expect a dyslexic person to write fluently or read fluently, so my expectations might be too high and then in that sense I am, I would opt for adjustments.
>
> (Netherlands class teacher, high school, urban area)

There were few 1st level themes that were specific to each country group.

Second level theme: 'enhanced staffing/resources'

One 1st level theme, making up this 2nd level theme, was used in each country group, 'better trained teachers'. It was also one of the more frequently used 1st level themes. Here are examples of this theme:

'better trained teachers'

> It's a really early stage, but I see that the most important thing to do now is giving the teachers the opportunity to learn and to make changes in their classrooms.
>
> (Netherlands head teacher, primary school, urban)

> And I think possibly one of the difficulties, one of the challenges in SEN is actually having the space and the time within the schools for awareness or knowledge in the field of SEN to get teachers with subject responsibilities to work out differentiating the curriculum, modifying what you do. On the other hand, I think steps have been taken to kind

of overcome or try and overcome some of that by providing guidance training and resources to modify the delivery of those strategies.

(English national administrator)

One other 1st level theme, making up this 2nd level theme, was used only by US and English participants ('more resources'). There were also few 1st level themes specific to each country.

Second level theme: 'systems development'

Though this was one of the less frequently used 2nd level themes, it was used more by US (16 per cent) and Netherlands (13 per cent) participants than English ones (6 per cent). One 1st level theme was only used by US and English participants, 'differentiation as management issue'. Here is an example of this theme:

'differentiation as management issue'

> Again it would need a significant shift in thinking, it would need a significant shift in resourcing and time tabling with the school day. I mean if it was done, adequately resourced, well staffed and done properly. I mean there's no proof that it would work but I think it might.
>
> (English class teacher, special school, urban area)

Of the five 1st level themes specific to US participants, one ('policy change') related to current US policy issues. Here is an example of this theme:

'policy change'

> It's getting worse with these high school assessments, with this No Child Left Behind, telling the teacher 'I don't care if he's got a seventy IQ, he's going to learn algebra'. We've got a real problem right now. . . . the first thing that's going to happen is teachers' heads are going to roll 'cause their first question is going to be 'why aren't you doing this, what are you doing wrong?' I think the whole system is going to have to crash and burn before people acknowledge that this was not wise. . . . Oh the pendulum, it's going to swing, there will be a resolution, but we're going to have to have a lot of victims, have a lot of casualties. . . . and no matter how hard the children try, they can't pass the test, and that's going to cause a backlash and then eventually it will be resolved.
>
> (US resource teacher, special school, rural district)

There were four 1st level themes specific to Netherlands participants and only one theme specific to English participants.

Other 2nd level themes

The 2nd level themes 'participation in decisions' and 'promote positive aspects of difference' were the least used 2nd level themes. Only the English participants used the latter theme at the 10 per cent level. Here is an example of the most frequently used 1st level theme making up this 2nd level theme:

'equal worth to different kinds of achievement'

> But also find different ways of reflecting those differences so that they can be more equally valued although they're not the same thing, so that they're not always automatically kind of lower status. I think it will always be difficult to change societies views about what constitutes achievement, if only because of the employment market valuing something higher than others, so that will always be there as a tension, but on the other hand I think the education community should have some kind of a duty to change people's thinking about what matters and what doesn't.
>
> (English national administrator)

Second level themes used to explain different resolution positions

Table 6.10 shows that the two most frequently used 2nd level themes 'balance common/different aspect' and 'curriculum and teaching flexibility' were used by US participants across the different resolution levels. For example, there was no difference in their use between those with marginal compared to significant resolution levels. However, for the third most frequently used 2nd level theme 'continuing issues', those with marginal resolutions used this more than those with significant resolutions (5/13 for marginal positions versus 0/11 for significant ones). The four participants who saw no resolution to the curriculum dilemma, used the same positive suggestions as those who saw some degree of resolution, but they did not use the 'continuing issues' 2nd level theme.

Table 6.11 shows for Netherlands participants a difference in the pattern of 2nd level theme use between those with marginal and significant resolution levels. Though participants with these two positions used all four of the most frequently used 2nd level themes, those with marginal positions made more use of the 'continuing issues' theme than those with significant positions (7/9 compared to 2/12). Also, those with significant resolution positions used a wider range of 2nd level themes (excluding the 'continuing issues'; four for marginal versus seven for significant resolutions positions).

Table 6.10 Second level themes used by US participants to explain resolution of curriculum dilemma

US 2nd level themes	Resolution level						
	Not at all	Marginal	Signifi-cant	Consider-able	Uncertain	Split response	Total
	N = 4	N = 13	N = 11	N = 3	N = 3	N = 8	N = 42
Balance common/ different aspect	2	**4**	**4**	1	0	**6**	17
Curriculum and teaching flexibility	1	**4**	**4**	2	1	**3**	15
Continuing issues	0	**5**	0	0	0	1	6
Priority to individual relevance	0	**2**	1	0	0	1	4
Enhanced staffing/ resources	0	**2**	**2**	**2**	**2**	0	8
Systems development	2	**2**	1	1	0	1	7
Priority to common aspects	0	1	0	0	0	0	1
Promote positive aspects of difference	0	1	0	0	0	0	1
Participation in decisions	0	0	0	0	0	0	0
Depends	0	0	0	0	0	0	0

Note
Most frequent use in rows in bold, if >1.

Table 6.12 shows for English participants that there are different patterns of 2nd level theme use between seeing no or a marginal resolution versus seeing a significant or considerable resolution. Fewer with lower resolution levels used the most frequent theme 'balance common/different aspect' than those with higher resolution levels (7/14 compared to 12/16). Also, more with lower resolution levels used the 'continuing issues' theme than those with higher resolution levels (10/14 compared to 5/16). However, it was not possible to see any difference in the pattern of 2nd level themes between the participants who were uncertain about their resolution level and those who saw some degree of resolution.

Table 6.11 Second level themes used by Netherlands participants to explain resolution of curriculum dilemma

Netherlands 2nd level themes	Resolution level					
	Marginal N = 9	Signifi-cant N = 12	Consider-able N = 1	Uncer-tain N = 1	Split response N = 5	Total N = 28
Balance common/different aspect	**7**	**6**	1	1	2	17
Curriculum and teaching flexibility	3	4	1	0	**5**	13
Continuing issues	**7**	2	0	1	1	11
Priority to individual relevance	4	3	1	0	1	9
Enhanced staffing/resources	0	2	0	0	1	3
Systems development	1	2	0	0	1	4
priority to common aspects	1	2	0	0	0	3
Promote positive aspects of difference	0	0	0	0	0	0
Participation in decisions	0	1	0	0	0	1
Depends	0	0	0	0	0	0

Note
Most frequent use in rows in bold, if >1.

Table 6.12 Second level themes used by English participants to explain resolution of curriculum dilemma

English 2nd level themes	Resolution level						
	Not at all N = 1	Marginal N = 13	Signifi-cant N = 15	Consider-able N = 1	Uncer-tain N = 9	Split response N = 5	Total N = 44
Balance common/different aspect	1	**6**	**12**	0	5	1	26
Curriculum and teaching flexibility	0	**8**	7	1	5	0	21
Continuing issues	1	**9**	4	1	1	2	18
Priority to individual relevance	1	3	4	1	**4**	0	13
Enhanced staffing/resources	0	1	3	1	0	**4**	9
Systems development	0	2	1	0	0	0	3
Priority to common aspects	0	**3**	2	0	1	0	6
Promote positive aspects of difference	0	**3**	2	0	0	0	5
Participation in decisions	0	0	0	0	1	0	1
Depends	0	0	0	0	1	0	0

Note
Most frequent use in rows in bold, if >1.

Chapter 7

Location dilemma

Consider a young man with severe emotional handicap who was in a prison vehicle with other youngsters: he killed them spontaneously. This youngster was in a specialised special ed centre. Would it be appropriate to have him in a general setting?

(US senior teacher, special school, urban area)

I've been in Connecticut and I saw how it is there and I saw children in the schools in Connecticut where I thought 'that child is not happy here'. The child is in the classroom but it's not a part of the classroom, and I think that's not good for a child, it feels 'I don't belong here, I have no friends, I have to do things, I don't understand what I'm doing' and that's not my choice, I think you have to try it, but if you can't offer what the child needs, you need a special school.

(Netherlands resource teacher, primary school, urban area)

I think there's up to a certain line where you think 'yes this child is coping and they may be blossoming'. But I think there is a line where actually we don't meet their needs and I think when we're talking about children in this realm, you actually do need something different, and that's not less good, it's just different. Why would they feel excluded? If they feel secure and happy where they are and they have a bit of an understanding that they're different, they're not any less valuable as human beings. Would they feel excluded? And would they want to be included anyway?

(English SEN co-ordinator, secondary school, rural area)

Introduction

This chapter is concerned with the location dilemma which is about where children with more severe disabilities receive their educational opportunities. As explained in Chapters 5 and 6 this location dilemma is seen as coming after the question of whether to identify and what to learn, the curriculum question. As in those chapters this one sets out the analyses of the evidence about the positions taken by participants across the three countries.

The curriculum dilemma took the following form:

- If children with moderate and severe disabilities (needing special education) are taught in general classrooms, then they are less likely to have access to scarce and specialist services and facilities.
- If children with moderate and severe disabilities (needing special education) are NOT taught in general classrooms, then they are more likely to feel excluded and not be accepted by other children.

Location recognition ratings

Table 7.1 shows that the most frequent recognition rating in each country group was 'significant'. However, the frequency of 'significant' ratings was higher for Netherlands (41 per cent) and English (42 per cent) participants than for US participants (24 per cent). This overall consistency of ratings was reflected in the non-significant chi-square analysis (chi-squared = 14.6, df = 10, p > 0.05). Taken overall, a majority of participants in each country recognised a dilemma to some extent – US (74 per cent), Netherlands (85 per cent) and English participants (78 per cent). These figures need to be set in the context of the number of participants who were uncertain about or split their responses. More US participants were uncertain about this dilemma (10 per cent) than the identification (2 per cent) and curriculum (0 per cent) dilemmas. No Netherlands participants were uncertain about this or the other dilemmas. About the same proportion of English participants were uncertain about this (6 per cent) and the curriculum dilemma (8 per cent). A minority of participants in each group split their responses.

The most frequent basis for splitting responses across the three country groups was the degree of severity of difficulties/disabilities. Some participants split their responses in terms of emotional/behaviour/relationship versus other difficulties, special versus ordinary schools, self versus others less willing to include and children versus parents/teachers. For the majority who split their responses the most frequent rating was 'significant' for the aspect where they recognised a dilemma.

Location resolution ratings

Table 7.2 shows that the most frequent resolution for the US (35 per cent) and English (42 per cent) participants was 'significant', while for the Netherlands participants it was 'marginal' (30 per cent). However, there were more Netherlands participants who split their resolution (37 per cent) responses than gave a marginal resolution (30 per cent). This difference did not reach statistical significance (chi-squared = 13.5, df = 10, p > 0.05). However, the cross-country pattern of resolution ratings was consistent with the frequency of resolution ratings in the split responses. For the US and

Table 7.1 Breakdown of location dilemma recognition ratings across the three countries

	USA		Netherlands		England	
Not at all	1 (2%)			5 (16%)		7 (14%)
Not at all/marginal	10 (20%) }		0	2 (6%) }	0	11 (22%) }
Marginal	2 (4%)		2 (6%)		11 (22%)	
Marginal/significant	**12 (24%)** }		**0**	**13 (41%)** }	0	**21 (42%)** }
Significant	2 (4%)		0		21 (42%)	
Significant/considerable	6 (12%) }		0	5 (16%) }	0	**21 (42%)** }
Considerable	8 (16%)		5 (16%)		4 (8%)	
Uncertain	5 (10%)		0		3 (6%)	
Split responses	6 (12%)		7 (22%)		3 (6%)	
Breakdown of pairs of ratings	**Not at all + significant** Marginal + considerable	**5**	1	**Not at all + significant** Not at all + considerable	**6** 1	**Not at all +** **significant** Marginal + considerable	**2** 1
Totals	50 (100%)			32 (100%)		50 (100%)

Notes
Bold represents most frequent ratings.
Uncertain – participants were reluctant to indicate a degree.
Split responses – participants interpreted issue by responding to different aspects.

Table 7.2 Breakdown of location dilemma resolution ratings across the three countries

	USA		Netherlands		England	
Not at all	1 (2%)		1 (3–4%)		1 (2%)	
Not at all/marginal	12 (24%) }		0 } 8 (25%)		0 } 12 (24%)	
Marginal	13 (26–30%)		**8 (25–30%)**		12 (24–28%)	
Marginal/significant	2 (4%) } 13 (26%)		0 } 5 (13%)		2 (4%) } 16 (32%)	
Significant	**15 (30–35%)**		5 (16–19%)		**18 (36–42%)**	
Considerable	1 (2%)		1 (3–4%)		0	
Uncertain	7 (14–16%)		2 (6–8%)		8 (16–19%)	
Split responses	6 (12–14%)		10 (31–37%)		4 (8–9%)	
Breakdown of pairs of ratings						
	Not at all + significant	1	**N/a + marginal**	**3**	**N/a + significant**	**2**
	Not at all + uncertain	1	N/a + uncertain	1	Marginal + significant	1
	Marginal + significant	**2**	N/a + not at all	1	Uncertain + uncertain	1
	Uncertain + significant	1	N/a + significant	1		
	Significant + considerable	1	N/a + considerable	1		
			Marginal + considerable	1		
			Marginal + significant	1		
			Not at all + significant	1		
Those recognising the dilemma	43 (86%)		27 (84%)		43 (86%)	
Those not recognising the dilemma	7 (14%)		5 (16%)		7 (14%)	
Totals	50 (100%)		32 (100%)		50 (100%)	

Notes
Figures in brackets: first figure, percentage out of all participants; second figure, percentage out of those who recognised the dilemma.
Bold represents most frequent rating.
Uncertain: participants were reluctant to indicate a degree.
Split responses: participants interpreted issue by responding to different aspects.
N/a: not applicable – when dilemma not recognised, resolution question is not applicable.

English participants who split their resolution position, most gave significant resolutions for aspects where a dilemma was recognised, by comparison with Netherlands split responders who gave more marginal resolutions. An overall majority across the country groups saw some degree of resolution (marginal, significant or considerable) – US 69 per cent, Netherlands 58 per cent and English 70 per cent. This finding has to be set in the context of the uncertain and split responses. More US (16 per cent) and English (19 per cent) participants were uncertain about their resolution position than Netherlands participants (8 per cent). However, the reverse pattern was found for the splitting of the resolution positions; more Netherlands (37 per cent) than US (14 per cent) and English participants (9 per cent) split their resolution positions.

Recognition and resolution ratings by professional role

For the US participants it was found (see Table 7.3) that the most frequent recognition level was 'significant' for the regular and special school professionals, in line with the overall level. However, the most frequent level for administrators was considerable and for support professionals not at all. US Administrators continued to have a different modal resolution level (uncertain) compared to the overall level (significant), as did the regular school

Table 7.3 Breakdown of most frequent location recognition and resolution ratings by role

		USA	Netherlands	England
Recognition	Administrators	Considerable	Significant	Significant
	Support professionals	Not at all	Split (significant)	Marginal/ significant
	Regular school professionals	Significant	Significant	Significant
	Special school professionals	Significant	Significant	Significant
	Overall	Significant	Significant	significant
Resolution	Administrators	Uncertain	Marginal	Significant
	Support professionals	Significant	Split (marginal)	Uncertain
	Regular school professionals	Marginal	Marginal	Marginal/ significant
	Special school professionals	Significant	Significant	Significant
	Overall	Significant	Marginal	Significant

Note
Brackets after split response – most frequent recognition and resolution ratings for aspect of dilemma.

professionals (marginal). The most frequent resolution level for support and special school professionals was 'significant', in line with the overall level.

Table 7.3 shows that most Netherlands role groups had the same modal recognition and resolution level as the overall levels. Support professionals mostly had split responses, but the most frequent level for aspects where a dilemma was recognised was 'significant', as in the overall level. The same was found for the split resolution responses. The most frequent resolution for aspects where a dilemma was recognised was 'marginal', the overall modal resolution level. Only one group differed from the overall modal resolution level, special school professionals, who were more confident about resolution with a modal significant level.

Table 7.3 also shows that most English groups had modal recognition and resolution levels in line with the overall levels. However, English support professionals mostly held marginal and significant recognition positions and were mostly uncertain about resolving the location dilemma. Regular school professionals also mostly held marginal and significant resolution positions. Overall this indicates that there was more variation between US role groups in their recognition and resolution levels than in the role groups of the other two countries.

Qualitative accounts of the recognition of the location dilemma

English participants used more distinct 1st level themes (74) to explain their recognition levels for this dilemma than the Netherlands (48) or US participants (56). Most participants in each of the country groups used between two and three themes each and the range of themes used per participant was highest for English participants (1–8).

Table 7.4 shows that the only 2nd level theme which was used by more than 30 per cent in all three country groups was 'tensions' – by US (62 per cent), Netherlands (88 per cent) and English participants (68 per cent). The next most frequently used 2nd level theme was 'other negative aspects of inclusion', 31 per cent of Netherlands and 46 per cent of English participants, but only by 14 per cent of US participants. The 2nd level theme 'resolved tensions' was also one of the more frequently used 2nd level themes, but only by 34 per cent of US compared to 19 per cent of Netherlands and 26 per cent of English participants. The two themes that questioned the validity of the location dilemma were used by a similar proportion of participants. The 'moderate/deny reduced specialist provision' theme was used by between 28 and 31 per cent of participants across the three country groups, while the 'moderate/deny feeling excluded' theme was used by more US (32 per cent) and English (20 per cent) than Netherlands participants (3 per cent). The 2nd level theme 'positive aspects

Table 7.4 Comparison of 1st level themes for recognising location dilemma across the three countries

	USA	Netherlands	England
	N = 31 (62%)[a]	N = 28 (88%)	N = 34 (68%)
Tensions	*Problems in building in-class support 7[b]	*Problems building in-class support 1	*Problems build capacity in regular class 18
	*Regular teachers not used nor trained for severe disability 3	*Regular teachers not used nor trained for severe disabilities 3	*Regular teachers not used nor trained for dealing with severe disability 1
	*Tension because of resource gap 3	*Tension because of resource gap 4	*Tension because of resource gap 5
	*Experienced tension 1	*Experienced tension 9	*Experienced tension 6
	*Poor teacher attitude to inclusion 2	*Poor teacher attitude to inclusion 3	
	*For some, hard to support in regular class 4	*Some – hard to support regular class 2	
	*Students conceal being at special schools 1	*Students conceal being at special school 1	
	*Severe disability not get what need in regular class 16		*Severe disability not get what need to in regular class 4
	*Noise affects learning for disabled students 1		*Noise affects learning 1
	*Least restrictive environment is hard decision 2		*Least restrictive environment, threshold hard decision 1
	Always need special school or self contained class 2	Regular school not capacity to meet individual needs 6	Some students with low literacy, not keep up 1
	Majority of students want to be back in local school 1	If in separate class not mix socially 1	Students with very low abilities not fit regular school 1
	For homogenous groups easier plan inclusion 1	Most parents want regular school 1	MLD students not get what need 1
	Parent–teacher conflict of view 2	Problem in regular school taking child back from special school 1	Build capacity in regular class, hard decision 1
	Negative attitudes, but see benefits too 2	Some regular teachers not cope 1	Problems creating calm in regular class 1
	Obstacles to more restrictive environment 1	Less severe disabilities feel excluded in separate setting 3	Some moderate disabilities not want special school 1
		Secondary class teachers not have time for individual support 3	

Other negative aspects inclusion		
Severe disabilities disrupt classrooms 2 Withdrawn for special services 1	Some students want to be in regular setting 1 Regular school not cope with IQ less 60 1 Severe EBD feel excluded in special class in regular school 1 Significant tension for parents 1 Problems increasing disability status in regular schools 1	Problems reintegrating from EBD unit 1 Dumping mild behaviour difficulties has negative impact 1 If apart can feel excluded 2 Parent can be dissatisfied support in the regular class 3 Teachers less willing accept behaviour difficulties 1 Severe EBD/disabled not suited in regular class 3.
N = 7(14%)	N = 10(31%)	N = 23(46%)
*Severe behaviour difficulties, harmful in regular class 1 *Severe disabilities unwelcome in general classes 3 *Peers accept them but not as friends 1 *Typical students not get what need 6	*Severe behaviour difficulties harmful in regular class 1 *Peers not accept children with moderate/severe disability 1 *Severe EBD feel excluded in regular school 2 Severe learning disabilities not connect to regular peers 1 Isolated from peers in neighbourhood 2 Moderate/severe disabled feel excluded in regular school 5 Severe EBD cannot participate in regular class 2 If so severe that cannot perform in society, need special school 1	*Behaviour difficulties harmful in regular class 4 *Regular schools not welcome severe disability 1 *Peers accept but not as friend 1 *Typical students not get what need 2 *Peers not accept if big attainment gap 1 *Severe EBD feel excluded in regular school 3 Not excluded but socially isolated 2 Full inclusion creates exclusion feeling and stigma 3 Located in mainstream, but excluded 5 Students stand out, are isolated in regular classes 3 Aware what cannot do in regular class 2 Regular teachers label/treat EBD differently 1 Query regular class provides caring relationships 2

Table 7.4 (Continued)

	USA	Netherlands	England
Resolved tensions	**N = 17(34%)** *Majority included, minimal separate setting 1 *Require services in resourced not local schools 3 *Separate class but mix socially age peers 2 Part-time in general class inclusion possible 10 Try regular class, if not work some separation 1 Getting special services outweighs stigma 2 Practise reverse inclusion 1	N = 6(19%) *Majority included, minority in separate setting 2 *Maximise time in regular class 2 Internalised EBD more accepted by regular schools 1 Some withdrawal, but belong in regular class 1 Progress in making special setting more inclusive 1	N = 13(26%) *Required services in resourced: not local schools 2 *Separate class, but mix socially 2 *Maximise time in regular class 2 Health more important than feeling excluded 1 Need intensive specialist teaching and regular settings 6 Severe disability most of time in regular class 1 In joint lessons, severe disabled take part in activities 1 Successful partnerships with special schools 2 Parents satisfied with resourced unit provision 1 No stigma associated with resource unit 1
Moderate/deny reduced specialist provision	N = 14(28%) *Some severe disability build capacity in regular class 11 Special services in regular class have improved 6 Teachers good at learning support 1	**N = 10 (31%)** *For some, build support in regular class 7 *Regular school provision easier in early years and primary stages 3	**N = 15(30%)** *Some, build support in regular class 10 *Easier to include diverse needs in primary 3 Most moderate disability supported regular classes 4

	N = 16(32%)	N = 1(3%)	N = 10(20%)
Moderate/deny feeling excluded	*Minority/none care about being apart 13 *Unaware of being separate 3 Only minority want to be other (regular) setting 4	*Minority/none care about being apart 1 *Unaware of separation 1	*Minority/none care about being in special school 1 *Unaware of separation 3 Query students feel excluded in separate provision 5 We work at having them feel accepted 1 Query providing individual programme affects sense of belonging 1

	N = 8(16%)	N = 12(38%)	N = 14(28%)
Positive aspects separation	*Severe disabled students like some separation 3 Separate does not deny opportunities 2 What miss when withdrawn, no harm 1 Separate attention for students with emotional problems 2 Not so marked out in special school 2	*Severe disability relieved, like and comforted in special setting 7 *EBD students feel good in separate school 1 *Access peer group more in separate settings 1 Others would like some separate setting 1 Behaviour improvement outweighs neighbourhood isolation 1 OK to go to special school 1 If severe disability in special school, accepted in neighourhood 1 Severe sensory disability need special school 1 Child does not feel disabled in separate setting 1	*Severe disabled students like some separation 3 *Severe EBD feel good in special school/unit *Access peer group more in separate settings 1 Complex health needs require separate setting 1 Need special class, unit or school 2 Separate provision different not less good 1 Students see withdrawal as positive 1 Moderate disabled like withdraw provision in regular school 1 Health and safety as important as educating 1 Progress in separate setting more inclusive 3 Inclusive involvement in education not regular class 1

Table 7.4 (Continued)

	USA	Netherlands	England
Positive aspects inclusion	N = 3(6%) Others and families accept disability 3	N = 0	N = 2(4%) Regular teachers welcome them 1 Some aware of difference, others respect her 1
Depends	N = 4(8%) Whether disabled feel excluded when separate depends 3 Teacher accommodate, times yes, times no 1	N = 3(9%) Decision depends on social(-)emotional adjustment and belonging 3	N = 5(10%) Depends on school facilities 2 Depends on professional advice 1 Depends on school's inclusive ethos 1 Severe disability in regular class depends on how many 1
Comments	**N = 18(36%)** *Varied parental views 1 *Severity level important 3 Goal full time inclusion 4 Disabled students want to be accepted 1 Tried inclusion, not worked 2 Separate schools as illegal 1 Students vary in understanding and ability 2 Full inclusion not least restrictive environment 4 No teasing, as they look after themselves, as tough 1 Parents of typical students check inclusion 1	N = 2(6%) *Parents varied views 2	N = 9(18%) *Varied parent views 1 *Severity level important 3 Cannot generalise 1 Query impact therapeutic services on educational outcomes 1 Parents want mainly in regular class 1 Teachers inclusion commitment varies 1 Isolated from peers in neighbourhood 1

Notes
a N: number of participants using 2nd level theme (% of all participants – in bold if more than 30%).
b * Indicates similar 1st level themes used in two or three of the countries (numbers after 1st level themes represent frequency of use of this theme).

of separation' was used mostly by Netherlands (38 per cent) and English participants (28 per cent) than by US participants (16 per cent). By contrast, much fewer participants across the three country groups used the 2nd level theme 'positive aspects inclusion', between 0 and 6 per cent across the three groups. Finally, though a low proportion used the 2nd level theme 'depends', there was relatively high use of the theme 'comments', especially by US (36 per cent) and English participants (18 per cent).

Second level theme: 'tensions'

Table 7.4 shows that just over a third of 1st level themes were shared with one or both other countries for Netherlands and English 1st level themes, while more than half of US 1st level themes were shared. These shared 1st level themes also tended to be the more frequently used ones, with the exception of one 1st level theme 'regular school not capacity to meet individual needs' which was used by six Netherlands participants. The table also shows that there were four 1st level themes which were used in each country group, 'problems in building in-class support', 'regular teachers not used nor trained for severe disability', 'tension because of resources gap' and 'experienced tension'.

Here are examples of the 1st level theme 'problems in building in-class support':

'problems in building in-class support'

> Well I wouldn't say they're less likely to have access, I would say that they wouldn't have because of what they need, and I can't see any way where even with all the money in the world you can actually do that in a mainstream classroom, and I'm thinking of primary and secondary.
>
> (English senior teacher, special school, rural area)

> Absolutely, yes, I mean my major dilemma is getting them in to school to begin with because that is limited and I know that we do have a lot of children that we believe firmly, and the Head will talk about this, and it works very much when you have that package that comes with the child. When you don't then it presents all sorts of difficulties for the class teacher who, with twenty-eight, thirty other children, cannot manage that child's needs when emotionally they can't access the class and they've got their head down on the table, or they're under the table kicking and screaming and throwing chairs, and we've experienced all this. But I would agree that if they're not taught in general classrooms then they do feel excluded, they do feel not accepted, but there's a huge amount of work to be done around social skills and acceptance to allow this to happen for them to be in class. So if you spoke to a class teacher

they would have very different views to mine. Because they are managing children within the classroom and they would say 'I do not have time to deal with the extent of this child's difficulty.'

(English SEN advisory teacher, urban area)

The 2nd level theme 'regular teachers not used nor trained for severe disability' was also used across the three country groups. Here are examples of this theme:

'regular teachers not used nor trained for severe disabilities'

The city does not plan properly. They do not have qualified teachers who work with these children. There is a lack of services and related services with enough people to provide them. We have to live with this, some cannot be mainstreamed.

(US senior teacher, special school, urban area)

Although most people, most teachers would approve of that, the situation changes when you really actually have this type of children in your own classroom because then it will cost a lot of extra time and energy and they can't really cope with it because they're not used to it, they've not been trained to do this. If you put a student just in an ordinary class the student will have fourteen or fifteen different teachers during the week and most of these teachers will not know how to deal with this type of children, so it's one thing for the government to give the money but what we need is the expertise, and so far I think we have got the expertise in our school but it's concentrated in two or three people.

(Netherlands senior teacher, secondary school, urban area)

Another 2nd level theme used across the country groups was 'tension because of resource gap'. Here are examples of this theme:

'tension because of resource gap'

With the resources, yes, it's mainly, because we have now children who are labelled who get the money from the government but it's not the same amount of money which they receive in special schools so it's a big problem, I really want to be an inclusive school because I (...) the vision behind it, but I need the funding, that's a big issue because you cannot expect the teachers who are having a classroom with twenty-five children without significant help.

(Netherlands senior teacher, primary school, urban area)

To become an inclusive school you also need the support from outside, there is a resource implication, there is a monetary implication, and inclusion to me does work, but only when you are also given those resources. And the tendency seems to be 'well you're doing very well, therefore you don't need anything additional'. They're on the autistic spectrum, but they will not have a statement because we're doing so well. So the significant dilemma is how to have those children in our classrooms, but access the resources, and for us it's a particular dilemma because we're half a mile away from a cluster, we belong to action zone clusters and we're in a smaller cluster of seven. Now if we were in the larger cluster, as the school half a mile away is, we would have access to drama therapists, we would have access to counselling, to learning mentors. But as a cluster of seven we have more limited resources, so to keep my young people here who have a huge level of need, I am constantly facing the dilemma 'who do I call in, what can I access?'.

(English advisory teacher, urban area)

The fourth 1st level theme used across the country groups was 'experienced tensions'. Here are examples of this theme:

'experienced tensions'

if they're in the general ed class room what are they doing? They're doing some kind of modification of the general ed curriculum. What should they be doing? Should they be learning how to get about in the community, doing some kind of transportation, mobility training, doing some independent living skills and so forth? And then of course are we limiting them by not providing them full access to that general ed curriculum with a content expert in the general ed classroom? And then, of course, if they don't have that kind of access to other kids, can they feel a part of the school community as a whole? So there's a considerable dilemma.

(US administrator, Federal Department)

It's certainly an issue and I would suggest it's a huge issue because what we're striving for all the time in our inclusive schools is for children to be educated with all their peers but also to receive the specialist individual teaching requirements they need. So that I think is a huge tension, how much can they cope with the mainstream classroom and how much specialist input do you give them? And the needs are different for each child.

(English local administrator, urban area)

There were three 2nd level themes which were used only by US and Netherlands participants, 'poor teacher attitude to inclusion', 'for some, hard to support in regular class' and 'students conceal being at special schools'. Here are examples of these themes:

'poor teacher attitude to inclusion'

> I think it is pretty scary for some classroom teachers and some classroom teachers just have a bad attitude, they're not willing, it's extra work. A lot of it is technology, the alpha smarts and software and different things that we can use, that's scary to them too. They might not feel like using it so they might not be very good. So it might be the risks and it might be the attitude. I think that there are some classroom teachers who will do things to not have those children in their classroom.
>
> (US class teacher, middle school, rural area)

'some are hard to support in regular class'

> I think that they're (parents) very realistic about the needs of their students. Well I have ten students and five of them are still in diapers or pull ups, we work on toilet training a lot of our day, well you know you can't do that in the mainstream, and this is, you know, real input in a classroom. So we really are doing a lot more on functional life skills for my population.
>
> (US special education teacher, resource area, middle school, rural area)

'students conceal being at special school'

> And there are children in this school who are feeling bad that they are going to a special school, some with Down Syndrome. They feel very sorry that they are here. . . . when they are at home they don't dare say 'I am at this school' because this school is very low.
>
> (Netherlands advisory teacher, urban area)

There were three 2nd level themes used only by US and English participants, 'noise affects learning', 'severe disability not get what need in regular class' and 'least restrictive environment is hard decision'. The last-mentioned theme will not be presented as the excerpts did not go much beyond the coded theme itself. Here are examples of the other themes:

'noise affects learning'

> because with a class of twenty-eight or whatever they've got in the mainstream these days, the sheer noise level for a lot of our kids would

be too much, let alone the distractions. I'm thinking of our kids with autism, probably most of them would find it almost impossible to be in the mainstream, for those that aren't concentrating in a class of eight with no distractions, within a more carefully controlled environment.

(English senior teacher, special school, rural area)

'severe disability not get what need in regular class'

Yes, like I said, from an education stand point I look at the fact 'are they getting the education that they need?' and if we here as general educators can't provide it in a regular school setting then, I don't think it's fair to keep the child here and deny them what they need.

(US class teacher, regular class, rural district)

There were fewer 1st level themes which were specific to US participants (8) than specific to Netherlands or English participants (both 12). Of the Netherlands specific themes, 'regular school not capable of meeting individual needs of severe disabled' was one of the most frequently used of all 1st level themes (6). Here is an example of this theme:

'regular school not capable of meeting individual needs of severe disabled'

It depends, if the school can cope with the children with severe learning difficulties I would prefer to keep them in a regular school, but if in the IEP the goals that are there can only be reached by placing outside the classroom then what's the difference between a regular school and a special school?

(Netherlands psychologist, urban area)

Second level theme: 'other negative aspects of inclusion'

The 2nd level theme 'other negative aspects of inclusion' was one of the more frequently used themes. It focused on other negative aspects of having children with more severe disabilities in ordinary classrooms and was used more by Netherlands (31 per cent) and English (46 per cent) than US participants (14 per cent). For US participants, all 1st level themes were used by participants in the other two countries, while for Netherlands and English participants only about a half of the 1st level themes were shared across the country groups. Below are examples of the only 1st level theme that was used in all three country groups, 'severe behaviour difficulties harmful in regular classes':

'severe behaviour difficulties harmful in regular classes'

> I think especially with the behaviour problems you have attacks on the children who are normal. The children couldn't cope with it when you have too much behaviour problems. And one or two behaviour problems in a group of twenty we can manage, but not more.
>
> (Netherlands senior teacher, primary school, rural area)

> I think there is a serious issue there, yes. I mean they have a job to do and they have thirty-odd children in each class and if one of them is behaving in a way that is affecting other people's learning, then that's a serious issue that's got to be dealt with.
>
> (English class teacher, behaviour unit, rural area)

Three 1st level themes were used by US and English participants only, 'typical students not get what they need', 'peers accept but not as friends' and 'severe disabilities unwelcome in general classes'. These were used more frequently by US than English participants. Here are examples of these 1st level themes:

'typical students not get what they need'

> It would mean mainstream schools looking more like special schools, which wouldn't necessarily meet the needs of mainstream pupils 'cause mainstream pupils need to learn to get on in a group of twenty-five or twenty-eight. And if you're bringing the class sizes down then they're going to lose that. You're not giving the majority, which is the mainstream, what they need, so you're cutting off their opportunities for ours.
>
> (English senior teacher, special school, rural area)

'peers accept but not as friends'

> I will tell you about a secondary school which is promoted for being inclusive, in a very inclusive authority. A young adolescent with Down Syndrome was taught in mainstream classes but still could not find her way around this two thousand strong school. She therefore has a learning support assistant. I've sat in a lesson when they were talking about their hobbies, this is a year eleven in a mixed ability group. The others were talking about the weekends, they came up to the centre, went shopping, went to discos, did things like this, and this sixteen-year-old talked about playing with her dollies because she was operating at nine-year level. I am sorry, she'll be accepted as far as they tolerate her but they weren't going to be friends with her, because she wasn't

capable of thinking like that. So children who are operating at a different chronological age probably will be accepted and tolerated, they might even play with them in the play ground, but they are different and that gap gets wider.

(English national administrator)

'severe disabilities unwelcome in general classes'

I mean the more severe the disability is the less likely they are to really be welcomed in the general ed classroom.

(US national administrator)

Two 1st level themes were used only by Netherlands and English participants, 'peers not accept children with moderate/severe disabilities' and 'those with severe emotional/behaviour difficulties feel excluded in regular school':

'peers not accept children with moderate/severe disabilities'

they had a study in Holland that asked teachers and parents of children with special needs in the general classrooms, 'what do you think of it?' The teachers and the parents were mostly optimistic, but the children in the classes not. The major conclusion was that these children were not accepted, they were not part of the classroom.

(Netherlands national administrator)

'those with severe emotional/behaviour difficulties feel excluded in regular school'

I speak with my mind here. The children who come here from other ordinary schools, they were not accepted in those schools, they experienced negative issues.

(English class teacher, special school, urban area)

There were no 1st level themes specific to US participants, but five specific to Netherlands participants and six specific to English participants. The most frequently used of the Netherlands specific themes was 'moderate/severe disabled feel excluded in regular schools' (5).

'moderate/severe disabled feel excluded in regular schools'

We did have some research on this subject and in the Netherlands it's not that if a child with a handicap is within a mainstream school or a mainstream class it's more accepted by his co pupils. What was found was that they were feeling more excluded if they were in the regular classroom. I think it's mostly to do with multiple handicaps and the mental handicaps, yes because blind and deaf children, they are accepted quite well . . . and Down Syndrome and things like that. . . .

(Netherlands national administrator/adviser)

Three of the English specific themes, which were amongst the more frequently used English 1st level themes, focused on feeling excluded in regular schools. Here are examples of these themes:

'full inclusion creates exclusion feelings and stigma'

And of course there's been the wholesale push for inclusion which happened in our authority. The director stopped all things that were going on including the building of a new school because there was questioning about whether we needed special schools 'cause the idea of inclusion I feel was ten years old, ten years out of date; the wholesale 'they all go in to mainstream schools', and that is going to work even less, that will create even more stigma because mainstream staff aren't trained, they haven't got the experience and they're frightened of the unknown, as we all would be, it's not their fault

(English senior teacher, special school,
rural area)

'located in mainstream but excluded'

What's difficult about it I think is that on the ground there is a bit of a patchwork quilt of provision and in some senses you can see children in mainstream schools that are excluded within the school. In a sense so they're not getting the benefits if you like of inclusion in real terms, they're not part, they don't feel part of the school community and have access to all of the experiences that children have within that setting.

(English national administrator)

Second level theme: 'resolved tensions'

'Resolved tensions' was also one of the more frequently used 2nd level themes across the three country groups, but was only used at more than the 30 per cent level by US participants. About half of the 1st level themes were used by other groups, but none were used across all three country groups. Only one 1st level theme was used by US and Netherlands participants, 'majority included, minority in separate setting'. Here is an example of this theme:

'Majority included, minimal separate setting'

> but you can use differentiated instruction in ordinary class almost ninety percent, maybe ninety-five percent of the children, the remaining ten percent you cannot.
>
> (Netherlands senior teacher, primary school, urban area)

Two 1st level themes were used by US and English participants only, 'require services in resourced not local schools' and 'separate class but mix socially'. Here are examples of these themes:

'require services in resourced not local schools'

> Now those children, it is obviously easier, pragmatically, and they might need specialised equipment, to cluster them. And those children will need to be in specialist provision, you may be able, if you had a lot of those in a local authority, be able to cluster them in one local school and resource it.
>
> (English national administrator)

'Separate class but mix socially'

> I really feel that educationally he is not going to get what he needs in my programme and I really feel that he would benefit more from being in the special ed programme because of his level of disability. A student in that programme is still not totally isolated, I mean we still send those students to music, they eat in the cafeteria.
>
> (US resource teacher, resourced middle school, rural area)

One 1st level theme was used only by Netherlands and English participants, 'maximise time in regular class'. Here is an example of this theme:

'maximise time in regular class'

> In our school children with special needs go three hours a week to the special classes, the rest of the week they are in their own classes with their own teacher.
>
> (Netherlands resource teacher, primary school, urban area)

There were fewer 1st level themes specific to US (4) and Netherlands (4) participants than English ones (7). Of these the most frequently used (10) by US participants was:

'part-time in general class, inclusion possible'

> but if you put them in the resourced school, they might spend fifty, I don't know, thirty percent of their time in a withdrawn setting, but then they can put the relevant services in to the general class in that resourced school.
>
> (US Federal administrator)

The 1st level theme 'need intensive specialist teaching and regular settings' was the most frequently used that was specific to English participants (6):

'need intensive specialist teaching and regular settings'

> I think there are benefits to both, there are benefits to children for being moved, you know, they will have more specialist attention, equipment, things like that.
>
> (English teacher, behaviour unit, rural area)

Second level theme: 'moderate/deny reduced specialist provision'

This 2nd level theme, which questions the validity of the dilemma, was used by about 30 per cent of participants in each country group. There was only one 1st level theme which was used in each country group and this was the most frequently used theme, 'for some severe disability build capacity in regular class'. Here are examples of this 1st level theme:

'for some severe disability build capacity in regular class'

> the intention is to include them, so from a policy perspective the schools are getting the specialists, the services and the resources and at the school level they're making decisions about how to best use those. What we see in the high flying schools is an ability to integrate those specialists with general education for all ranges of performance levels for students.
>
> (US State administrators)

> I think the system at this moment depends on the teachers, so when there is a good teacher the identified children stay in a regular school. At the moment they are not as good as the parents want, so they decide to let the child go to a school for special needs. So this issue depends on the teachers, and there are some schools where they have a very good

climate, where every teacher can give attention to the children that has special needs, but not all schools.

(Netherlands psychologist, urban area)

There are some excellent mainstream provisions where they've actually identified unit provision – enhanced resources within those mainstream schools and hand in hand with that the specialist services and facilities are actually aligned to support the group of children that are there. So in those cases no they're not less likely to have access to those services.

(English national administrator)

Another 1st level theme was used by Netherlands and English participants, 'regular school provision easier in primary stages'. Here is an example of this theme:

'regular school provision easier in primary stages'

I think it's mostly to do with multiple handicaps and the mental handicaps, yes because blind and deaf children, they are accepted quite well . . . and Down Syndrome and things like that, and mostly in primary education it works but secondary education it's much more difficult, because you have girl friends and boy friends and things like that and it's more difficult for these pupils . . . .

(Netherlands national administrator/adviser)

There were two 1st level themes specific to US participants, 'special services in regular class have improved' and 'teachers good at learning support'. The former one was one of the more frequently used (6) 1st level themes:

'special services in regular class have improved'

I used to teach in elementary school. Having children with SEN in the class frustrated teachers as usually they did not get services that they needed. Things have changed since then. I understand that it can work if done well, if there is team work. Things have improved.

(US counsellor, special school, urban area)

There were no 1st level themes specific to Netherlands participants and only one for English participants, 'most moderate disabilities supported in regular classes'.

Second level theme: 'moderate/deny feeling excluded'

The other 2nd level theme which denied one of the consequences in the location dilemma, 'moderate/deny feeling excluded' was used by about the same proportion of US and slightly less for English participants (20 per cent) as the previous 'moderate/deny reduced specialist provision' theme. By contrast, Netherlands participants used the 'moderate/deny feeling excluded' theme much less (3 per cent) than the 'reduced specialist provision' theme (31 per cent). Nevertheless, there were two 1st level themes which were used across all three country groups, 'minority/none care about being apart' and 'unaware of being separate'. The former theme was the most frequently used US 1st level theme (13), but only used by one participant in each of the other two groups. The latter 1st level theme was used by fewer participants. Here are examples of these themes:

'minority/none care about being apart'

> they get math, they get their math, they get their reading, we include them in the trips we take and they take their own trips, but I don't think they feel like they are, they're being excluded. I really don't.
>
> (US senior teacher, middle school, urban area)

> I don't believe that a severe mentally handicapped child knows about not being accepted when he goes to this school in comparison to the regular school. And I think all the children here are very happy, most of them are happy to be here, they're not wondering 'why am I not in a regular school?' it's not in their mind.
>
> (Netherlands advisory teacher, urban area)

Some of the 1st level themes that were specific to country groups were amongst the more frequently used themes. For example:

'only minority want to be other (regular) setting' (US theme)

> No, no problem, for the most part most of them, you may get a handful, I'm not going to say all of them, you may get a few that don't want to be, you know, noticed by other kids.
>
> (US teaching assistant, special school, urban area)

'query students feel excluded in separate provision' (English theme)

> I'm not really sure because why would they feel excluded? If they feel secure and happy where they are and they have a bit of an understanding that they're different, they're not any less valuable as human

beings but they have got different needs would they feel excluded? And would they want to be included anyway?

(English SEN co-ordinator, secondary school, rural area)

Second level themes: positive aspects of separation

This 2nd level theme was also used across the three country groups, but more so by Netherlands (38 per cent) and English (28 per cent) participants than by US participants (16 per cent). The one 1st level theme which contributed to this 2nd level theme across the three country groups was 'severe disabled students like/relieved in special setting'. Here are examples of these:

'severe disabled students like some separation'

I've even had children say it to me like 'when is it my time to leave? When am I going to go to Mrs whoever's room? How many more minutes?' because whatever their disability may be it is difficult work.

(US class teacher, elementary school, rural area)

I work one day a week in a special school and when children are referred the first moment they come in to the special school is 'phew!' They are relieved.

(Netherlands psychologist, urban area)

Netherlands and English participants used a similar 1st level theme, which focused particularly on those with severe emotional/behaviour diffi-culties. Here is an example of this theme:

'severe emotional and behaviour difficulties feel good in special school/unit'

I think in terms of EBD it's over played, it actually, the pupils them-selves, I mean I have spent my whole life talking to the pupils, do they feel devalued? No, in fact what they'll say is 'see I can actually, you let me play for this school football team, I would never have got selected'.

(English head of behaviour unit, rural area)

The other 1st level theme was used only by Netherlands and English participants only. Here is an example of this theme:

'access peer group more in separate settings'

They are more likely to feel excluded at the school because it's always better to be in the school situation which is a regular situation, but accepted by other children. What I hear from school, from teachers here is that children meet other children who have the same problem so it makes them feel more accepted because they are similar.

(Netherlands senior psychologist, expertise centre, urban area)

There were varied 1st level themes specific to US (4), Netherlands (6) and English participants (8) that made up this 'positive aspects separation' 2nd level theme. Of the themes specific to English participants, 'progress in separate setting more inclusive' was the most frequently used (3) and represents an interesting perspective on inclusion:

'progress in separate setting more inclusive'

Well I feel I am being more inclusive by withdrawing them, I do the same curriculum in here. Because at the beginning of the session the child cannot follow it, his language level is so delayed. I think by withdrawing him and doing that at his own level in a small group, it is more inclusive than him sitting there staring in to space.

(English specialist unit teacher, first school, rural area)

Other 2nd level themes

It is notable that the 2nd level theme 'positive aspects inclusion' were rarely used across the three country groups; US (6 per cent), Netherlands (0 per cent) and English (4 per cent). The 'depends' 2nd level theme was also used by less than 10 per cent across the three country groups, though there were differences in what the positions were reported as depending on. For the US and Netherlands participants who used this theme it was seen as depending on the students' personal and social adjustment, whereas for the English participants it was on school ethos, facilities and the number with severe disabilities. More participants across the three country groups used the 'comments' 2nd level theme, though this was mostly by US participants (36 per cent). In each group there was some reference to 'varied parents views' and in the US and English groups to 'severity level was important'. US participants also made notable comments about inclusion, either that the 'goal was full time inclusion' or that they had 'tried inclusion, but it had not worked'. Several also remarked that 'full inclusion was not the least restrictive environment'.

Second level themes used to explain different recognition positions

Table 7.5 shows, as expected, that the most frequently used US 2nd level theme 'tensions' was used mostly by participants with a significant recogni-

Table 7.5 Second level themes used by US participants to explain recognition position for the location dilemma

US 2nd level themes	Recognition level						Total
	Not at all	Marginal	Significant	Considerable	Uncertain	Split response	
	N = 7	N = 11	N = 12	N = 8	N = 5	N = 6	N = 50
Tensions	4	**5**	**11**	4	1	**5**	30
Resolved tensions	2	**5**	**5**	1	**4**	0	17
Other negative aspects inclusion	1	**3**	1	1	1	0	7
Moderate/deny reduced specialist provision	0	**4**	2	2	**4**	2	14
Moderate/deny feeling excluded	**4**	1	2	1	**5**	3	16
Positive aspects separation	3	**4**	1	0	0	0	8
Positive aspects inclusion	1	1	1	0	0	0	3
Depends	0	1	1	0	0	2	4
Comments	2	**4**	2	2	**5**	3	18

Note
Most frequent use in rows in bold, if >1.

tion level (11/12 participants). Lower proportions of those not recognising (4/7) or with marginal recognition (5/11) used the theme. However, only half of those with the highest level of recognition 'considerable' also used this theme.

The 2nd level theme 'resolved tensions' was used across the different recognition levels, there being no clustering towards the lower recognition levels. However, the related themes 'other negative aspects inclusion' and 'positive aspects separation' were used more by participants not recognising or with marginal recognition levels (3/7 with marginal and 7/8 with not at all/marginal positions used these themes, respectively). Similarly, the two 2nd level themes that question the validity of the dilemma were used more by participants with low or uncertain recognition of the dilemma – for 'moderate/deny reduced special provision' by 4/11 with marginal positions and 4/5 with uncertain positions; 'moderate/deny feeling excluded' was used by 4/7 with no recognition and 5/5 with uncertain recognition.

Table 7.6 also shows a tendency for those Netherlands participants with higher recognition levels to use the most frequent 2nd level theme 'tensions' – 12/13 with significant and 5/5 with considerable recognition levels. As with the US participants the 'resolved tensions' theme was used across the

Table 7.6 Second level themes used by Netherlands participants to explain recognition position for the location dilemma

Netherlands 2nd level themes	Recognition level					
	Not at all	Marginal	Significant	Consider-able	Split response	Total
	N = 5	N = 2	N = 13	N = 5	N = 7	N = 32
Tensions	2	2	12	5	7	28
Resolved tensions	2	0	1	0	3	6
Other negative aspects inclusion	3	1	5	1	0	10
Moderate/deny reduced specialist provision	4	1	3	1	1	10
Moderate/deny feeling excluded	1	0	0	0	0	1
Positive aspects separation	4	1	1	0	6	12
Positive aspects inclusion	0	0	0	0	0	0
Depends	1	0	0	1	1	3
Comments	0	1	1	0	0	2

Note
Most frequent use in rows in bold, if >1.

recognition levels. So was the 'other negative aspects of inclusion' – by 3/5 not recognising and 5/13 with significant recognition. By contrast, 'positive aspects of separation' was mostly used by those not recognising the dilemma – 4/5 not recognising it. The table also shows that 6/7 with split responses also used this 2nd level theme. This theme was used for that aspect where no dilemma was recognised; for the aspect where a dilemma was recognised (mostly significant level), the 'tensions' theme was used (7/7 with split responses). Only one of the two 'moderate/deny' themes was used more frequently, 'moderate/deny reduced specialist provision'. For this theme, though used across different levels, the tendency was, as expected, for more use at lower recognition levels (4/5 not recognising dilemma compared to 3/13 with significant recognition).

Table 7.7 shows that for English participants the 'tensions' theme tends also to be used more by those with higher levels of recognition (10/18 with not at all/marginal compared to 18/26 with significant/considerable levels). The 'resolved tensions' theme is used more by those with lower recognition levels (9/18 with not at all/marginal compared to 4/26 with significant/considerable levels). 'Other negative aspects of inclusion' was used across the recognition levels, with no clear clustering according to level. 'Positive

Table 7.7 Second level themes used by English participants to explain recognition position for the location dilemma

English 2nd level themes	Recognition level						Total
	Not at all	Marginal	Signifi-cant	Consider-able	Uncertain	Split response	
	N = 7	N = 11	N = 22	N = 4	N = 3	N = 3	N = 50
Tensions	4	**6**	**14**	4	3	3	34
Resolved tensions	4	**5**	2	2	0	0	13
Other negative aspects inclusion	4	**6**	**9**	1	1	2	23
Moderate/deny reduced specialist provision	1	**6**	4	0	2	2	15
Moderate/deny feeling excluded	**4**	**3**	1	0	1	1	10
Positive aspects separation	**4**	**3**	4	0	1	2	14
Positive aspects inclusion	**2**	0	0	0	0	0	2
Depends	1	**3**	1	0	0	0	5
Comments	1	1	4	0	2	1	9

Note
Most frequent use in rows in bold, if >1.

aspects of separation' tended to be used more by those with lower recognition levels (7/18 with not at all/marginal compared to 4/26 with significant/considerable levels). Similarly, for both 'moderate/deny' themes there was a tendency for them to be used by those with lower recognition levels – for 'moderate/deny reduced specialist provision', 7/18 with 'not at all/marginal' compared to 4/26 with 'significant/considerable' levels; for 'moderate/deny feeling excluded', 7/18 compared to 1/26.

Qualitative accounts of the resolution of location dilemma

The number of distinct 1st level resolution themes across the three country groups was between 46 and 68, with most for the English participants (68). Most participants used between one and two themes and the ranges across the three countries were between one and six to ten themes. Table 7.8 shows the ten 2nd level resolution themes used to analyse the 1st level themes. This table shows that the 'balance included/separate provision' was the most frequently used 2nd level theme in each of the three country groups, though it was used most by Netherlands (63 per cent), then English (56 per cent) and least by US participants (38 per cent).

Table 7.8 Comparison of 1st level themes for resolving location dilemma across the three countries

	USA	Netherlands	England
Balance included/ separate provision	**N = 19(38%)**[a]	**N = 20(63%)**	**N = 28(56%)**
	*Mixed model 10[b]	*Mixed model 7	*Mixed model 19
	*Reduce numbers in special settings 2	*Reduce numbers in special settings 3	*Reduce numbers in special settings 3
	*Include in regular class for part of period 1/short term separate placements 1	*Part-time and temporary placement in separate settings 1	*Withdrawal may be temporary 1
	*Flexible withdrawal arrangements needed 1		*Flexible withdrawal arrangements 2
		*Better special and regular school collaboration 4	*Better special–regular school links 2
		*Try resourced inclusion, if not work separate provision 6	*Try resourced inclusion, if not work separate provision 1
		*Have mainstream special classes/units 3	*Mainstream units for behaviour difficulties 3
		*Reverse inclusion 1	*Reverse inclusion 1
	Severe disabilities in regular classes inappropriate for some subjects 2	Regular class inclusion easier	LRE implies separate provision minimised 2
	Separate settings not noticed in regular school 1	In primary stage 2	Off-site units to support in mainstream 1
	Some students in regular, severe disabled in separate class/ school 5	Parents decide–accept advantages/ disadvantages 2	Ask how to meet needs in least restrictive environment 2
		Transfer resources from special to regular schools 1	All students at least some inclusion experience 1
		Federate special and regular schools 1	Co-locate special schools 1
			Joint regular–special school activities if all benefit 1
			Focus more on how than on where 2
			Current maximising inclusion right policy 2

	N = 17 (34%)	N = 12 (38%)	N = 15 (30%)
Enhance flexible services and staffing	*Improve training of teachers and administrators 5 *Additional resources for regular schools 1 *Co-teaching needed 2 *Better staffing, resourcing and planning 10 Improved staff communication and collaboration 4 Opportunity for regular teacher to develop confidence 1 Use methods derived from those with experience 2 Regular teacher accommodate their needs 1 Work round problems in co-teaching 1	*Improve training for teachers and administrators 7 *Additional resources regular schools 4 *Better staffing, resourcing and planning 2 *New support arrangements 2 *Differentiated teaching programmes 1 Teachers becoming more capable 1 Arrange volunteer support for learning 1 Have internal learning support department 1 Try to give needed learning support 1 Regular schools become more flexible 1	*Improve training teachers and administrators 4 *Appropriate specialist services in regular schools 7 *More collaborative teaching 1 *New support arrangements 1 *Differentiated teaching programmes 1 What done in special school, done in regular schools 1 In-class support strategies 1 Better multi-agency work 3 Severe disability, specialist services in the regular class more flexible and relevant curriculum 1 Better understanding by school SEN management 1
	N = 8 (16%)	**N = 12 (38%)**	**N = 15 (30%)**
Continuing issues	*Hard issue 5 *Way forward not realistic 3	*Hard issue, continuing issue 7 *Way forward unrealistic 1 Ideals formed separate from economics 1 Gap between theory/ideals and practice 5	*Hard issue – ongoing issue 10 Issues in co-located special schools 1 Special school students required to fit regular school programmes 1 Problems with special–regular school link scheme 3 Unknowns about more inclusive for severe disabled 2 Understanding what is involved in inclusion 1

Table 7.8 (Continued)

	USA	Netherlands	England
Limits to inclusion	N = 5(10%)	N = 14(44%)	N = 10(20%)
	*Sticking point will and commitment 2 *Some willing, others will not change 1 *Regular teachers not meet needs 2	*Sticking point will/commitment 2 *Some willing, others will not change 3 *Limit to what regular school can do 2	*Regular teachers not meet their needs 1 *Limit to what regular schools can do 1
	Cost of regular class special services excessive 1 Teachers choose, not to impose inclusion 1 Time for differentiation planning not available 2	If mainly out of regular class, then need special school 1 Most regular schools not cope 1 Some severe disability not fit regular setting 4 Maybe limit to what regular can provide 1 Some severe EBD not fit in regular schools 1 Cannot reduce numbers in special schools 1 Many teachers not willing change 1 Inclusion slow process 1	Some severe disabled students not survive in regular settings 4 Honest about needs of the system 1 Factors external to school important too 2 Inclusion as process may never get there 2 Supporting inclusion long scary process 1 Separate setting threshold if mostly out of regular class 1
Student and parent participation in decisions	N = 5(10%)	N = 0	N = 3(6%)
	Support for students who want regular class 2 Improved parental involvement 3		Need to consult child and parents 2 Special school decision made after long discussion and parents agree 1 OK if consulting child and parent led to increase in special schools 1

	N = 8(16%)	N = 11(34%)	N = 9(18%)
Systems/local change needed	*Smaller classes 1 Have teachers who want to teach 2 Monitor inclusive developments 3 Principal supportive 1 Staff support inclusion 1 Improve social background of children 1 Need higher expectations of students 1	*Smaller classes 3 Schools commitment to restructure for inclusion 2 Need for more pilot inclusion trials 1 Legislation for more inclusion 2 Support for schools to make more inclusive 3 Integrate services under one authority 1	*Smaller classes 3 Resolve by commitment to restructure 3 LA and schools work together on inclusion 1 Remove school targets and league tables 2 Trust teachers and schools more 1 Restructure education system as long term matter 2 Reconsider size of regular schools 1 Consensus in school about inclusion 1 Convince others of import inclusion 1
	N = 6(12%)	**N = 3(9%)**	**N = 5(10%)**
Accept separate specialist provision	Access to general education curriculum in separate setting 1 Some disabled need to be with like students 1 Reasons for special schools to continue 2 Normalise special schools: promote positive image for special schools 2	Place in special school depends on being happy and feeling sense of belonging 2 Special school can support development of personal skill 1 Special school if students not feel accepted 1	Separate provision is OK 1 Retaining specialist expertise 1 Right to specialist separate provision 1 Some need special school to make progress in their education 1

Table 7.8 (Continued)

	USA	Netherlands	England
Promote positive contacts	N = 2(4%)	N = 0	N = 5(10%)
	Prepare typical student about disability 2		Promote positive attitudes in peers 2 Not made to feel excluded in separate provision 2 Regular students mix more with disabled students 1
Depends	N = 6(12%)	N = 0	N = 6(12%)
	*Depends on individual student 5 *Extent of inclusion depends on outcomes 1		*Depends on individual student 3 *Focus on outcomes in decisions 1 Depends on school's level of development 1 Local context important 2 Depends on teachers involved 1
Comments	N = 8(16%)	N = 5(16%)	N = 1(2%)
	Moderate disability in regular classes 4 Severe disabled included for social reasons in early years 1 In class support strategies can be used for others 2 Provision depends on category, not need 1 Problems in co-teaching 1	Uncertain students feel excluded in special classes 1 Numbers in special schools rising 2 Some parental moves towards inclusion 1 Not ignore other students 1	Much progress to inclusion recently 1 Some parents anxious regular school setting 1

Notes

a N: number of participants using 2nd level theme (% of all participants – in bold if more than 30%).

b * Indicates similar 1st level themes used in two or three of the countries (numbers after 1st level themes represent frequency of use of this theme).

Another 2nd level theme, 'enhance flexible services and staffing' was also used by more than 30 per cent of participants in each country group. A third 2nd level theme, 'continuing issues' was also used by 30 per cent or more of participants, but only by Netherlands (38 per cent) and English participants (30 per cent). The 2nd level themes 'limits to inclusion' and 'systems/local change needed' were also used more by Netherlands (44 per cent and 34 per cent) than US (10 per cent and 16 per cent) or English participants (20 per cent and 18 per cent). This pattern of using 2nd level themes can be related to the modal resolution rating shown earlier in this chapter in Table 7.2. The most frequent Netherlands resolution rating was 'marginal' compared to 'significant' for the US and English participants. This corresponds to the greater use by Netherlands participants of the 2nd level themes 'continuing issues', 'limits to inclusion' and 'systems/local change needed'.

Second level theme: 'balance included/separate provision'

This most frequently used 2nd level theme included three 1st level themes which were used in each of the country groups, 'mixed model', 'reduce numbers in special settings' and 'include in regular class part-time/short term' (the exact wording of the latter theme differed across the countries). The first of these 1st level themes 'mixed model' was the most frequently used 1st level theme in each country group. The 1st level themes which were used across the country groups, in all three or just two groups, made up about half the 1st level themes and tended to be the more frequently used ones. Here are examples of the first of these themes common to each country (excerpts for the other two merely restate the 1st level themes):

'mixed model'

It's a mixed model and with the goal of the kid as much as possible, being socialised appropriately. . . . so, it's not in the regular classroom, that's not always practical . . . .
(US administrator, Federal Department)

Mostly in regular schools, so it's a kind of mix. There is inclusion, in fact there is effective inclusion but the question is how far can we go? So full inclusion in Holland is not an option. I don't think that the resolution is choosing for full inclusion or for no inclusion. It's a kind of mix, what will the school, the regular schools, what can they handle, what do they want to handle? That's a part of it.
(Netherlands national administrator)

I just see a solution really, I mean we've got the ideal solution here, it's what parents have said, it's the best of both worlds 'cause they've got access to their peers in mainstream for some things where it's appropriate and they've got a high staffing ratio for one to one working here and they've got play time, and I wish you'd have seen one of our play times where apart from the different colour of the t-shirts, you wouldn't know any difference. And I wish you'd have been here yesterday lunchtime when one of the mainstream children was over talking to our children after the lunch, which is normal, wow you know, that blows you away, so that's why I'm saying yes there is a tension there but there is a solution and we are living it.

(English senior teacher, special school, rural area)

The 1st level theme 'flexible withdrawal arrangements' was used only by US and English participants. Four 1st level themes, 'better special and regular school collaboration', 'try resourced inclusion, if not work separate provision', 'reverse inclusion' and 'have mainstream special classes/units' were used only by Netherlands and English participants. Some of these 1st level themes were amongst the more frequently used themes in these country groups. Here are examples of three of these themes:

'better special and regular school collaboration'

I run a session with the comprehensive school in their fitness gym. I teach children who have extreme difficulties in terms of movement and understanding. They don't have full body control and it's a repetitive to learn. They work alongside some year eleven students who are doing leadership qualifications and there's definite benefits to all parties in the room.

(English class teacher, special school, urban area)

'try resourced inclusion, if not work separate provision'

That depends, I can't say in general but I think that there are really some children, when you are able with some help to be in a 'normal' school, I say to you normal when it can, but when it has to be special then it must be special.

(Netherlands senior teacher, special school, urban area)

'have mainstream special classes/units'

Well I think there has been progress with kind of units on site, units on mainstream sites to take behaviour problems. I think that's been a great success, that's a very good intermediate step. They're still in the mainstream school environment and they're getting the extra support but they're not being excluded from their peers.

(English class teacher, behaviour unit, rural area)

There were fewer themes specific to US participants (3) and Netherlands participants (4) than English ones (8). The following theme was amongst the more frequently used specific US 1st level themes:

'some students in regular setting: severe disabilities in separate settings theme'

We'd still have a resource model. This year we put resource back in place with a pull out model. For the previous five years we've used resource teachers, resource teachers scheduled themselves to visit the classes where their students are and service them there. Unfortunately it did not work well at all, so this year we went back to the pull out model.

(US class teacher, regular school, urban district)

Second level theme: 'enhance flexible services and staffing'

This 2nd level theme was also used by 30 per cent or more of the participants in each country group, though to a lesser extent than the previous 'balance' one. In each group the shared 1st level themes were just less than half of all 1st level themes used in each group. As before, the shared 1st level themes were also the more frequently used ones. There were two 1st level themes that were used across the three country groups, 'improve training of teachers and administrators' and 'additional/appropriate resources in regular schools'. Here are examples of the former theme:

'improve training of teachers and administrators'

Professional development, I would think professional development for regular ed teachers and special ed teachers. Kind of that problem-solving approach that we talked about before where it might not be through a professional development but just pooling resources that we have maybe outside of buildings and coming up with alternatives inside of buildings.

(US advisory teacher, rural area)

It's difficult, if you would resolve it you should have to give the regular school more options and more possibilities, more education of the teachers, and it would also make the job more interesting.

(Netherlands resource teacher, special school, urban area)

One 1st level theme was used only by US and English participants, 'more co-teaching or collaborative teaching' and also one 1st level theme was used only by US and Netherlands participants, 'better staffing, resourcing and planning'. Here is an example of the latter theme:

'better staffing, resourcing and planning'

> you would need a common planning time with that special educator so that you could sit down and make sure that you're working towards the same goals.... 'here's how we're going to do this, here's how we're going to include this child in this activity or in this group'. So that's, as a classroom teacher that would be my biggest concern, having two teachers that are willing to do that. You know, if you put someone in there that says 'yes I'll go in the classroom' but then they don't want to communicate with you, it's not much help to us.
>
> (US class teacher, regular school, rural district)

There were a similar number of 1st level themes (5) that were specific to each country group.

Second level theme: 'continuing issues'

The third most frequently used 2nd level theme recognised the persistence of issues in finding a resolution, 'continuing issues'. However, this was used more by Netherlands (38 per cent) and English (30 per cent) participants than by US participants (16 per cent). The most frequently used 1st level theme was one that was used across all three country groups, 'hard issue – continuing issue'. Here are examples of this theme:

'hard issue'

> I think that's a difficult question because the same question, what do we do with all the people? Put them in a house! And so are we prepared to accept people that are different and do we want to have them in our society or do we pretend that we want it and people pretend that we want it, so we put all the children in the classroom and nothing happens. So I think I don't know how to ....
>
> (Netherlands national administrator/adviser)

> I think there will always be an issue. I think so because you can never, I don't believe that you can lump, I can't think of a more appropriate word really, these children with disabilities together under one umbrella, they are all individual and what works for one child isn't going to work

for another and there will continue to be a need for some children to be educated within a special school environment.

(English SEN advisory teacher, urban area)

There was another 1st level theme which was used only by US and Netherlands participants, 'way forward not realistic'. There were no US specific 1st level themes, but two Netherlands specific themes, 'ideals formed separate from economics' and 'gap between theory/ideals and practice'. By contrast there were five 1st level themes specific to English participants which were focused on particular English issues, e.g. 'issues in co-located special schools' and 'problems with special–regular school link scheme'.

Second level theme: 'limits to inclusion'

A related 2nd level theme to the 'continuing issues' one was 'limits to inclusion', though with more focus on specific obstacles to inclusion. This was used much more by Netherlands (44 per cent) than US (10 per cent) and English participants (20 per cent). There were no 1st level themes, making up this 2nd level theme, which were shared across all three country groups, but two related 1st level themes were used by US and Netherlands participants, 'sticking point is will and commitment' and 'some willing, others will not change'. A third 1st level theme was used by US and English participants, 'regular teachers not meet needs', while a fourth 1st level theme was used by Netherlands and English participants, 'limit to what regular school can do'. None of these shared themes were the more frequently used ones. First level themes specific to each country related to a range of factors – US (3), Netherlands (8) and English participants (6).

Second level theme: 'systems/local change'

This 2nd level theme was also used more by Netherlands (34 per cent) than US (16 per cent) or English participants (18 per cent). Only one 1st level theme was used across the country groups, 'smaller classes'. All others were specific to each group with some reflecting national contexts, especially Netherlands (e.g. 'need for more pilot inclusion trials' and 'legislation for more inclusion') and English themes (e.g. 'remove school targets and league tables').

Second level theme: 'accept separate specialist provision' and remaining themes

This 2nd level theme was used by between 9–12 per cent of participants in the three country groups and none of the 1st level themes were shared across the groups. The way in which this 2nd level theme ('accept separate specialist provision') was interpreted reflected some country specific aspects. Some US specific themes focused on special schools continuing (e.g. 'normalise special schools' and 'promote positive image for special schools'). By contrast, Netherlands specific 1st level themes focused on accepting separate provision for social-emotional reasons (e.g. 'place in special school depends on being happy and feeling sense of belonging' and 'special school can support development of personal skill'). English specific 1st level themes focused on the specialist aspects of separate provision (e.g. 'retaining specialist expertise' and 'right to specialist separate provision').

'Promote positive contacts' was the least used 2nd level theme, being used only by US (4 per cent) and English participants (10 per cent).

Second level themes used to explain different resolution positions

Tables 7.9, 7.10 and 7.11 show no consistent relation between using the 'continuing issues' theme and low resolution ratings. The 2nd level themes did not consistently differentiate in any country group between participants

Table 7.9 Second level themes used by US participants to explain resolution of location dilemma

US 2nd level themes	Resolution level						
	Not at all	Marginal	Signifi-cant	Consider-able	Uncertain	Split response	Total
	N = 1	N = 13	N = 15	N = 1	N = 8	N = 6	N = 43
Balance included/ separate provision	0	**4**	2	0	1	1	8
Enhance flexible services and staffing	0	**9**	7	0	2	1	19
Continuing issues	0	1	**3**	1	1	0	5
Limits to inclusion	1	**2**	1	0	1	0	5
Student and parent participation in decisions	0	1	**2**	1	1	0	5
System/local change	0	0	2	0	**3**	1	8
Accept separate specialist provision	0	**3**	**3**	0	0	0	6
Promote positive contacts	0	0	0	1	1	0	2
Depends	0	2	**3**	0	0	1	6
Comments	0	**4**	3	0	1	0	8

Note
Most frequent use in rows in bold, if > 1.

Table 7.10 Second level themes used by Netherlands participants to explain resolution of location dilemma

Netherlands 2nd level themes	Resolution level						
	Not at all $N = 1$	Marginal $N = 8$	Signifi-cant $N = 5$	Consider-able $N = 1$	Uncertain $N = 2$	Split response $N = 10$	Total $N = 27$
Balance included/ separate provision	1	**4**	**4**	1	2	**8**	20
Enhance flexible services and staffing	0	**5**	1	1	1	**4**	12
Continuing issues	1	**4**	1	1	1	**4**	12
Limits to inclusion	0	**4**	**4**	1	1	**4**	14
Student and parent participation in decisions	0	0	0	0	0	0	0
System/local change	0	**2**	**2**	1	**2**	**4**	11
Accept separate specialist provision	0	0	0	0	0	**3**	3
Promote positive contacts	0	0	0	0	0	0	0
Depends	0	0	0	0	0	0	0
Comments	0	0	**2**	0	0	**3**	5

Note
Most frequent use in rows in bold, if > 1.

with marginal and significant ratings. For example, one of the most frequently used 2nd level theme in each country group, 'balance included/ separate provision', was used by participants across different resolution levels. This was also found for the other more frequently used 2nd level theme 'enhance flexible services and staffing', though for Netherlands participants, there were more users of this theme by those with 'marginal' (5/8) than 'significant' ratings (1/5).

Future role of special schools

Another topic which arose in the interviews as an emergent one, mainly from the location dilemma, but also with the other two dilemmas, was whether there was a future for special schools in provision for students with SEN/disabilities. This theme arose less for US participants than for those from the Netherlands and England (see Table 7.12). This is partly because special schools featured less in provision in the two US school districts, especially the rural one, than in the other countries. Also, the first interviews were the US ones and once it had arisen, the topic was addressed in the subsequent interviews in the other countries.

Table 7.11 Second level themes used by English participants to explain resolution of location dilemma

English 2nd level themes	Resolution level					
	Not at all	Marginal	Significant	Uncertain	Split response	Total
	N = 1	N = 12	N = 13	N = 8	N = 4	N = 38
Balance included/ separate provision	1	**10**	**12**	3	2	28
Enhance flexible services and staffing	0	5	**7**	2	1	15
Continuing issues	0	4	**7**	4	0	15
Limits to inclusion	0	**5**	3	2	0	10
Student and parent participation in decisions	0	1	0	1	1	3
System/local change	0	2	**6**	0	1	9
Accept separate specialist provision	1	1	**3**	0	0	5
Promote positive contacts	1	0	**4**	0	0	5
Depends	0	2	2	0	2	6
Comments	0	0	1	0	0	1

Note
Most frequent use in rows in bold, if >1.

Table 7.12 shows the 1st level themes which arose in relation to this topic and the 2nd level themes under which these were organised. General comments about the future of special schools were organised in terms of five general 2nd level themes: 'rationale', 'change in numbers', 'organisation', 'depends' and 'comments'. This table shows that almost all of those commenting on this topic favoured some future role for special schools. Only in the USA was there one participant who did not. The following excerpt illustrates this participant's position against special schools, in this case focusing on deaf students:

> for example in xxx county we have a high school, elementary, middle and high school that has a critical mass of deaf kids, but they're in a regular school, and so I don't think its necessarily all in the classroom or all in a resource room but if I were to say any one thing strongly its 'you don't want to have specialised schools. You do not.'
>
> (US administrator, Federal Department)

Table 7.12 Breakdown of 1st and 2nd level themes relating to perspectives on the future of special schools

2nd level themes	USA 31/50 participants commented on this theme	Netherlands 31/32 participants commented on this theme	England 47/50 participants commented on this theme
Favouring some future role for special schools	30/31 (97%)	31/31 (100%)	47/47 (100%)
Rationale	3 (10%)	1 (3%)	8 (17%)
	*Reluctant future for special schools 3	*Reluctant future for special schools 1	*Reluctant future for special schools 5 No special schools as aim 3 Special schools future seen in wider context 1 Aim to maximise social inclusion 1
Change in numbers	1 (3%)	18 (58%)	13 (28%)
	No specialised schools 1	*Reduced number 16 *Retain same number special schools 2	*Reduced numbers for more complex need 10 *Same number or more 2
Organisation	0	12 (39%)	10 (21%)
		*Merge special and regular schools 2 *As part of continuum of provision 7 Unsure about merging or closing special schools 3	*Co-located special schools 8 *Part-time special school placements 2 Not have pupil referral units 1

Table 7.12 (Continued)

2nd level themes	USA 31/50 participants commented on this theme	Netherlands 31/32 participants commented on this theme	England 47/50 participants commented on this theme
Depends	0	4 (13%)	2 (4%)
		*Continue only if quality of their education improves 1 *Continue until schools and teachers willing 3 *If close, then improve regular school 2	*Future depends on special schools maximising learning progress 1 *Depends on appropriate provision in regular schools 1
Comments	4 (13%)	2 (6%)	1 (2%)
	*Two sides to debate 3	*Two sides to debate 1 *Feel tension – heart versus mind 1	*Hard question 1
	Opposed special school, now see need 1	School teachers favour keeping special schools 1	Special services in regular schools costs more 1

Reasons for special schools:

	13 (42%)	14 (45%)	20 (43%)
Children's characteristics	*Significant care needs 6 *Severe emotional-behaviour students, need counselling and small groups 4 *Significant medical needs scary for teachers 2 Social/family needs met better 1	*For very severe and complex difficulties 5 *Very low intellectual levels 2 *For severe emotional and behaviour problems 5 *Challenging behaviour is threat to others 1 *Children not fit in anywhere 6 Children not happy nor feeling they belong in regular school 2 For severe sensory impairments 1 For older children with Down Syndrome who have tried regular school 1	*For profound disabilities 1 *Students with severe emotional and behaviour difficulties 5 *Students' challenging behaviour threat to others 1 *For those not survive in regular setting 5 *Daily complex medical care 2 Needs so significant 3

	9 (29%)	5 (16%)	12 (26%)
Provision available	*Justified if they can move back 3 *Safer environment 2 If not fit self contained class/backup more restrict environment 4	*Justification if return after fixed period 2 *Safe environment 1 Make adaptations not possible in regular school 1	*Justified because children go back to regular setting 2 *Happy safe environment 3 Calm structured and welcoming ethos 4 Provision for level below what regular school can 2 Separate but mix socially at times 2

Table 7.12 (Continued)

	USA 31/50 participants commented on this theme	Netherlands 31/32 participants commented on this theme	England 47/50 participants commented on this theme
	Rigidity in regular school system 1	Fresh start away from neighbourhood 1 To link with mental health services 1	Curriculum breadth compared to regular school, unit or class 1 Somewhere where they feel they belong 1 Smaller classes and more staffing 1 Grow more in confidence and are with peer group 1 Where residential therapy approach needed 1
Professional and school specialisation	5 (16%) *Technical training and support roles 3 *Specialist professionals available 3 Scarce specialist staff in regular schools 1	5 (16%) *Outreach to regular schools 2 *Professionals with specialist knowledge 2 Special schools are very specialised 1	12 (26%) *Training support role for regular schools 8 *Special professionals and facilities are available 7 As hubs for regular school outlets 1
Stakeholders' interests	2 (6%) *Some parents want them 2	3 (10%) *Some parents want them 1 Child can benefit 1 Regular teachers not want disabled children in or back in class 1	5 (11%) *Parents want special school 2 Support professional culture and continuity 2 Better than not being at any school 1
Economic factors	2 (6%) *Excessive cost for provision in regular schools 2	1 (3%) *More economic use resources 1	1 (2%) *Special school economy scale 1
Stigma	1 (3%) Less stigma associated with special schools 1	0	0

Notes
Figure in brackets is percentage out of those commenting on emergent theme.

In terms of the rationale for special schools, there was some reference to a 'reluctant future for special schools' across the three country groups. It is notable that the three US participants who were reluctant to accept special schools were administrators at either district or Federal level. As one US participant put it, it was 'an unfortunate necessity'. Here is a Netherlands and English example of this theme:

'reluctant future for special schools'

> Yes, accept special schools at this moment with this society, with this way of thinking, with this way of looking at special groups of people in our society at this moment, but my vision and I like to work on it in my way with my influence, so I'd never say in this way 'I can't decide', because I can, every day I can decide about those things by having initiatives in making a discussion about them, that's my drive.
>
> (Netherlands senior teacher, special school, urban area)

> I struggle with this, I would like to be an inclusionist, but from my experience I see it is not feasible.
>
> (English national/regional administrator)

Only English participants (3) saw 'not having special schools as an aim'. Here is an example of one of them:

'not having special schools as an aim'

> If there is a place for self contained classrooms or special schools, I'm not persuaded there is but if there is it's to do with children who have significant emotional problems. I think we could do that, I think we could put children's health care needs into mainstream classrooms, I think we would have to cut the numbers of children we have in classrooms.
>
> (English senior psychologist, rural area)

As regards a change in the number of special schools, this did not emerge with US participants but many Netherlands and English participants preferred a reduced number to the number staying the same or increasing. As regards the organisation of special schools in future, only Netherlands and English participants explained their perspectives. More Netherlands participants referred to special schools as part of a continuum of provision rather than the merging of special and ordinary schools. By contrast, English participants referred more to co-located special schools than provision connected to a continuum. Both Netherlands and English participants also explained how their support for special schools depended on factors in special and ordinary schools: special schools had to provide quality provision that maximised learning progress, on the one hand, and, on the other, more inclusion depended on appropriate provision in ordinary schools, including teachers who were willing to accommodate exceptional needs. Some of the comments made by participants in each country group on this topic also revealed that tensions in decisions were evident. In the USA and the Netherlands this was captured by the 1st level theme that there were 'two sides to the debate'.

The reasons for a future role for special schools were analysed in terms of six 2nd level themes. The most frequently used 2nd level reason was 'children's characteristics'. There was some agreement across the country groups on the kinds of characteristics. There were references by participants in each country group to those with severe, profound or complex disabilities. In the USA this was referred to as 'significant care needs', in the Netherlands as 'very severe and complex difficulties' or 'very low intellectual levels' and in England as 'profound disabilities'. Distinct from this was reference to children with severe emotional and behaviour problems. For US participants there was some reference to the need for small groups and counselling, while for Netherlands and English participants, there was reference to 'challenging behaviour that is a threat to others'. In these countries some participants made general references to 'children not fitting in anywhere' and 'for those not surviving in regular settings' without being more specific. There were also some US and English participants who referred to children with medical care needs. There was one specific US theme and one specific English theme about children's characteristics.

The second most frequently used 2nd level reason for special schools was about the 'provision available'. There were two 1st level reasons related to available provision that were used across the country groups, 'justified if they can move back to regular settings' and 'safer/happy environment'. There were fewer US specific themes (2) and Netherlands specific themes (3) than English specific themes (8). However, none of these country-specific themes were related to specific national aspects of policy and practice.

Another 2nd level reason for special schools was in terms of 'professional and school specialisation'. There were two 1st level reasons related to this 2nd level theme which were used across all three country groups. One was about the special school outreach and support roles for ordinary schools, which was expressed slightly differently in each country analysis. The other was about special schools having 'specialist professionals'. There was also one additional specific reason under this 2nd level theme in each country group. For the USA, it was to emphasise the scarcity of specialist staff, 'scarce specialist staff in regular schools', for the Netherlands it was to emphasise the specialist nature of special schools, 'special schools are very specialised', and for England it was to refer to special school linked to a cluster of ordinary schools, 'as hubs for regular school outlets'.

'Stakeholder's interests' was another 2nd level theme used to justify special schools, though not a frequently used one. The only 1st level theme used across the country groups was 'some parents want them'. Though there were no other US 1st level themes, there were Netherlands and English themes relating to teacher and children's interests. For the Netherlands, there was reference to 'regular teachers not wanting disabled children in or back in their class' and that the 'child can benefit' from special school. By contrast for England there was reference to special schools 'supporting professional culture and continuity' and for children special schools being 'better than not being at any school'.

The other two 2nd level themes were about 'economic factors', that special schools were a more economic use of resources (though this was used by very few participants) and about 'stigma' a theme only used by one US participant, that 'less stigma was associated with special schools'.

Chapter 8

Conclusions

I suppose I do get treated differently now and again, I think that's a good thing and sometimes I feel it's a bad thing. I mean obviously, I want to be treated the same, but then sometimes I'd like to be treated differently ... I like to be asked.

14-year-old boy with a degenerative neuromuscular condition
(Asprey and Nash, 2005)

Introduction

This final chapter starts with a summary of the key findings from each of the three previous chapters. In the next section these will then be compared with how participants in the USA and England responded to the dilemmas in the 1993 study. This will lead onto the third section that analyses responses to the dilemmas in relation to specific national aspects of the policy and practice. The fourth section will explore the extent to which the findings fit the assumption about dilemmas of difference and the final section discusses the strengths and limitations of the study and its significance.

Summary of positions taken to the three dilemmas across the three countries

Identification dilemma

Though a majority of participants in each country recognised the identification dilemma to some extent (marginal, significant or considerable ratings), the most frequent position was different in each country. Most US participants recognised only a marginal dilemma by contrast to Netherlands participants who mostly recognised a significant dilemma. English participants were split in their most frequent positions, between those who did not recognise a significant dilemma and those who did. This English split could be linked to role differences, where administrators and support professionals mostly recognised a significant dilemma, while regular and special school professionals mostly did not. Analysis of role differences for Netherlands participants showed that two of the four role groups, administrators and special school professionals, identified a considerable identification dilemma, even higher than the modal level. This contrasted with US administrators who by comparison with the overall modal US position, mostly did not recognise this dilemma. US special school professionals were split into those who held the overall modal position, 'marginal', and those who saw a significant dilemma. Overall there were no clear associations between role and recognition positions across the three countries.

However, the most frequent resolution level for participants in each country group was significant, though there were some variations about this level for different role groups in each country. The least variation was for Netherlands participants, where only regular school professionals were less optimistic about a resolution, seeing only a marginal resolution. Two US role groups, support professionals and special school professionals, were less optimistic about a resolution than the overall US resolution level. English resolution levels were the most varied between role groups. Administrators mostly held significant or split resolution levels, support professionals were uncertain and special school professionals mostly held split positions.

Analysis of the most frequent 2nd level themes used to explain recognition positions shows a similar mix of themes in each country; reference to tensions and a questioning of the devaluation consequence. Where there were differences in 2nd level theme use, this can be linked to overall modal recognition levels. For the US group which had the lowest recognition level (marginal), one of the most frequent 2nd level themes also questioned the resource consequence. For the Netherlands group with the highest recognition level, one of the most frequent 2nd level themes was one which saw other positive consequences of identification ('identification required for positive outcomes'). For the English group split into those who did not recognise the dilemma and those who did at a significant level, the most frequent 2nd level themes also included one that saw a tension but considered that there was already a resolution of it ('need outweighs stigma') and another that expressed a 'it depends' view.

Analysis of these most frequent 2nd level themes also showed about half of the 1st level themes (49–59 per cent) making up these most frequent 2nd level themes were shared with one or both other country groups. This indicates a moderate level of commonality across these country groups in how recognition of the identification dilemma is viewed. Further analysis showed the expected relationships between different recognition levels and kinds of explanations used in each country group. Those with higher recognition levels tended more often to use themes relating to tensions, while those with lower or no recognition of the dilemma tended to use the themes which questioned the negative consequences in the presented dilemma and/or which saw some resolution to an assumed tension.

Analysis of the most frequent 2nd level resolution themes showed a similar mix across each country group: the need for national and local developments and to change attitudes to SEN/disability. That there were continuing issues about identification was also one of the most frequent 2nd level themes for US and Netherlands participants. Enhanced communication with parents and students was one of the most frequent Netherlands resolution themes, as was going beyond negative labelling for English participants. Analysis of these most frequent 2nd level resolution themes in each country also showed that about half of the 1st level themes (45–63 per cent) were shared with one or both other country groups. This also indicates a moderate level of commonality across these country groups in how resolution of the identification dilemma is viewed.

These findings have relevance to Anita Ho's theoretical analysis of the dilemma of labelling in the USA and United Kingdom (Ho, 2004) and her suggested resolution of this dilemma. Her proposed resolution was to assume that all children learn in unique ways and that the school system be designed to reflect this assumption, so that flexible measures can be adopted. She also argued against 'pathologising academic difficulties as much as possible' (Ho, 2004: p. 90). Participants across the three country groups showed some similarities to her approach in their suggested resolutions – reducing special education identification and adopting national and local developments which involve improving the general education system so that it becomes more inclusive. However, another resolution that emerged from this study diverged from her position in also suggesting that attitudes to SEN and disabilities needed to become more positive and, for some, that this involved finding ways to go beyond negative labels. This departs from her position because these approaches assume that we are dealing with difficulties and disabilities. Second, some participants in this study (between one in five and one in three depending on the country) believed that despite these positive resolutions, there were continuing issues about identification.

Curriculum dilemma

Compared to the identification dilemma the most frequent recognition level for the curriculum dilemma was consistently 'significant' across the three country groups. For those who split their responses to this dilemma, the most frequent recognition level was 'not recognise' for one aspect and 'significant recognition' for the other. A majority of participants (60–70 per cent) in each country group recognised this dilemma to some extent. There was also less variation from the overall most frequent position for different roles compared to the identification dilemma. The most frequent recognition level for all US role groups was the same as the overall level (significant), while for English participants only support professionals showed some variation (marginal and significant as most frequent recognition levels). Only for the Netherlands support professionals, was the most frequent recognition level (marginal) less than the overall level. The most frequent resolution levels were 'significant' for Netherlands and English participants, but at a lower marginal level for US participants.

There was also more variation of the most frequent levels for different roles across each country group for resolution than recognition levels. Regular and special school professionals in Netherlands had 'marginal' as a most frequent resolution level. English support professionals continued to have 'uncertain' as their most frequent resolution level, while administrators and special school professionals had split responses. Though the overall most frequent US resolution level was 'marginal', support professionals and regular school professionals had 'significant' as their most frequent resolution levels.

For the US group, which had a lower recognition level than the other two groups, the most frequent 2nd level explanations were in terms of seeing tensions, seeing tensions which had been resolved and questioning that curriculum differences implied lower status. Though English participants had an overall higher significant recognition level for this dilemma, they had a similar mix of 2nd level explanations. For Netherlands participants, with the same significant level of recognition, explanations were mostly in terms of seeing tensions and seeing tensions which had been resolved. For both US and Netherlands participants there were also some comments about curriculum matters specific to each country. Unlike the other two dilemmas there was very low use of the 2nd level themes that questioned the validity of this curriculum dilemma in terms of either the lower status or the relevance to individual needs arguments. Analysis also showed that less than half of the 1st level themes (43–53 per cent), making up these most frequent 2nd level themes, were shared with one or both other groups. This indicates a moderate level of commonality across these country groups in how recognition of the curriculum dilemma was viewed. However, further analysis of the different orientations within the 'resolved tensions' theme showed that Netherlands participants made more use of themes emphasising commonality or differentiation/relevance than the US or English participants. They also used themes focusing on a balance between commonality and differentiation/relevance less than the US and English participants.

Analysis of the most frequent 2nd level resolution themes showed a similar mix across each country group, balancing common and different aspects of the curriculum and having flexibility in the curriculum and teaching. The US group, being less optimistic about resolving the curriculum dilemma, referred to the need for systems development (such as, the need for 'policy change'), which was a 2nd level theme where the 1st level themes were mainly specific to this country. One of the other most frequent 2nd level resolution themes for the US group was to enhance staffing resources. It is interesting that despite the US group being less optimistic about resolving the curriculum dilemma, it was the Netherlands and English participants who mostly recognised continuing issues in resolving this dilemma. Analysis of these most frequent 2nd level curriculum resolution themes in each country also showed that about two-fifths of the 1st level themes (38–45 per cent) were shared with one or both other country groups. This indicates a low to moderate level of commonality across these country groups in how resolutions of the curriculum dilemma are viewed. That the frequencies of shared resolution themes are lower than for curriculum recognition might reflect that resolutions are more country specific than the recognition of the curriculum dilemma. Further analysis showed the expected tendency for participants using the 'continuing issues' theme to have lower resolution levels in each country group. For English participants only, there was also a tendency for those with higher resolution levels to use the most frequent theme about balancing common and different aspects of the curriculum.

Location dilemma

The most frequent recognition level for the location dilemma was consistently 'significant' across the three country groups. For those who split their responses to this dilemma, the most frequent recognition level was 'not recognise' for one aspect and 'significant recognition' for the other. A large majority of participants (76–86 per cent) in each country group recognised this dilemma to some extent, more than for the other two dilemmas. There was little variation from the overall modal level for different roles. For US administrators the most frequent recognition level was higher (considerable) than the overall level. All four Netherlands role groups had the same most frequent recognition level as the overall level 'significant'. English support professionals also had 'marginal' as their most frequent recognition level. The most frequent resolution level was 'significant' for US and English groups, but only 'marginal' for the Netherlands group. There was more variation of the most frequent resolution levels for different roles than for recognition levels across each country group. US administrators were mostly uncertain and regular school professionals less optimistic about resolving this dilemma. By contrast, special school professionals in the Netherlands were more optimistic than the overall marginal level in this country group. English support professionals continued to be uncertain, while regular school professionals were mostly 'marginal' and 'significant' about their resolution levels.

The only 2nd level explanation for the significant recognition levels in each country group was the most frequently used one about tensions. Explanations in terms of resolutions of assumed tensions (resolved tensions) were used frequently in the US but not in the other country groups. However, explanations in terms of questioning the implication of reduced specialist support in regular class placement and seeing positive aspects of separation, were used mostly by Netherlands and English participants. Linked to the significant recognition level of Netherlands participants was the more frequent use of explanations about other negative aspects of placing the children with more severe SEN/disabilities in regular classrooms. Analysis of these most frequent 2nd level themes showed that about two-fifths of the 1st level themes (39–43 per cent), making up these most frequent 2nd level themes, were shared with one or both other country groups. This indicates a low to moderate level of commonality across these country groups in how recognition of the location dilemma was explained.

Analysis of the most frequent 2nd level resolution themes showed a similar mix across each country group, balancing included and separate provision and enhancing flexible services and staffing, while recognising that there are continuing issues in resolving this dilemma. Though the 2nd level explanation about the need for systems change was used in each country group, only US participants used it more frequently. Only Netherlands participants used the 2nd level theme about limits to inclusion more frequently. This can explain the overall lower marginal resolution level in this country group. Analysis of these most frequent 2nd level location resolution themes in each country also showed that about two-fifths of the 1st level themes (35–46 per cent) were shared with one or both other country groups. This indicates a low to moderate level of commonality across these country groups in how resolutions of the location dilemma are explained. Further analysis also showed the expected tendency for participants using the 'continuing issues' theme to have lower resolution levels across the three country groups.

The emergent analysis of participants' views about the future of special schools showed that all those who presented a view, with one US exception, saw some future role for special schools. For the Netherlands and English participants this meant a reduced number of special schools, the merger of special and regular schools and that this depended on the quality of provision. Reasons for special schools were consistent across the three country groups, in terms of children's significant needs, the kind of provision available in separate settings, professional and school specialisation, stakeholders' interests and economic factors.

Comparison of US and English findings: 1993 and 2005 studies

Caution is required in drawing conclusions from a comparison of the findings from the 1993 and the 2005 studies for English and US participants. Though similar materials, with some changes, were used across the 12 years, participants came from different areas in each country. Also, the participants in both countries included a range of administrative roles in the 2005 study (local and national) that were not included in the 1993 study. An urban and rural school district were involved in both studies, being in neighbouring States on the east coast of the USA and in different regions in England. The qualitative analyses were also more extensive and intensive in the 2005 study. Nevertheless, it has been possible to re-analyse the resolution themes from the 1993 study in terms of the 2005 2nd level resolution themes (Norwich, 1993b). The most frequent recognition level in the 1993 study for all the dilemmas was 'significant' in both country groups (see Table 8.1). This compares with the 2005 study where the most frequent US identification recognition level was 'marginal'. For English participants the most frequent 2005 identification recognition level was mostly 'significant' for those outside schools (administrators and support professionals), and mostly 'not at all' for those inside schools (special and regular school professionals). These differences for the identification dilemma were not found for the other two dilemmas.

One interpretation of the change in recognition of the identification dilemma in both countries is that there has been a change in social and education beliefs about SEN/disability from less to more positive images. The qualitative data in the 1993 study related mostly to the resolution rather than the recognition of the dilemma, so differences in recognition explanations cannot be compared. But, the themes used in the 2005 study to explain the US 'marginal' and English dual 'significant/not at all' recognition levels, show some questioning of the negative consequences of disability identification, for example, through 1st level themes, such as, 'stigma has reduced', 'disability has positive image' and 'labels do not lead to devaluation'. These findings are consistent with the development of more positive social and educational images of disability in the USA and England over the last decade. This can be interpreted as reflecting the impact of disability rights legislative and policy initiatives and developments in the USA and the United Kingdom over this period, discussed in Chapter 3. The difference in the most frequent identification levels within the English 2005 group between those inside (not at all) and those outside schools (significant) might be related to their frame of reference. School insiders tended to question the validity of the dilemma in terms of whether identification leads to devaluation inside schools, while those outside school tended to recognise tensions about the wider negative consequences of labels. The use of the other 2nd level theme 'moderate/deny resource consequences' by about 20 per cent of US participants can also help explain the mostly marginal US identification recognition level in 2005. These participants were indicating that there were alternative forms of additional provision without special education identification.

The most frequent resolution levels were 'significant' for all three dilemmas across both countries in 1993 and remained so for the identification and

Table 8.1 Most frequent ratings for US and English recognition and resolution levels and associated 2nd level resolution themes in the 1993 and 2005 studies

	USA		England	
	1993 study	*2005 study*	*1993 study*	*2005 study*
Recognition				
Identification	Significant	Marginal	Significant	Significant + not at all
Curriculum	Significant	Significant	Significant	Significant
Location	Significant	Significant	Significant	Significant
Resolution				
Identification	Significant • *National/local developments • *Change attitude to SEN/disability • Go beyond negative labels	Significant • *National/local developments • *Change attitude to SEN/disability • Continuing issues	Significant • *National/local developments • Go beyond negative labels	Significant • *National/local developments • Change attitude to SEN/disability • Go beyond negative labels
Curriculum	Significant • *Balance common/different aspects • *Enhanced staffing/ resources • Continuing issues • Priority to individual relevance	Marginal • *Balance common/different aspects • Curriculum and teaching flexibility • Systems development • *Enhanced staffing/resources	Significant • *Balance common/different aspects • Enhanced staffing/resources • Continuing issues	Significant • *Balance common/different aspects • Curriculum and teaching flexibility • Continuing issues
Location	Significant • *Enhance flexible services and staffing • *Balance included/separate provision • *Continuing issues	Significant • *Balance included/separate provision • *Enhance flexible services and staffing • *Continuing issues • Systems /local change	Significant • *Enhance flexible services and staffing • *Balance included/separate provision	Significant • *Balance included/separate provision • *Enhance flexible services and staffing • Continuing issues

Note:
* Indicates shared 2nd level themes between 1993 and 2005 studies.

location dilemmas in the 2005 study. The most frequent English curriculum resolution level remained 'significant' over this period as well. But, this was not so for the US curriculum resolution which changed to 'marginal'. This can be interpreted to reflect less current optimism about resolving the curriculum dilemma. Comparing the most frequent explanations for these resolution levels over this period indicates some similar 2nd level themes – 'enhanced staffing/resources' and 'balance common and different aspects'. But, there were notable differences. In the 1993 study some participants used the theme 'priority to individual relevance', which reflects a way forward that emphasises relevance over commonality. Also, in the 2005 study, some participants used the 'systems development' theme, which for these participants meant 'a policy change' (1st level theme, see Table 8.2) about the No Child Left Behind legislative system. Participants also used the 2nd level theme about 'curriculum and teaching flexibility' more frequently in the 2005 study. For US participants this mostly meant a 'different curriculum for severe disabilities', 'more flexibility for teachers' and 'collaboration between special education and regular teachers'.

Country specific analyses: recognition and resolution of the three dilemmas (2005 study)

US findings and policy context:

The most frequent recognition level was lower (marginal) for the identification dilemma than for the curriculum and location ones (significant). This difference can be associated with the most frequent themes used to explain these positions (see Table 8.2). The 'marginal' identification level was mostly explained in terms of themes which either questioned the validity of the identification dilemma in some way ('in-class support reduces stigma', 'stigma has reduced' and 'how alternatives to special education identification work') or saw a resolved tension ('needs outweigh stigma'). By contrast, the significant recognition of the curriculum dilemma was seen mainly in terms of curriculum tensions ('academic curriculum not meet needs', 'current tensions', 'problems using same standards and tests') and one resolved tension ('modifying general curriculum for all'). The significant recognition of the location dilemma was mainly seen in terms of location tensions ('severe disability not get what they need in regular class' and 'typical students not get what they need').

Another notable finding was that about a quarter of US participants explained their recognition positions in terms of students with severe disabilities being 'unaware of being separate, different or stigmatised'. Netherlands and English participants, by contrast, used this emergent theme much less frequently. It is interesting that about the same proportion of US participants, but not English ones, in the 1993 study also used a

Table 8.2 Breakdown of most frequent US recognition and resolution levels (2005) and associated 1st level themes (top three where n>2)

	Identification	Curriculum	Location
Recognition level	Marginal	Significant	Significant
Explanations	In-class support reduces stigma Stigma has reduced Needs outweigh stigma How alternatives to SE identification work	Academic curriculum not meet needs Current tensions Problems using same standards and tests Modifying general curriculum for all	Severe disability not get what they need in regular class Typical students not get what they need
Resolution level	Significant	Marginal	Significant
Explanations	Make alternative provision More training Develop inclusive approach Communicate positively with students Show sensitivity about labelling	Hard to resolve Modify general curriculum to meet individual needs Need policy change	Better staffing, resourcing, planning Mixed model: include as much as possible Depends on individual student

similar theme to explain their recognition of the location dilemma. This continuity in US explanation that questions the validity of these dilemmas indicates a particular kind of explanation that is specific to some US teachers in these studies.

Though these findings cannot be easily generalised to other districts in the State or to other States in the USA, it is clear that for these participants the identification dilemma presented less tensions than the other two dilemmas. It is notable that the role analysis shows that the administrators in the group who represented a small number of district, State and Federal level administrators mostly saw no identification dilemma at all. US support professionals were split into two groups, those who saw no dilemma and those with the overall most frequent level (marginal). This role analysis reinforces the significance of the overall marginal recognition level, as no sub-groups had their most frequent recognition levels above the marginal level. As the excerpts in Chapter 5 indicate, these participants saw stigma as having been reduced in their settings, that disability had a more positive image and that positive action had been taken to address these image issues. These explanations of reduced stigma and more positive disability images are consistent with the change in the most frequent recognition level of the identification from 'significant' to 'marginal' over the decade since the 1993 study. Though there were no resolutions to the identification dilemma that referred to specific US policy and practice matters, one of the most frequent 1st level resolution themes was about 'the use of alternative provision' as a way of reducing special education identification. This theme reflected the views of several US participants about improving early intervention and the use of the three-wave model as a way of improving general education and linking it to special services. These practices reflect Federal IDEA legislation which supports early intervention (Katsiyannis *et al.*, 2001).

Table 8.2 also shows that resolution levels varied across the three dilemmas for the US participants, with the resolution level being lower for the curriculum dilemma (marginal) than the identification and location dilemmas (significant). The significant resolution of the identification dilemma was seen mainly in terms of reducing special education identification ('make alternative provision'), national and local developments ('more training' and 'develop an inclusive approach'), better communication ('communicate positively with students') and going beyond negative labels ('show sensitivity about labelling'). The significant US resolution of the location dilemma was seen mainly in terms of enhancing flexible services and staffing ('better staffing, resourcing and planning'), balancing included and separate provision ('mixed model: include as much as possible') and some reference to factors on which resolutions were dependent ('depends on individual student'). By contrast, the marginal resolution of the curriculum dilemma was seen in terms of a mix of themes, such as systems development ('need policy change'), balancing common and different aspects ('modify general curriculum to meet individual needs') and continuing issues ('hard to resolve'). As mentioned in the previous section, the need for policy change was about the standards agenda implemented through the No Child Left Behind legislative system (see Chapter 3 for details). The other resolution themes which clearly linked to the constraints seen in this legislative framework were the 2nd level theme about 'curriculum and teaching flexibility', a 'different curriculum for severe disabilities' and 'more flexibility for teachers'. These themes are related to the conclusions of the US National Research Council report on students with disabilities and the standards agenda, discussed in Chapter 3 (McDonnell *et al.*, 1997). These authors noted that for a small percentage of those with low incidence disabilities, goals which are mainly academic will not be relevant to their life goals. They also questioned whether academic content and performance levels might take time away to teach what many regard as more valuable skills. Similar issues were noted in participants' explanations of their recognition of the curriculum dilemma, in specific 1st level themes, such as 'academic curriculum not meet needs' and 'problems in using the same standards and tests'.

Netherlands findings and policy context

Table 8.3 shows that the most frequent recognition level across the three dilemmas for the Netherlands participants was 'significant'. The most frequently used 1st level themes to explain these recognition levels were mostly in terms of tensions specific to each of the three dilemmas. For the identification dilemma the most frequently used 1st level themes were about 'tensions experienced' and 'special education labels as negative'. The comment that some parents wanted, while others did not want labels, was also a frequently used one. This significant overall recognition of the identification dilemma by Netherlands participants contrasted with the US and English approaches to this dilemma. This difference could be interpreted to reflect a relatively less well-developed inclusive ethos and relatively less well-developed practices in ordinary schools in the Netherlands.

For the curriculum dilemma the significant Netherlands recognition level was explained in terms of 1st level themes about 'current tensions' and 'maximising common curriculum', which was interpreted as a resolved tension. Maximising implies a priority towards common curriculum options but some recognition of limits in the form of some curriculum differentiation. For the location dilemma the significant recognition level was explained in terms of 1st level themes about 'experienced tensions' and 'regular schools not being capable of meeting individual needs of those with severe disability', on the one hand, and 'students with moderate/severe disabilities feeling excluded in regular schools', on the other. This 'feeling excluded in the regular school' theme was interpreted as another negative

Table 8.3 Breakdown of most frequent Netherlands recognition and resolution levels (2005) and associated 1st level themes (top three where n>2)

	Identification	Curriculum	Location
Recognition level	Significant	Significant	Significant
Explanations	Tensions experienced SE labels as negative Parental reasons for labelling	Current tensions Maximise common curriculum	Experienced tensions Regular school not capable of meeting individual needs of severe disability Students with moderate/severe disability feel excluded in regular schools
Resolution level	Significant	Significant	Marginal
Explanations	Open positive communication Show potential for progress Positive image disability Develop positive school ethos/practices	Modify general curriculum for individual needs Flexible adaptive class teaching for all	No 1st level explanations were used more than twice, but 2nd level ones were: Balance included/separate provision Continuing issues Limits to inclusion Enhance flexible services and staffing

aspect of including those with severe disabilities. This theme arose as many Netherlands participants were opposing one of the consequences in the presented dilemma, that being educated in a separate setting led to students feeling excluded.

The most frequent resolution level for the identification and curriculum dilemmas was 'significant'. The most frequently used 1st level themes for this resolution level of the identification dilemma were about better communication ('open positive communication'), about changing attitudes to SEN/disability ('show potential for progress' and promote 'positive images of disability') and about national and local developments ('develop positive school ethos and practices'). Though some of these most frequent Netherlands resolutions were similar to US identification resolutions, there was no notable use of 1st level themes about reducing special education identification, such as 'make alternative provision'. This omission can be interpreted to indicate less awareness among Netherlands participants of alternative systems of additional provision not needing special education identification, as used in the USA and United Kingdom. The most frequent themes for the significant resolution of the curriculum dilemma were about balancing common and different aspects of the curriculum and about curriculum and teaching flexibility.

Where the Netherlands participants departed from significant resolutions was in the location dilemma, for which the most frequent resolution rating was 'marginal'. This can be interpreted in terms of their most frequently used 2nd level themes. Though many supported a balance between included and separate provision for students with more severe disabilities, enhanced flexibility of services and staffing and changes to the system, there were also prominent 2nd level themes about continuing issues and the limits to inclusion. These themes about continuing issues and limits were used more than in the other two countries. These findings are consistent with the historical system of separate provision in the Netherlands, which has not been challenged and reformed to the extent found in the USA or England, as discussed in Chapter 3 (Vislie, 2003). Other analyses reinforce this interpretation of the positions held by the Netherlands participants. Though the most frequently used 2nd level location recognition theme in all three countries was 'tensions', indicating a common perspective on the issues about placement of children with more severe SEN/disabilities in ordinary classrooms, the percentage of Netherlands participants using this theme was higher than for US and English participants. Netherlands participants also had a relatively high use of other 2nd level themes, about positive aspects of separate provision and negative aspects of ordinary class inclusion. Nor were there any Netherlands participants who used the 2nd level theme 'positive aspects of inclusion', which included 1st level themes such as 'others and families accept disability' and 'regular teachers welcome them', which were used by at least some US and English participants. That the moves towards more inclusion were less developed than the other two countries was also evident in the more frequent use of the 2nd level resolution theme about systems and local change. This theme involved greater schools' commitment to restructure for inclusion, the need for more pilot inclusion trials, more legislation for inclusion and support for schools to be more inclusive, all of which were seen by about a third of the Netherlands participants as part of the resolution of the location dilemma.

English findings and policy context

Table 8.4 shows that the curriculum and location dilemmas were most frequently recognised at a significant level by English participants. The most frequent 1st level themes associated with the significant recognition of the curriculum dilemma were, on the one hand, about 'current tensions' and about the 'National Curriculum being over-prescriptive', and on the other, about giving 'priority to what is relevant', which was interpreted as emphasising relevance while recognising curriculum commonality. These themes reveal that, despite the moves in England from the original 1988 National Curriculum towards greater flexibility and the national adoption of inclusive curriculum and teaching principles, tensions between commonality and differentiation and relevance are seen to persist. The most frequent 1st level themes associated with the significant recognition of the location dilemma were also about tensions ('problems in building capacity in regular classes'), but included some questioning of the validity of the reduced specialist provision consequence (for some, 'can build capacity in regular class'). Though English participants continued from the 1993 to the 2005 study to see a significant location dilemma, it is evident from the 2005 1st level themes that progress has been seen in making specialist provision available in regular classrooms for some children with more severe disabilities.

The most frequent identification recognition level for English participants was split between 'significant', which was mostly held by those working outside schools, and 'not at all', mostly held by those working inside schools. Themes explaining the significant positions were about the 'tensions experienced' and 'labels can lead to stigma', on the one hand, and about other positive consequences of identification and how the consequences depended on school inclusiveness, on the other. For those who did not recognise the dilemma, the 1st level themes were about questioning the validity of the devaluation consequence ('label not lead to devaluation' and 'parents want label') and having resolved the balance between need and stigma in favour of need ('need outweighs stigma').

The most frequent resolution levels adopted by English participants was 'significant' for all three dilemmas. For those who recognised the identification dilemma to some extent, the most frequent resolutions were about national and local developments ('training and education' and 'developing

Table 8.4 Breakdown of most frequent English recognition and resolution levels (2005) and associated 1st level themes (top three where n>2)

	Identification	Curriculum	Location
Recognition level	Significant	Significant	Significant
Explanations	SEN/disability label can lead to stigma Tensions experienced Identification required for positive outcome Depends on how inclusive the school	Current tensions Priority to what is relevant National Curriculum over-prescriptive	Problems in building capacity in regular classes For some build capacity in regular class
	Not at all		
	Label not lead to devaluation Parents want label Need outweighs stigma		
Resolution level	Significant	Significant	Significant
Explanations	Training and education Develop inclusive approach Open positive communication with parents	Modify general curriculum to individual needs Same general areas, different programmes Work from individual needs	Mixed model Ongoing issue Improve teacher and administrator training

an inclusive approach') and about enhanced communication ('open positive communication with parents'). The most frequent resolutions of the curriculum dilemma were about having a balance between common and different curriculum aspects ('modify general curriculum to individual needs' and 'same general areas, different programmes') on the one hand, and giving priority to individual relevance ('work from individual needs'), on the other. These resolutions can be interpreted to indicate as with the recognition themes, that despite greater priority being given to curriculum relevance in the brief history and development of the English National Curriculum (see Chapter 3 for more details), that many participants still saw the need for even more emphasis to be given to relevance over commonality.

The most frequently used 1st level themes used to explain the significant resolution of the location dilemma were about having a balance between included and separate provision ('mixed models'), about enhancing flexible services and staffing ('improve teacher and administrator training') and about there being continuing issues about providing specialist services in regular classes for children with more severe SEN/disability. This conjunction of a balanced resolution with the recognition of continuing issues resembles the most frequent Netherlands explanations, though the English resolution levels were mostly at 'significant' and not at the Netherlands marginal level. Both English and Netherlands participants saw continuing issues and limits to inclusion (as 2nd level themes) in relation to the location resolution, though this was to a greater extent for the Netherlands participants. These differences might help to explain the higher modal resolution level for the English group relative to the Netherlands group.

Evidence in relation to the dilemmatic framework

Evidence from both the 1993 and the current 2005 studies show that the assumption about dilemmas of difference can be subjected to empirical scrutiny. Had the participants across the three countries responded to the presented dilemmas by mainly denying tensions, there would have been some evidence to question the validity of the assumption. Analysis of the 2005 recognition ratings showed that for all three dilemmas in the three countries there was some recognition of the dilemmas. A majority (between 56 and 86 per cent) across the three countries recognised dilemmas to some degree across the three presented dilemmas. Resolution levels were similarly high across the three dilemmas in the three countries. In terms of those who recognised dilemmas, a majority reported that they saw some resolution of these dilemmas. These percentages are even higher when split responses are taken into account, that is, when participants distinguished between two aspects of the three dilemmas. Most of these distinctions were made to differentiate between aspects where no dilemma was recognised and another aspect where a dilemma was recognised.

The qualitative analyses of the 2nd level themes in terms of the 1st level themes are also consistent with implications of the dilemmatic framework. Some of the 2nd level themes were derived from the dilemmatic framework. The first implication was that there would be 1st level themes expressing tensions of various sorts ('tensions'). The second was that there would be some 1st level themes which question the negative consequences that followed from one or both of the presented consequences ('moderate or deny' a negative consequence). The third was that there would be some 1st level themes that reflected opting for a position after balancing or weighing up the tension ('resolved tension'). These three kinds of recognition explanations were found to be relevant to analysing many of the 1st level themes across all three dilemmas. Other 2nd level themes were also generated that related to other negative and positive aspects and consequences of the options under consideration. These were expected in the original design because the presented dilemmas were framed for presentational clarity purposes in terms of single and not multiple consequences.

The associated explanations for the recognition positions also corresponded to a marked extent with the different recognition levels in all three countries across each dilemma. Of the nine comparisons between 'not at all' and 'significant' recognition levels for the three dilemmas across the three countries (3 dilemmas × 3 countries), there was a strong tendency for non-recognition positions to be mostly explained by resolved tension themes or ones which questioned some aspect of the negative consequences. There was also a strong tendency for significant recognition positions to be mostly explained in terms of tensions. For example, US participants with a significant modal recognition level for the curriculum dilemma mostly referred to tensions in their explanations with some reference to resolved tensions. By contrast, the minority of US participants who did not recognise the curriculum dilemma mostly used resolved tensions explanations and explanations which questioned the validity of the negative consequences.

The dilemmatic framework also had implications for the kinds of resolution expected. One implication was that resolutions would involve some balancing between the contrary options. There was much evidence of this across the three dilemmas in each country group. In the identification dilemma, some resolutions were about using alternative approaches to special education identification, but these themes were less frequent than ones that assumed that special education identification was required. Here the resolutions were about going beyond negative labels and changing attitudes to SEN/disability to become more positive as part of national and local developments. The most frequently used themes to explain resolutions of the curriculum and location dilemmas were also about balancing, for curriculum the balance between common and different aspects of the curriculum, and for the location dilemma, the balance between included and separate settings. The other implication of a dilemmatic framework for resolutions was that there would be reference to continuing issues in resolving these dilemmas. It was found that in seven of the nine areas (3 countries × 3 dilemmas), there were references to continuing issues. This pattern of evidence is consistent with the dilemmatic assumption.

This overview of the findings about resolutions to the dilemmas also shows that Minow's attempt to transcend dilemmas of difference by questioning the bases for identifying differences in the first place is not strongly reflected in the explanations held by participants in this study (Minow, 1990). As explained in Chapter 2, her position was that by recognising that differences arise in relationships in social contexts, it is possible to introduce new possibilities which put the onus on organisations like schools to accommodate differences in the general system and so avoid providing distinct provision that can become stigmatised. Some of the suggested resolutions presented by participants across the three country groups did focus on alternative systems of provision that recognise differences as relevant to all children. In response to the identification dilemma, some participants indicated that by improving general education and adapting provision for all, not just those with learning difficulties and disabilities, special education identification could be reduced. In relation to the curriculum dilemma some, but not many, participants recognised that the tensions they saw in relation to children with disabilities were relevant to other differences, such as lower attaining children. Many participants across the three country groups also saw a resolution to the curriculum dilemma in terms of modifying the general curriculum to individual needs and some saw this going beyond learning difficulties and disabilities. But, other resolutions clearly showed that most participants still believed that some differentiation was needed, whether in terms of identification as requiring special education services, or for modified and/or alternative curriculum programmes in some separate settings for some of the time. As explained above and shown in Chapters 5–7, participants also saw that there were continuing tensions and issues over these kinds and forms of differentiation.

Implications and general conclusions

Caution is required in generalising the findings of this study to other professionals and administrators in these three countries. As explained in Chapter 3, the scale of the study was partly set by pragmatic factors, but nevertheless the depth of analyses and the range of participants provide enough of a base to illustrate how informed professional positions in some areas of these three countries are consistent with a dilemma of difference framework. Those participating in this study were not 'paralysed' (a word used by Minow, 1990: p. 375) by their recognition of these dilemmas, but sought ways of finding some balance between commonality and differentiation while avoiding stigma and reduced opportunities and services. So, it can be

concluded that the dilemmatic assumptions not only provide a useful theoretical framework for considering policy and practice in this field, but also a
rich source of ideas about policy directions.

These resolution ideas will be summarised in terms of the three dilemma
areas. But first it is important to explain that there may be other versions of
difference dilemmas and that there is no definitive statement of these
dilemmas. The three areas that were focused on in this study aimed to illustrate dilemmas in three key areas of educational provision. It is also important to emphasise that these general resolutions relate to settings in this
study. Starting with the identification dilemma, there was some evidence
across each country group, if only from one or two participants, that
tensions about identification could be resolved by finding alternative ways
of providing additional provision. This was seen as a way of reducing the
extent of special education identification. This might involve improving
general education, either by preventing difficulties through more adaptive
provision and/or by additional provision organised through more general
and less separate systems. However, where identification for special education was still required, efforts would be focused on going beyond negative
labelling, changing attitude to SEN/disabilities and enhancing communication between professionals, parents and children/students. All this would
depend on various national and local developments and as some suggested
might involve student choice about additional provision. Though there were
country-specific versions of this generalised set of resolutions, there were
no country-specific differences in general resolution directions.

As regards resolving tensions involved in the curriculum dilemma, tensions over the commonality–differentiation of the curriculum were generally and mainly seen to require some balancing between these aspects.
However, this is where national differences were evident, with the US and
English participants showing more consensus about balancing these aspects,
while Netherlands participants did so less and had a larger minority with
opposed views – either emphasising relevance/difference or commonality.
Connected to the balancing question is the suggested need for more curriculum and teaching flexibility. Here again there were several national differences, such as the Netherlands specific position that special schools make
curriculum flexibility more possible. National developments to support
these curriculum positions were also recognised in each country group, but
again with national differences.

Resolutions of tensions across the country groups about the placement of
students with more severe SEN/disabilities in terms of ordinary class–separate settings were mostly about finding a balance between included and
separate provision. This balancing involved enhancing flexible services
and staffing, which was seen to be dependent on systems changes at national
and local levels. Some US and Netherlands participants also saw the need
for parents and students/children to participate in decisions about setting.

However, there was a general recognition that resolutions only went so far, that there were limits to placement in regular classes for those with the more severe disabilities, though mostly in the Netherlands group. There were some participants in each country group who believed that specialist separate provision should be accepted. These views about the future of separate specialist settings were clearly expressed in general positions about special schools having a future, though for most who expressed a view, a reduced number of special schools. Some participants admitted being reluctant to hold these views, while others continued to see two sides to the debates about separate settings. These responses can be seen to reflect expressions of the continuing tensions experienced in relation to this location dilemma. The general reasons across the country groups for having special schools were in four broad areas:

i   children's functioning levels (mostly for significant care and medical needs, needs associated with severe emotional, behavioural and intellectual difficulties/disabilities);
ii kind of provision available (safe, calm, flexible programmes, temporary, part-time, links and movement between ordinary/general and separate settings);
iii specialisation offered (specialist facilities, specialist and scarce professionals);
iv stakeholders' interests (parental and teachers' preferences).

The significance of these resolutions in relation to those with more severe SEN/disabilities is highlighted by the use of themes, especially by some US and English participants, that most of those with moderate SEN/disabilities can be supported in regular classes.

This chapter and the book concludes by reflecting on the relationship between recognising and resolving dilemmas of difference and the explanations given in resolving these dilemmas in this three country study. This relationship will be discussed in relation to the responses of English participants to the location dilemma, but other dilemmas and other country groups could be used as well.

Most English participants recognised a significant location dilemma and also saw a significant resolution of it. However, 56 per cent of them opted for a 'mixed model' of provision in their resolution, which balanced included and separate settings, while about 10 per cent accepted separate specialist provision and settings – by contrast to a 'full inclusion' model. Also, 30 per cent of them saw continuing issues about placing children with severe disabilities in ordinary classrooms and 20 per cent saw limits to inclusion – therefore not seeing final solutions, but resolutions based on balancing. These explanations might be interpreted as indicating less than a significant resolution, though, of course, this depends on the interpretation that participants put on a term like 'significant'. In the Netherlands, most participants used the term 'marginal' to describe their resolution, and this may be because of their historical and current special education policy context. However, no English participants saw a considerable resolution of the location dilemma. So, perhaps it is this finding – no considerable resolutions – that suggests that the use of 'significant' is compatible with seeing the persistence of tensions about inclusive placements. This suggests that most of these teachers and administrators proposed resolutions that were not final solutions, but ways forward in which tensions persisted.

As explained in Chapter 1, this study was conducted because it was evident that despite much talk about dilemmas, tensions and issues in the field, there has been little interest in a dilemmatic perspective. The reason for conducting this particular study of professional perspectives to dilemmas of difference a decade after an earlier study, was to find out if there was still evidence for the recognition of such dilemmas. Despite interesting country-specific variations and indications of some changes over the last decade, it is concluded that there is still some evidence that professional beliefs fit this kind of framework. But the lack of interest in a dilemmatic approach may have deeper roots. As some political theorists have noted (Berlin, 1990), recognising value tensions and conflicts – in the terms of this study, adopting a dilemmatic position – involves accepting some crucial losses. The key losses are about social arrangements that are less than perfect and giving up a certain kind of purist hope for the future. In all the research and theorising about special needs and inclusive education over the last 12 years since the initial 1993 study, I have not found much receptiveness to the dilemmatic framework. One conclusion to draw from this lack of interest, which is sometimes expressed by a lack of criticism, is that it probably originates from the challenge posed to cherished commitments by acknowledging value and policy dilemmas of difference. However, despite this, I contend that acknowledging and taking account of dilemmas provides a realistic and authentic approach to hope about an inclusive and humane education. It is form of hope based on being creative about options, analysing, clarifying and examining these options, finding ways of having it both ways as far as possible in a morally acceptable and decent way. The teenager with a degenerative neuromuscular condition, quoted at the start of this final chapter, said that he wanted to be treated the same as others, but then sometimes he would like to be treated differently. There is no better way to summarise the main point of this book than to refer to the balancing he was calling for and the consultation with those involved, including children and young people, in finding these balances.

References

Arnove, R.F. (2001) Facing the 21st century: challenges and contribution. Presidential Address. *Comparative Education Review*, 45 (4), 477–503.

Artiles, A.J. (1998) The dilemma of difference: enriching the disproportionality discourse with theory and context. *Journal of Special Education*, 32(1), 322–36.

—— (2000) *The inclusive education movement and minority representation in special education: trends, paradoxes and dilemmas*. Paper to ISEC International Conference, University of Manchester, UK.

Asprey, A. and Nash, T. (2005) *Including young people with degenerative neuromuscular disease in mainstream education*. Barnstaple: Children's Hospice Southwest.

Audit Commission (2002a) *Statutory assessment and statements of SEN: in need of review?* London, Audit Commission.

—— (2002b) *Special educational needs: a mainstream issue*. London: Audit Commission.

Berlak, A. and Berlak, H. (1981) *Dilemmas of schooling: teaching and social change*. London, Methuen.

Berlin, I. (1990) *The crooked timber of humanity*. London: Fontana Press.

Bernstein, B. (1970) *Theoretical studies: towards a sociology of language, vol. 1*. London: Routledge, Kegan, Paul.

Billig, M., Condor, S., Edwards, D., Gane, M., Middleton, D. and Radley, A. (1988) *Ideological dilemmas: a social psychology of everyday thinking*. London: Sage.

Booth, T., Ainscow, M., Black-Hawkins, K., Vaughn, M. and Shaw, L. (2000) *Index for inclusion: developing learning and participation in schools*. Bristol: CSIE.

Burbules, N.C. (1997) A grammar of difference: some ways of rethinking difference and diversity as educational topics. *Australian Education Researcher*. http://faculty.ed.uiuc.edu/burbules/papers/difference.html (accessed 19 October 2006).

Campbell, C. (2002) Conceptualisations and definitions of inclusive schooling, in Campbell, C. *et al.* (eds) *Developing inclusive schooling: perspectives, policies and practices*. London: Institute of Education, Bedford Way Papers.

Campbell, C, Gillborn, D., Lunt, I., Sammons, P., Vincent, C., Warren, S. and Whitty, G. (2002) Strategies and issues for inclusive schooling, in Campbell, C. *et al.* (eds) *Developing inclusive schooling: perspectives, policies and practices*. London: Institute of Education, Bedford Way Papers.

Clough, P. (2006) Review of 'Moderate learning difficulties and the future of inclusion', *European Journal of Special Needs Education*, 21(2), 227–29.

Clough, P. and Corbett, J. (2000) *Theories of inclusive education: a student's guide.* London: Paul Chapman.

Cole, B. (2005) Good faith and effort? Perspectives on educational inclusion. *Disability and Society*, 20(3), 287–307.

Croll, P. and Moses, D. (2000) Ideologies and utopias: education professionals' views of inclusion. *European Journal of Special Needs Education*, 15(1), 1–12.

Dahl, R.A. (1982) *Dilemmas of pluralist democracy: autonomy and control.* New Haven, CT: Yale University Press.

DES (1978) *Warnock Committee Report.* London: HMSO.

DfE (1994) *Code of Practice on the identification and assessment of special educational needs.* London: DfE.

DfEE (1997) *Excellence for all children: meeting special educational needs.* London: HMSO.

DfES (2002) *SEN Code of Practice.* London: DfES.

—— (2003a) *Data collection by type of special educational needs.* London: DfES.

—— (2003b) *Targeting support: choosing and implementing interventions for children with significant literacy difficulties.* Management guidance DfES 0201/2003.

—— (2004) Children's Trusts: *Developing Integrated Services for Children in England, National Evaluation of Children's Trusts, Phase 1 Interim Report.* London: DfES.

—— (2005) SEN in England 2005. *National Statistics, First release.* London: DfES.

Disability Rights Commission (2003) *Code of Practice for Schools.* London: DRC.

Drasgow, E., Yell, M.L. and Robinson, T.R (2001) Developing legally correct and educationally appropriate IEPs. *Remedial and Special Education*, 22(6), 359–73.

Drisko, J.W. (2000) *Qualitative data analysis: it's not just anything goes!* Charleston, SC: Society from Social Work and Research Conference, 30 January, 458.

Dyson, A. (2000) Inclusion and inclusions: theories and discourse in inclusion, in Daniels, H. and Garner, P. (eds) *Supporting inclusive in education systems.* London: Kogan Page.

Dyson, A. (2001) Special needs in the twenty-first century: where we've been and where we're going. *British Journal of Special Education*, 28(1), 24–29.

Dyson, A. and Millward, A. (2000) *Schools and special needs: issues in innovation and inclusion.* London: Sage.

Edwards, D. and Mercer, N.M. (1987) *Common knowledge: the development of understanding in the classroom.* London: Methuen.

European Agency for Development of Special Needs Education (2004) *Netherlands overview.* www.european-agency.org/nat_ovs/netherlands/index.html (accessed 24 July 2006).

Eurydice (2004) Summary sheet on education systems in Europe: the Netherlands. www.eurydice.org (accessed July 2006).

Florian, L. and Rouse, M. (2001) International perspectives on school reform and SEN (editorial). *Cambridge Journal of Education*, 31(3), 285–89.

Ford, A., Davern, L. and Schnorr, R. (2001) Learners with significant disabilities: curricular relevance in an era of standards based reform. *Remedial and Special Education*, 22(4), 214–22.

Fulcher, G. (1989) *Disabling policies? A comparative approach to educational policy and disability.* Lewes: Falmer.

Gewirtz, S. (2002) *The managerial school: post-welfarism and social justice in educa-tion*. London: Routledge.

Giddens, A. (1994) *Beyond left and right: the future of radical politics*. Cambridge: Polity Press.

Goodhart, D. (2004) Too diverse? *Prospect*, February, 30–37.

Gray, J. (1989) *Liberalisms: essays in political philosophies*. London: Routledge.

Hamstra, G (2000) *'Just different': special education in an experimental setting in Almere*. Paper to ISEC International Conference, University of Manchester, UK.

Ho, A. (2004) To be labelled or not to be labelled: that is the question. *British Journal of Learning Disabilities*, 32, 86–92.

House of Commons Select Committee on Education and Skills (2006) *Special educa-tional needs, Volume 1*. London: TSO.

Howe, K.P. and Welner, K.G. (2002) School choice and the pressure to perform: déjà vu for children with disabilities. *Remedial and Special Education*, 22(4), 212–21.

Huefner, D.S. (2000) The risks and opportunities of the requirements under IDEA 1997. *Exceptional Children*, 33, 195–204.

Hursh, D. (2005) The growth of high-stakes testing in the USA: accountability, markets and the decline in educational equality. *British Educational Research Journal*, 31(5), 605–22.

Ignatieff, M.(1998) *Isaiah Berlin, a life*. London: Chatto and Windus.

Judge, H. (1981) Dilemmas in education, *Journal of Child Psychology and Psychiatry*, 22, 111–16.

Katsiyannis, A., Yell, M.L. and Bradley, R. (2001) Reflecting on the 25th anniver-sary of the Individuals with Disability Education Act, *Remedial and Special Education*, 22(6), 324–33.

Kaufman, J.M. (1989) The regular education initiative as Reagan–Bush education policy: a trickle down theories of education of the hard-to-teach. *Journal of Special Education*, 23(3), 256–78.

Kaufman, J.M. and Hallahan, D.P. (1995) *The illusion of full inclusion: a compre-hensive critique of a current special education bandwagon*. Austin, TX: Pro-ed.

Kaufman, J.M., McGee, K. and Brigham M. (2004) Enabling or disabling? Observations on changes in special education. *Phi Delta Kappan*, April, 613–20.

Kennedy, R. (1999) Facing the dilemmas of difference, in Lowe, E.Y. (ed.) *Promise and dilemma: perspectives on racial diversity and higher education*. Princeton, NJ: Princeton University Press.

Kohlberg, L. (1984) *Essays on moral development. Vol. 2, The psychology of moral development: the nature and validity of moral stages*. San Francisco, CA: Harper & Row.

Layder, D. (1998) *Sociological practice: linking theory and social research*. London: Sage.

Levitas, R. (1990) *The concept of utopia*. London: Philip Allen.

Linn, R.L. (2005) *Fixing the NCLB accountability system*. CRESST Policy Brief, UCLA Center for the Study of Evaluation.

Lipsky, D.K. and Gartner, A. (1996) Equity requires inclusion; the future for all students with disabilities, in Christensen, C. and Ritzi, F. (eds) *Disability and the dilemmas of education and justice*. London: Open University Press.

Lunt, I. and Norwich, B. (1999) *Can effective schools be inclusive?* London: Institute of Education, Bedford Way Series.

MacBeath, J., Galton, M., Steward, S., MacBeath, A. and Page, C. (2006) *The costs of inclusion.* Report for the NUT. University of Cambridge.

McDonnell, L.M., McLaughlin, M.J. and Morrison, P. (1997) *Educating one and all: students with disabilities and standards based reform.* Washington, DC: National Academy Press.

McLaughlin, M. and Henderson, K. (2000) Defining US special education into the twenty-first century, in Winzer, M.A. and Mazurek, K. (eds) *Special education in the 21st century: issues of inclusion and reform.* Washington, DC: Gallaudet University Press.

McLaughlin, M.J., Dyson, A., Nagle, K., Thurlow, M., Rouse, M., Hardman, M. *et al.* (2006) Cross-cultural perspectives on the classification of children with disabilities. Part II. Implementing classification systems in schools. *Journal of Special Education,* 40(1), 46–58.

Marshak, D. (2003) No Child Left Behind: a foolish race to the past. *Phi Delta Kappan,* November, 229–31.

Mead, G.H. (1934) *The works of George Herbert Mead. Vol. 1, Mind, self and society.* Chicago, IL: University of Chicago Press.

Meijer, C.J.W. (2000) Funding and inclusion, in SEN Policy Options Steering Group (eds) *Developments in additional resource allocation to promote greater inclusion.* Tamworth: NASEN.

Minow, M. (1985) Learning to live with the dilemma of difference: bilingual and special education, in Bartlett, K.T. and Wegner, J.W. (eds) *Children with special needs.* Boulder, CO: Transaction Books.

—— (1990) *Making all the difference: inclusion, exclusion and American Law.* Ithaca, NY: Cornell University Press.

—— (2005) The dilemma of difference, in Adams, D.M. (ed.) *Philosophical problems in the law,* 4th edition. Belmont, CA: Wadsworth.

National Disability Council (1989) *The education of students with disabilities: where we stand?* Washington, DC: Government Printing Office.

Neill, M. (2003) Leaving children behind: how No Child Left Behind will fail our children. *Phi Delta Kappan,* November, 225–28.

Netherlands Ministry of Education (2006) *Special needs education statistics for the Netherlands* (personal communication).

Nilholm, C. (2006) Special education, inclusion and democracy. *European Journal of Special Needs Education,* 21(4), 431–45.

Norwich, B. (1990) *Reappraising special needs education.* London: Cassell.

—— (1993a) Has 'special educational needs' outlived its usefulness? in Visser, J. and Upton, G. (eds) *Special education in Britain after Warnock.* London: David Fulton Publishers.

—— (1993b) Ideological dilemmas in special needs education: practitioners' views. *Oxford Review of Education,* 19(4), 527–45.

—— (1994) Differentiation: from the perspective of resolving tensions between basic social values and assumptions about individual differences. *Curriculum Studies,* 2(3), 289–308.

—— (2002) *LEA inclusion trends in England 1997–2001.* Bristol: CSIE.

Norwich, B. and Kelly, N. (2004) *Moderate learning difficulties and the future of inclusive education*, London: Routledge.

OECD (2000) *Special needs education: statistics and indicators*. Paris: OECD.

Office of National Statistics (2001) *National census data 2001*. London: ONS.

Ofsted (2004) *Special educational needs and disability: towards inclusive schools*. London: Office for Standards in Education.

Pijl, S.J. and Meijer, C.J.W. (1991) Does integration count for much? An analysis of the practices of integration in eight countries. *European Journal of Special Needs Education*, 6(2), 100–11.

Pijl, Y.L and Pijl, S.J. (1995) Ontwikkelingen in de deelname aan het speciaal onderwijs [Developments in participation in special education]. *Pedagogische Studien* [Educational Studies], 72, 102–13.

Pijl S.P. and Van den Bos, K. (2001) Redesigning regular education support in the Netherlands. *European Journal of Special Needs Education*, 16(2), 111–19.

Pijl, S.P. and Veneman, H. (2005) Evaluating new criteria and procedures for funding special needs education in the Netherlands. *Educational Management and Administration and Leadership*, 33(1), 93–108.

Pugach, M.C. and Warger, C.L. (2000) Curriculum matters: raising expectations for students with disabilities. *Remedial and Special Education*, 22(4), 194–96.

Qualifications and Curriculum Agency (2003) *Planning, teaching and assessing the curriculum for pupils with learning difficulties*. London: QCA.

Raveaud, M. (2005) Hares, tortoises and the social construction of the pupil: differentiated learning in French and English primary schools. *British Educational Research Journal*, 31(4), 459–79.

Reezigt, G.J. and Pijl, S.J. (1998) The Netherlands: a springboard for other initiatives, in Booth, T. and Ainscow, M. (eds) *From them to us: an international study of inclusive education*. London: Routledge.

Rodbard, G. (1990) Going Dutch! A perspective on the Dutch system of special education. *European Journal of Special Needs Education*, 5(3), 221–29.

Sailor, W. and Roger, B. (2005) Rethinking inclusion: schoolwide applications. *Phi Delta Kappan*, March, 503–9.

Scheepstra, A., Nakken, H. and Pijl, S.P. (1999) Contacts with classmates: the social position of pupils with Down Syndrome in Dutch primary schools. *European Journal of Special Needs Education*, 14(3), 212–20.

Sen, A. (1992) *Inequality re-examined*. Oxford: Clarendon Press.

Smith, T.E.C. (2000) Section 504, the ADA and the public schools. *Remedial and Special Education*, 22(6), 335–43.

Stocker, M. (1990) *Plural and conflicting values*. Oxford: Oxford University Press.

Terzi, L (2007) Beyond the dilemma of difference: the capability approach to disability and special educational needs, in Florian, L. and McClaughlin, M. (eds) *Categories in special education*. London: Sage.

Thomas, G. and Feiler, A. (1988) *Planning for special needs: a whole school approach*. Oxford: Blackwell.

Thomas, G. and Loxley, A (2001) *Deconstructing special education and constructing inclusion*. Maidenhead: Open University Press.

Thurlow, M. (2002) Positive educational results for all students. *Remedial and Special Education*, 23(4), 195–202.

Triano, S. (2000) Categorical eligibility for special education: the enshrinement of the medical model. *Disability Studies Quarterly*, 20(4), 399–412.

UNESCO (1994) *The Salamanca statement and framework for action on special needs education*. Paris: UNESCO.

US Department of Education (1997) *Nineteenth annual report to Congress on the implementation of the IDEA*. Washington, DC: Office of Special Education Programs.

—— (2002) *Twenty fourth annual report to Congress on the implementation of the IDEA*. Washington, DC: Office of Special Education Programs.

—— (2003) *Twenty fifth annual report to Congress on the implementation of the IDEA*. Washington, DC: Office of Special Education Programs.

Van Houten, D. and Bellemakers, C. (2002) Equal citizenship for all. Disability policies in the Netherlands: empowerment of marginals. *Disability and Society*, 17(2), 171–85.

Vislie, L (2003) From integration to inclusion: focusing global trends and changes in the western European societies. *European Journal of Special Needs Education*, 18(1), 17–35.

Warnock, M. (2005) *Special educational needs: a new look*. Impact.

Weber, C. (1997) *'De Rugzak' komende veranderingen in het speciaal onderwijs* [*'The backpack': Impending changes in special education*]. Bilthoven: NVA (Dutch Autistic Society).

Will, M.C. (1986) Educating children with learning problems: a shared responsibility. *Exceptional Children*, 52, 411–16.

Ysseldyke, J.E., Olsen, K. and Thurlow, M. (1997) *Issues and considerations in alternative assessments*. Minneapolis University, National Center for Educational Outcomes. ERIC Document Service, No. ED 415–616.

Index